D0464629

DATE DUE

GAYLORD			PRINTED IN U.S.A.

BLACK ACES HIGH

Also by Robert K. Wilcox

Wings of Fury
Scream of Eagles
Japan's Secret War
Fatal Glimpse
Shroud
The Mysterious Deaths at Ann Arbor

BLACK ACES HIGH

The Story of a Modern
Fighter Squadron at War

Robert K. Wilcox

Thomas Dunne Books / St. Martin's Press ✹ New York

To Bego, love forever.

THOMAS DUNNE BOOKS.
An imprint of St. Martin's Press.

www.stmartins.com

Book design by Michael Collica

ISBN 0-312-26916-1

First Edition: October 2002

10 9 8 7 6 5 4 3 2 1

Contents

Acknowledgments

There are over five thousand men and women with various jobs on an aircraft carrier such as the *Roosevelt*. Each of them has a function that is most vital. Every crew member of the *Roosevelt* helped in making this book possible. Unfortunately, I couldn't write about every one of them. I couldn't even spotlight every one of the three hundred or so men and women who make up the roster of the Black Aces, nonflying people behind the scenes who do the administrative work, repair the airplanes, and cook the food that feeds those on the ship, especially the aviators. Nevertheless, I wish to thank all of them for providing the setting, the function, and the working machines, and for all the other things they did that contributed to this story. They are unsung in these pages but not unappreciated.

When I first decided to write this book, several outstanding naval aviators I knew got me started with information about what was going on in the Kosovo air war and then put in a good word about me with those who received my request. These were Vice Adm. John B. Nathman, who was director, Air Warfare, for the navy at the time; Capt. Mark Fox, skipper of VFA-122 at Lemore, California; and Dale Snodgrass, a retired captain who now flies his planes at air shows across the country. All were kind and instrumental, and I am grateful for their help.

At the Pentagon, Comdr. Jeff Gradeck, Navy Office of Legislative

Affairs, and Rear Adm. Tom Jurkowski, chief of Navy Information, helped me get approval for my trip out to the *Roosevelt*. Capt. Mike Denkler and Lt. Bob Mehal also aided. In Italy, Lt. Garrett Kasper helped while I waited for a ride to the carrier. That was a five-day ordeal. I was with a group of other journalists also waiting, and we were a low priority. We'd wait all day at the airport in Bari, Italy, and the lieutenant would then suggest places to stay in town. He was always trying to make up for the delays that he could do nothing about. A large, cavernous helicopter finally took us out.

Finally, I'd like to thank the staff of the *Hook*, the journal of carrier aviation, for letting me research in their files; my editor at Thomas Dunne Books, Peter Wolverton, whose suggestions have helped make the book better, and, as always, my longtime agents, Jim Trupin and Elizabeth Trupin-Pulli of Jet Literary Associates, for placing the book. They, as usual, worked diligently and smartly, and I am very grateful.

KOSOVO AND SURROUNDING AREAS

Typically, planes would take off and rendezvous at tankers waiting for them somewhere off the tip of the "boot" of Italy. After tanking, they'd head in mass across Adriatic on routes depending on where their targets were. Once near the target, they'd have a final rendezvous and "push" in battle formation to the actual target.

HUNGARY

★ Belgrade

YUGOSLAVIA

Vicenza

SERBIA

Adriatic Sea

Montenegro   KOSOVO

Tivat Djakovica

Bay of Kotor   Pristina

BULGARIA

Podgorica Urosevac

Prizren ★ Skopje

ITALY

MACEDONIA

Brindisi

ALBANIA

N

GREECE

Ionian Sea

USS Roosevelt

Sigonella

Mediterranean Sea

0   500 Kilometers

0   500 Miles

Map by James Sinclair

Introduction

When the U.S. War on Terrorism heightened to actual air strikes against the Taliban government in Afghanistan on October 7, 2001, one of the navy squadrons selected to lead the early bombing raids was VF-41, a fighter squadron flying F-14A Tomcats and nicknamed the Black Aces. VF-41 crews were assigned some of the most heavily defended Taliban targets and dropped over two hundred bombs in three weeks of night operations, a prodigious amount, scoring an unprecedented hit rate of nearly 90 percent.

The squadron, part of Airwing 8, the carrier's approximately eighty-plane, multisquadron air arm, should have been home at NAS (Naval Air Station) Oceana, Virginia Beach, Virginia, when the Taliban bombing began. The *Enterprise* had finished a nearly six-month cruise in the Persian Gulf, had been relieved by another carrier, and was on a leisurely route back to the United States via some exotic ports of call where its five-thousand-plus officers and enlisted personnel planned to unwind and have a good time. But when Islamic fanatics hijacked four U.S. airliners on September 11 and flew two of them into the International Trade Center in New York and another into the Pentagon in Washington, D.C., killing thousands of American civilians, those plans changed abruptly. The *Enterprise* was ordered to turn around and quickly return to the Gulf.

Airwing 8 and particularly the Black Aces were uniquely suited for what was suddenly anticipated after September 11—a fact strong in the minds of military leaders who ordered it back. Although changed somewhat by normal attrition and replacement, a strong core of the squadron had fought in early 1999 in America's last air war, the Kosovo War, and possessed expertise that was suddenly needed. In 1999, Airwing 8 had been on the USS *Theodore Roosevelt*. Because the *Roosevelt* and the air wing were beginning a cruise and were heading for the nearby Mediterranean, it was not much of a diversion to extend the carrier's destination to a position off Kosovo and substitute training exercises for the real thing.

Kosovo presented a new kind of conflict for modern fighter squadrons, a precursor to what would happen later in Afghanistan and other terrorist countries the United States, in its subsequent War on Terrorism, might bomb. It wasn't a conventional conflict in which fighters battled other airplanes for control of the skies and air operations supported ground invasion and conquest. In Kosovo, fighter squadrons, usually pristine in their role as air fencers, got down and dirty and dropped bombs. Kosovo marked the first time in the history of warfare that victory was won without the introduction of troops on the ground.

Airplanes reigned supreme—but not as easily as has been portrayed in the press or by the pundits.

The Black Aces probably played a greater part in that 1999 victory than did any air squadron in theater, whether air force or navy. Because of its superior performance, sophisticated equipment, and two-man crews, who took it upon themselves to do something extra, the Tomcat and its flyers distinguished themselves. Basically, they proved in Kosovo to be the one U.S. asset that could both find hiding enemies and destroy them with smart bomb accuracy.

And doing that eventually became the main mission of the navy there—despite daunting problems.

Flying aging Tomcats and faced with having to locate Serb fighters operating covertly in a mountainous land, much like Afghanistan, and with almost no help from ground spotters, VF-41 aviators spearheaded for the navy the creation of new ways to pinpoint, identify, and destroy enemy troops and weapons. These were tasks that fighter crews had seldom had to do before. The Aces had to break rules and frequently go in harm's way in order to be successful. In the beginning, there had been resistance to their taking license. But they eventually had done so well that for the first time in aviation history, a fighter squadron—theirs—had been awarded the Wade McClusky Trophy, the navy's premier bombing honor. The award, named for a World War II dive-bomber pilot and post–World War II admiral, had been won previously only by bombing squadrons.

The award was quite a coup, but like the purely symbolic Superbowl or World Series trophies, it was hardly indicative of the hard work, missteps, pain, sacrifice, and dedication needed to win it.

The experience of the Aces in fighting over Kosovo—what they did and how they did it—is what this book is about.

I had always wanted to write a book about a fighter squadron at war. A fighter squadron has its own inherent drama and human interest. Fighter pilots and fighter crews are in themselves intriguing. They must be smart and talented to safely operate their intricate, awesome, and deadly dangerous machines. In the sky, they are often at the very edge of their abilities and of human endurance. Many of them like that. Competition is what most of them are about. And there is no crucible like danger and battle. Both reveal character. It is almost impossible to fake courage or knowledge in the middle of an emergency. There is only honesty—often brutal, sometimes inspiring. Every decision, every action can have a monumental effect, especially in the air.

War just heightens those aspects.

Someone is trying to kill you.

I realized that, from the squadron's commanding officer, who must lead, to the newly winged junior lieutenant who must learn but also perform from day one, the dynamics of a squadron fighting at war make an interesting story. September 11 would make that story timely and pertinent as well.

When the Kosovo War started, I saw a chance. It didn't seem like a very big or even interesting war. But war alone wasn't what I sought. I sought to portray a fighter squadron *at* war. And that was there.

Because of several books I'd written on fighter pilots, the navy agreed to let me go on a carrier. There were no strings attached. After a lot of waiting, I finally made it out to the *Roosevelt* as the war was ending. It was a good time to arrive. Tensions were lessening. We were somewhere in the middle of the Ionian Sea between Italy and Greece. The air-wing commander, or CAG, was generous. He said I could interview any squadron. I wanted his guidance. I asked him which squadron would be the best. He said I might want to talk to the Black Aces. "They're doing some interesting things."

I'm glad I followed his advice. Eventually, after many interviews conducted then and later, a story of fear and courage, mishap and success, fighting spirit and military innovation, unfolded. *Black Aces High*. It's a human story that goes behind the smiling, sunglass-wearing facade of aviators flashing a V, the sterile, seemingly slow-motion target video that has become a staple of Pentagon briefings, and the rock 'n' roll cowboy image of fighter crews seen in the movies.

It is a story, I hope, that shows something of who these aviators really are and what they do beyond what the public is told, a story that probably will be repeated again and again as our carriers continue to deploy in this new kind of war our nation is fighting.

In a phrase, *Black Aces High* is the story of a modern American fighter squadron in a twenty-first-century war.

Book 1
FEAR AND TREPIDATION

One

Lt. Marcus "Lupe" Lopez wrenched his Tomcat hard and low into the path of the MiG-29 as it roared past their merge. The fight was on. He shot a look back to see the point-nosed Fulcrum's afterburners blowing fire in the start of a high climbing turn—a first move in gaining an advantage. The 29, its retreating silhouette gleaming lethally in the Mediterranean sun, could actually increase its speed going up—a phenomenal feat normally reserved only for rockets.

Scarily, the guy driving the Fulcrum was one of the best MiG-29 pilots in the world—a burly senior German officer call-signed "Hooter," who had missing teeth and a beard, and liked to wear an eye patch and pirate bandanna when off duty drinking or riding his motorcycle. Besides being a biker, he was a professional dogfighter who spent nearly all his considerable airborne hours practicing air-combat maneuvering, or "ACM" in the jargon, in perhaps the best dogfighting jet in the world.

In contrast, Lupe—a slight, clean-cut, youthful twenty-seven, with dark-haired good looks and a genial personality, had only been in the VF-41 Black Aces squadron for a little over five months and hadn't been in a turning fight since he'd left the F-14 training squadron the previous spring. Lupe was a rookie, or "nugget," as they call a new pilot in the navy, shiney barred and untested, with at most a half-dozen one-versus-one (1v1) dogfights on his résumé.

He was also in one of the navy's oldest jets, the F-14A, which had made its debut back in 1972, nearly three decades before. While it was fitted with new avionics and other upgrades that made it, among other things, a better turner than many newer Tomcat models, it was still an aging fighter that, on paper, did not match up well in a turning fight against the newer Fulcrum.

The MiG even had a Star Wars–type missile-firing system that allowed its pilot to launch merely by pointing his helmet at the intended target. If Hooter could get the Tomcat in a position only forty-five degrees off his MiG's nose—which was a heck of a lot easier to establish than the Tomcat's narrower, ten-to-twenty-degree nose-on requirements—and at the proper distance, Lupe was dead meat.

No question the young lieutenant had his hands full this August day in the beautiful sun-splashed fight skies off Italy. And he knew it.

But he had a plan.

He and his backseater, Lt. Comdr. Louis "Loose" Cannon, a quiet, thoughtful Desert Storm veteran flying RIO, or radar intercept officer, with Lupe specifically because of his experience, had decided they would, at first, just try to keep the fight even, doing their best to stay out of the maneuverable, smaller MiG's kill envelopes while threatening it enough to keep it at bay. The tactic would buy them time, and if Hooter made a mistake, they'd pounce.

Maximum performance was the key. As long as they could continue turning well enough to keep their nose threatening the 29, Hooter would have to respect them. He wouldn't go for the kill until he thought they were in trouble. Since they didn't have the MiG's power, they'd use gravity to help them turn. Turning bled speed, or "energy," as it was also called in the dogfighting world. Without speed, any fighter is vulnerable. Maneuvering becomes harder. But roaring down, with gravity aiding them, they'd be regaining energy lost in the hard turning.

It was a chess game, the cobra and the mongoose. If Lupe and Loose kept sight of the MiG so that they knew where it was and therefore what to anticipate, and kept elusive so that the MiG had harder shooting angles, and if Lupe flew the jet at its optimum turning speed—around 310-to-320 knots—where it would curl fastest and in the shortest radius, they would have a chance.

It only took one mistake to give them an opening.

The Tomcat was now seconds into its descending turn. Lupe was tugging the stick as hard as he could, his feet coordinating the rudders, keeping the jet steady at the six and one half Gs at which it curved the best.

A "G" stands for a unit of force roughly equivalent to a man's weight. One G can feel like 180 pounds on the body; six Gs, like a crushing half ton. Gs on an airplane are exerted by gravity. They are similar to, but much greater than, the centrifugal force experienced in a car careening around a corner. Too many Gs and blood drains from the brain. Unconsciousness, or blackout, ensues. Aviators wear inflating G-suits, or "speed jeans," to keep blood from draining. But the more Gs they experience, the harder that task becomes—as their grunting and groaning often indicate.

First color fades. Then vision tunnels. Unconsciousness comes next. And it isn't a sweet drift into sleep. It's a sometimes-nauseous, painful, scary feeling that no pilot or RIO wants or likes.

But at this point unconsciousness wasn't a factor. Perhaps there was only a little graying at the edges. Both Lupe and Loose were locked on the MiG, their perceptions supercharged as they roared to optimum knot speed.

In a second or two, Loose would start snatching glimpses at instruments in the cockpit in order to keep Lupe advised of airspeed, Gs, and other data he needed in order to fly without having to take his eyes off the Fulcrum. Years prior, when backseaters were first introduced to modern navy jet fighters, the RIO was resented by pilots who didn't feel they needed somebody else's help.

But Vietnam changed that. Backseaters more than proved their worth as a second pair of eyes for finding MiGs that looked like gnats in the huge sky, and for reducing the complicated workload, including running the radar and locating bombing targets. Such tasks were increasingly demanded in the cockpits of the sophisticated new jets. By the time the Tomcat became the main carrier fighter, RIOs, because of their worth, expertise, and proven leadership, were increasingly being given command of fighter squadrons, even though they rode in the backseat without a stick.

In fact, at this very moment, the Black Aces were commanded by a RIO, Comdr. Joseph "Joey" Aucoin, a graduate of the Navy Fighter Weapons School, which was better known as "Top Gun." Joey, like

Loose, was a Desert Storm combat veteran with thousands of hours in the backseat.

But none of this was on their minds right now—if it ever was. Lupe and Loose were only thinking of the fight.

Suddenly, Hooter did the unexpected—well, not totally unexpected, because Lupe and Loose knew the Fulcrum tactics and had discussed just such a move. But the fight had begun as they wanted, and, in the heat of battle, they had hoped it would continue that way.

Both jets at this instant were at the beginnings of what is called a "two-circle" fight. At the merge, they had turned into each other, the MiG going high, the Tomcat low. In order to bring their noses around to threaten each other, each fighter would have to travel a full circle, or 360 degrees; hence the two circles. Two-circle was what Lupe and Loose wanted because if they could hold the optimum six-and-a-half-G turn as they were, they felt they could traverse the circle about as fast as the Fulcrum.

They'd remain even.

But now they saw Hooter do a sudden reversal, a quick change of direction from the circle he was previously flying to the beginnings of one in the opposite direction. He'd suddenly gone counterclockwise, which would change the fight into what is called a "one circle." While a two-circle could be envisioned as a figure eight in the sky, with both jets roaring clockwise on the opposite spheres of the eight—eventually, after 360 degrees of turn, to meet in the middle—a one-circle fight flipped one jet out in the opposite direction so that it only needed to turn 180 degrees to meet the other.

One-circle meant that in an instant Hooter had cut in half the curling distance he had to travel.

Hooter probably figured that Lupe, being as green as he was, wouldn't know what was happening and would continue along his 360-degree trek. With Lupe and Loose rounding the bottom of the eight, the 29 would quickly be aiming at the Tomcat like a submarine fixed on an unsuspecting freighter.

But Lupe and Loose had kept sight of Hooter and seen his maneuver. Lupe instantly knew he had to counter. In a millisecond, he also reversed, in effect forcing the fight back to a two-circle. It was a violent reversal, smashing both men against the cockpit as Lupe rammed the stick forward to "unload," or "divest Gs," so he could reverse more quickly, and then snapped it back sharply in the other direction while simultaneously pumping the rudders. Lupe's reaction not only nullified Hooter's reversal, but because of a design flaw in the Fulcrum, gave him a chance to pounce.

The MiG had a blind spot behind its cockpit. Unlike the Tomcat crew, which sat fairly elevated in a cockpit that gave them clear 360-degree vision, Hooter sat low, a large seat back obstructing his view. When he made his reversal, it flipped the rear of the Fulcrum at the F-14, causing him to momentarily lose sight. In that millisecond, Lupe made his reversal. When Hooter came out of the maneuver, he was expecting to see the Tomcat in a chunk of sky near where he'd left it.

But it wasn't there!

In addition, because he was going up, the reversal cost Hooter airspeed. "He pulled for everything he was worth," recalls Lupe. "He doesn't care about energy. . . . He just wants to bring his nose around faster. That's what the MiG-29 does best. Maneuverability. But as soon as he does, he's bleeding airspeed. He's trading energy for nose position. He'll do that to get the one-circle because with the one-circle he can get the quick kill."

But because of the blind spot, he didn't see the Tomcat reverse. He burst from his reversal, fangs out. But instead of finding the Tomcat a mile below, bottoming around a two-circle turn, he saw nothing but an empty piece of sky.

"Lose sight, lose fight," is the dictum.

Now *Hooter* had to be scared.

And with good reason. Since the Tomcat was headed down when it reversed, it had hardly lost any speed. Lupe and Loose, their jet primed, were quick-turning up on the other side of the MiG, barely three thousand feet away, and preparing to shoot. The MiG teetered helplessly, nose up, trying to regain some maneuvering speed, its pilot desperately trying to find his target.

But it was too late.

As the Tomcat closed the gap and Lupe called "Fox One," meaning a radar missile had been locked and was on its way, Hooter finally located them. It's not clear whether he heard the Fox One call, got warning indications of the radar lock on his cockpit alert gear, or simply spotted them against the azure Mediterranean sky. But he realized instantly that he was in trouble. Hooter did the only thing he could do. In an effort to bring his nose back around and at least try to threaten the Tomcat, he again pulled hard with everything he had and over-stressed the Fulcrum.

"His nose is still stuck up high, and I'm down low," recalled Lupe. "So he's trying to bring his nose down there as fast as he can, and he probably pulls the stick in his lap."

The MiG-29 is a nine-G jet, meaning that's the limit the manufac-turer says the pilot can put on it. Anything more is dangerous and can break the plane. "I'm sure he pulled so hard he hurt himself," said Lupe. "You can feel it. It's a seat-of-the-pants thing . . . very painful . . . He knew he'd overstressed the jet."

This was a training fight and had to be called off. The jet might have been damaged in the overstress, rendering it unsafe to fly hard any longer. Lupe and Loose had already won anyway because the Fox One they had called was a kill shot, verified by their onboard equip-ment. Had they been in a real dogfight, Hooter, not the rookie, would have bought the farm.

"That was nice," said Lupe. "We had to fly back slow and easy, check his jet, and make sure nothing was broken. We were happy as can be and ready for the German O club."

And it had all happened in less than a minute.

Make no mistake—had he not damaged his jet, Hooter most likely would have returned and in the next fight waxed the rookie. Experi-ence counts. It counts the most. But for this day, Lupe was the victor, and Loose was probably less impressed because he'd seen it so much more.

But for a fighter pilot, ACM was traditionally what distinguished the good from the not so good. Things had changed in the nineties. Bomb-ing, which most fighter pilots regarded as grunt work, was definitely making a comeback. But ACM was still how a fighter pilot made his reputation and secured his place in the pecking order, his right to stand at the bar with his mate, hands flying, telling great stories.

So Lupe was feeling his oats. But he was no fool. He knew the fight could just as easily have gone the other way.

What he was really happy about was that he had upheld his squad-ron's honor. By a chance draw, he had been matched against the MiG squadron's best—and on the very *first* day of the squadron's one-versus-one fights. The squadron was like a family, a fraternity. It was an elite brotherhood of men he liked and respected. Some he might have even idolized. The demands of the squadron meant that a pilot or RIO spent more time with its members than with his wife or girlfriend. It was an intimate, revealing camaraderie. You can't fake who you are at six hundred knots, with your life liable to be snuffed out in a millisecond. Pilots and RIOs flew and sometimes tragically died together. They trusted each other, depended on each other. They were handpicked, recruited like professional athletes or elite social-club pledges. A squadron wanted the best, demanded the best.

Because of all this, Lupe was proud that he'd held his own. He'd just been through a war with the Black Aces and contributed more than he had expected, and this was further proof that he was fitting in.

But he hadn't always felt this way. Five months earlier, in April 1999, he'd been as apprehensive as any nugget pilot. Not just because he was joining his first squadron and going on his first cruise. But because the Black Aces, one of two F-14 squadrons on the carrier USS *Theodore Roosevelt*, were going to war.

Two

Comdr. Joseph "Joey" Aucoin, skipper of the VF-14 Black Aces, had last experienced abject fear during Desert Storm in 1991. On his very first combat mission, he was launched as a young lieutenant backseater in an F-14 on a MiG sweep. The Tomcat was running interference for a carrier night strike on Basra. They'd entered Iraq through a violent lightning storm over Iran and then, approaching the target, had been engulfed by a savage Basra night sky filled with antiaircraft fire.

"It was just the general things inherent in combat," he said about that baptism. "The confusion, the plan falling to pieces, not being able to communicate, the screaming on the radios. Boy, they were really trying to kill us. You could die. Just that realization. It's not like we can say, 'Okay, stop that.' It really takes some courage."

That's why this early evening he'd called the All Officers Meeting, or "AOM," as he and his officers referred to it. Ironically, the North Carolina native (he'd actually been born in Germany but called North Carolina home) had been a junior officer in the same Black Aces when he'd seen that first combat in Desert Storm. Junior officers didn't always come back to skipper their old squadrons. But Aucoin, call-signed "Joey," had come back. Now he wanted to talk to his aircrews and support officers about what they were soon to experience and what he would expect of them.

The Aces, some three hundred officers and enlisted support men and women, including thirty aviators, aboard the large nuclear carrier, were racing through the Mediterranean to a secret point south of Italy in the Ionian Sea. There, the following day, their aircrews would begin strikes on Serbian targets in Kosovo. They were readying themselves to take part in the newly declared war of the North Atlantic Treaty Organization (NATO) on the former Yugoslavian republic. Aucoin, forty-two, and one of his senior officers, Louis "Loose" Cannon, the squadron's only black aviator, were the sole combat veterans in the squadron. None of the others had ever experienced the chaos of war.

Aucoin looked on as the low-slung, dull gray ready room began to fill with green flight-suited pilots and RIOs and khaki-and-jerseyed support officers either taking the name-tagged leather seats reserved for flight-crew members or standing, arms folded, around the sides and in the back. Few, if any, could detect Aucoin's concern. Fit and lanky, quick to smile, he was always low-key but purposeful at such meetings. He had a down-to-earth, easy-talking leadership style, seldom got angry, and was known as a skipper who cared about his men, especially the enlisted troops. His father had been an enlisted man. That's how he'd been born in Germany. Several junior officers, or "JOs," as they were called in the squadron, had even gotten mad at him for what they perceived as his favoritism toward enlisted sailors. It wasn't true, but their irritation didn't bother Aucoin. He didn't worry how he was perceived. He had little egotism for a man in his profession, and was mainly interested in what worked and worked well. He believed in the power of the team. Stars alone weren't going to produce success. It took every player.

But the pressure was building.

Behind them was the struggle they'd all endured to get ready for this deployment these past months during "work-up," the year-plus period between cruises, also called "turnaround," when a fleet fighter squadron returned to its land base, regrouped, and began training again for its next extended cruise.

It took that long, after a deployment, to get back to a fighting peak.

The turnaround, which included Aucoin's assuming command of the Aces, hadn't been easy.

Far from it.

•   •   •

Maintenance had been a mess when Aucoin had become skipper in 1998 after serving as the squadron executive officer, or XO, as skippers-to-be normally did. Bad management had caused a deterioration in the quality of jet technicians and their noncommissioned managers, which had resulted in the squadron's airplanes being mostly grounded and in need of repair. The situation had gotten so bad that the squadron's previous cruise had been scornfully dubbed "the Love Boat Cruise" by its aviators because of the lack of flying time the broken airplanes had caused them. The nickname referred to the extra time in ports they had because they couldn't fly. Most of them had hated the situation.

Making matters worse, they had had to borrow airplanes during the cruise from their sister squadron, VF-14, the Tophatters. They were "sisters" only because they were both in Airwing 8, one of the few air wings that had two Tomcat squadrons. Most air wings only had one. The borrowing had been humiliating. If a fighter squadron is anything, it is a fiercely competitive organization that prides itself on being ready, reliable, and the best. But how good could the Aces really be if they had to depend on another squadron's maintenance department?

Morale was low. Readiness was shot.

The situation had been especially galling to Aucoin, who felt he knew how to change it but who, as a dutiful XO, had had to support his skipper's policies.

The first thing he did when he assumed command was to begin changing squadron atmosphere.

The problem boiled down to leadership style. Aucoin believed that every member of the squadron, from himself up top to the lowliest toilet scrubber at the bottom, had to be made to feel that he was a part of the team. In the previous regime, there had been a distance between officers and noncoms. They had seldom mixed, had little in common. Workers had just punched the clock and gone home. Aucoin began showing he cared about them by inviting them for beers, listening to their gripes and suggestions, and showing them he thought them important to the workings of the squadron. "That little guy has got to feel you need him," he said. "Then he'll do what is needed to make sure we succeed."

As part of the change, he'd filled squadron leadership slots by recruiting some old friends who basically felt the same way he did—key officers whom he believed would be instrumental in helping him turn things around, especially in "maintenance and operations," the two key squadron departments.

All navy fighter squadrons depend mainly on maintenance and operations to function. Maintenance, the largest department in a squadron, takes care of the airplanes, making sure they are fixed and running well so that the squadron can fly and do its business. Maintenance itself is sectioned into multiple "divisions": "administration" for paperwork; "aircraft" for repair of the engines and body; "avionics and ordnance" for electronics and weapons; and the "line" division for prep, such as fueling, before flight. The Aces, like most Tomcat squadrons, had fourteen jets for about thirty aviators, who flew as two-man crews. They took eleven on cruise. Operations, not as big as maintenance, uses the jets that maintenance has ready to schedule the squadron's almost daily flying, which, in peacetime, is mainly to train for war, and, in war, is mainly to fly combat missions. It's a job of logistics and supply, of juggling planes available for priority work, of deciding who flies and who doesn't, and why. Other important, but smaller, squadron departments are "administration," "safety," and "personnel."

The skipper oversees everything. His executive officer, while second in command and readying to take over, basically does the skipper's grunt work, the myriad of unglamorous, but essential, squadron-running tasks that the skipper hasn't got time to do, from writing up award recommendations to making sure the showers in the hangar or aboard ship are working. The XO is the skipper's confidant and adviser, his representative when he's not available. And since he's eventually going to take over, he must be a proven leader.

As his executive officer, Aucoin had recruited Comdr. Jim "Dog" Bauser, an ambitious, hard-charging upstate New Yorker and former U.S. marine who'd been enticed to switch to the navy when they'd promised to send him to flight school during a 1980s pilot shortage. Bauser, who loved a good Cuban cigar and sometimes chewed tobacco ("Don't tell my wife"), was a personable and respected fighter pilot — tough, wily, and erudite. He had the same affinity for the troops that Aucoin had, which was one of the reasons Aucoin had recruited him. Dog had been Joey's roommate on a 1986 cruise and had worked for him as a maintenance division head in VF-84 when Joey had taken his own turn as a squadron maintenance officer, or "MO," as they called it. He'd had to pull strings to get Dog.

Ditto for his own MO. He'd fought and won a battle with navy detailers, who assigned personnel, to get Lt. Comdr. Brian "Bru" Brurud, an inspiring, blond-headed former Oklahoma State footballer who resembled the late movie actor Pat O'Brien, known for his portrayals of warm, but righteous, Irish priests and cops. Bru, a pilot who had distinguished himself in the F-14's growing role as a bomber, had a country wit and disarming manner that belied a shrewd tactical mind and an indomitable, sometimes volatile, will. He too had served in maintenance under Joey in a previous squadron and was a fierce advocate for the troops. Because the Aces already had enough senior officers in existing slots, meaning he'd have more senior officers than most squadrons, Aucoin was forced to cash in some coveted markers to get Bru, but was "so glad I'd done it."

To head operations and become his "Ops O," as they called the operations officer, Aucoin had brought in Lt. Comdr. Steve "Wog" Carroll, a silver-haired, sharp-tongued New Jersey native who'd had a problem with his previous skipper and needed a good billet. Wog was a RIO, and Joey, being the same, had been one of Wog's early instructors. "I jumped at the chance of getting him," said Joey. Wog was an intrepid administrator and problem solver, oblivious to obstacles and quick to admonish those he felt were wrong. He jokingly liked to characterize himself as the bad cop in what he called the "good cop/bad cop 'Wog and Bru show,' " which the two new department heads, who were rooming together on this cruise, created to help them get things done.

"I wanted guys who were hardworking maintenance guys, guys who rolled up their sleeves and got the job done and didn't worry about the image thing," Aucoin later said about his staff. He himself was the same type. Although he was a 1980s graduate of the famous "Top Gun" school and probably had more hours in the F-14 (over four thousand) than any other aviator in the navy, the sun-glassed Hollywood-fighter-pilot look was not his style. He didn't own a motorcycle or sportscar and had recently married, settled down, and fathered a baby boy.

He knew the job got done at very basic levels.

To help Brurud in maintenance, Aucoin recruited Roger Elkins, a Cincinnati-born chief warrant officer who was the kind of hands-on airplane expert and manager of technical talent the squadron needed. Quiet, hardworking, a natural with machines, Elkins had been a technician for the famed Blue Angels, the navy's premier flight-demonstration team.

"When Joey brought me in here," said Elkins, "there wasn't any long-range plan in place. Everything had been knee-jerk reaction. Nobody had been asking what we were going to be doing next month and the month after that. Our people had been working on things they shouldn't have. So I got on the computer and developed a spreadsheet that showed us where we needed to be and what we needed to do to get there."

Under Brurud's guidance, Elkins became a recruiter himself. "It's a matter of getting good people first." He'd been a manpower officer at a fighter wing prior to coming, so he had good contacts with the detailers. When he found the talent he was looking for, it was fairly easy to get them sent over. Calling up a prospective technician, he'd say, " 'Hey, I've got a great deal here. I'm sitting pretty. I want you to come over.' When you call a guy like that, show some interest, their head swells. They feel pretty good. It's just a matter of working out the details."

Elkins knew who to go after. Mainly, he recruited chief petty officers who would do the actual field supervising. "If you don't have a good chief's community within the squadron, you're gonna have problems," he said. "It's going to force division officers and people like me to get involved to get the maintenance done, and you don't want that. You want the chiefs to be out there with the experience showing these kids when they need it."

The squadron already had some good chiefs, but they'd become gun-shy from the previous regime. Joe Knight, a senior chief responsible for quality assurance, was one of those they wanted to keep. "We knew he could do the job, but we had to convince him to step up to the plate," said Elkins. "It took myself and the MO a couple of weeks to convince him that things were going to be different. We told him he was one of the guys who could make us better."

Knight stayed.

With the newly installed management, talented technicians, and cooperative spirit, morale had begun to lift to where it had been in the earlier days of the storied squadron.

In 1981, for instance, two Black Aces aircrews had been the first Americans since the Vietnam War to register dogfight victories, not to mention the first-ever F-14 kills. They'd done so against a pair of Libyan Sukoi-22 jets that had challenged them over the Gulf of Sidra. A wooden plaque showing the New York Times stories recounting that triumph hung near the ready-room entrance being trafficked this very moment. And in 1995, over Bosnia, the Aces had become the first Tomcat squadron to deliver precision, laser-guided bombs in an official armed conflict.

But there was only so much that could be done with the squadron's aging Tomcats. The Aces were flying F-14As — not later-model Bs, or the souped-up newest Ds — but literally the first Tomcats made and delivered to the fleet. They were early-1970s vintage, nearly thirty years old. The ancient Tomcats were still formidable warplanes — agile, fast, able to deliver the firepower of several World War II bomber-and-fighter squadrons combined. They had great range. But they were in constant need of tune-ups, upgrades, and overhauls — like rare, mammoth classic cars still entered in crucial competition. And years of shrinking military budgets in the 1990s and consequential navy policy decisions had made replacement and upgrade parts and outsourced specialized labor extremely hard to get. Sometimes they'd had to resort to cannibalization of one plane to supply another.

And as deployment grew closer, the pressure to be ready had only heightened.

Then a figurative bombshell had been dropped on the squadron. The Black Aces were selected to be the first Tomcat squadron to undergo extensive upgrades to their aging aircraft. Upgrades are great — but not when you are rushing to get all your training done and to get the airplanes in top shape to go on cruise. There was enough to do without upgrades. "I was very mad about it, and so was Bru," said Aucoin. "We complained, but [their parent, Airwing 8] said, 'Hey, you guys can handle this.'" Subsequently, the air wing realized what a massive job the upgrades forced on the squadron and later began hiring contractors to do it for other squadrons going through the upgrades. But at the time, the Black Aces were the test case and had to do it themselves. "It was miserable," said Joey.

All eleven of the squadron's Tomcats had to undergo the following extensive modifications: Flight control systems on each had to be changed from analog to digital, a massive project that promised to give pilots quicker and more-precise stick-and-rudder response. Cockpits had to be adapted for night-vision goggle use; chaff systems, used to decoy missiles, had to be revamped and new decoy-dissemination apparatus installed; and a night targeting system called LANTIRN (Low Altitude Navigating and Targeting Infrared for Night) had to be added, which meant changes inside and outside the cockpit. LANTIRN was a must for precision laser bombing; the same that provided TV viewers with those sensational videos of pinpoint guided bombs zipping into grainy, waiting buildings and traveling vehicles. They were grainy and seemingly in slow motion because of the great distance of the lens from the target.

In some cases, the modifications took months. And all of them took much-needed manpower. As it was, the squadron, because of the downsizing in the 1990s, was greatly undermanned.

"We were staffed for nine airplanes, not fourteen," recalled Brurud. "We had a 50 percent deficit from the get-go. It meant that everybody had to work twice as hard and twice as long."

The extra work played havoc with training and qualification flights. The aircrews had little, if any, time for training, and when they managed to squeeze some out, there weren't any planes. An aircrew needing a mandatory hop in bombing proficiency in order to progress to the next mandatory level could not do so in an airplane that was gutted and in the midst of one of the modifications. And once all the modifications were completed, they had to be tested, usually in flight, and then debugged, if need be, which could take another month or two.

Time was running out. Time became an enemy.

As departure for cruise grew closer, Aucoin and his staff instituted double and triple work shifts, twenty-four hours a day, seven days a week. Aucoin required that officers as well as enlisted men pitch in and work overtime. This involved a tremendous sacrifice in time and effort not only by all squadron members but also by their families. The squadron, after all, was working so hard because it was about to go out to sea for six months. The time they had left was the last that each would be able to see his or her family. Now that too had been taken away.

"These people were dealing with all kinds of problems," said Brurud, "some getting divorced. Just trying to register their automobiles was a monumental headache."

What Aucoin got from his personnel was a major sacrifice and could not have been possible had not Aucoin and his recruited team instilled a new esprit de corps. It wasn't phony. They all expected real combat along with their training when they got out on cruise. They didn't know where — probably over Iraq. Navy carriers had been bombing Iraq increasingly in recent deployments. Saddam Hussein, the Iraqi dictator, had violated treaties signed when his country was defeated in the Gulf War. He'd been shooting at U.S. planes charged with enforcing no-fly zones.

Kosovo had been heating up, too.

They knew their lives depended on how well they did their jobs.

About six months into the reclamation, they saw the first tangible results.

"We came together as a team in Fallon [Nevada]," recalled Elkins. Fallon was the site of the navy's chief air-wing training base. With thousands of square miles in and above the uninhabited Nevada desert to practice in, the navy brought its air wings there to fly on simulated strikes, drop bombs, and hone their skills as carrier air arms.

"Even before Fallon," said Elkins, "I think people began to realize, 'Hey, this is a new regime here, and, no kidding, we're not gonna stick around and do our work just because we have to. We need to produce airplanes, good airplanes, because once we're done, we're going to have fun.' . . . Everybody started going in the same direction. . . . And then Fallon marked the first time we didn't have to fly any of [VF-14's] airplanes. That was one huge step."

The best proof, however, of the maintenance turnaround, he said, was that when the squadron left the four-week Fallon training session, all nine Tomcats they'd brought there left with them. "Every one of them taxied and launched at the same time. . . . People started to look at us, 'Holy shit, Forty-one flew all their airplanes away! What's going on?' "

Prior, he said, the squadron would have left a bunch that couldn't fly.

Even so, because of the mandatory upgrades, some of which had to be performed at facilities away from their squadron headquarters at

NAS (Naval Air Station) Oceana, Virginia, six of the squadron's eleven Tomcats going on cruise had only been delivered back to Oceana sixty days before the Aces had sailed. It wasn't enough time to do everything needed. The last modified jet had actually been returned, unpainted, a day before the *Roosevelt* had left Norfolk—March 23, 1999. Just one day before! Luckily, the squadron had had a week of no flying as they'd sped across the Atlantic. The carrier, by then on emergency orders to proceed as fast as possible because of the Kosovo situation, didn't want to slow down to turn into the wind for launching as it would have on a more leisurely trip. Airplanes need the lift that launching into the wind provides. The respite had given maintenance enough time to do essentials. But they were still behind. All checks and training hadn't been completed. They didn't even have manuals for some of the new modifications. Would major problems arise as they readied for combat? Or worse, when they were *in* combat?

The possibility worried Aucoin. A poor performance could ruin his career, but that wasn't his main concern. He'd like to be a CAG (air-wing commander) someday (the acronym derives from the earlier term *carrier airgroup commander*), such as he was serving under now. But his main concern was performing, getting the job done, and keeping his men safe. The admiral and the CAG had picked him to lead the first strike because he was the senior qualified strike leader in the air wing. He was honored and grateful for the chance. But there was nothing more he could do now except lead, drawing on the years of experience and accomplishment that had gotten him here. They would be launching the next evening. You went with what you had. That was the job.

"My strength was my ready room. I had a lot of talent in the senior pilots and RIOs," he said, referring to Dog, Bru, Wog, Loose, and the other O4s (the numerical designation for lieutenant commander Aces, often used instead of saying the actual rank). "They can teach the young guys."

The squadron's new pilots and RIOs, six nuggets in all and a few JOs, were his main personnel worry.

"There are some guys. . . . A skipper, after awhile, you sort of know. . . . Our job is inherently dangerous, landing on aircraft carriers. Landing at night is pretty close to combat. Pretty dangerous. There are some guys that you can tell don't like that, shy away from it. That's one indicator, and I already knew there were [a few like that]."

All these things were part of the squadron's history as Aucoin waited for his meeting to start.

Approximately thirty-five officers were now crowded into the cavernous, carrier-gray room. The meeting was a preliminary to the upcoming larger strike briefing that would be attended by crews from all the squadrons, fighter and not, in the air wing. This was only for the Aces. Unfortunately, Aucoin's executive officer wasn't there. Dog had left the carrier as it had started across the Atlantic, sent by the CAG to liaison with the various participants in the newly declared war—Sixth Fleet, the carrier's immediate superior, and the U.S. Air Force, which was basically running the war, code-named "Operation Allied Force," for NATO under Gen. Wesley K. Clark of the U.S. Army. These higher commands had compounds around the Mediterranean, including a headquarters called Combined Air Operations Center (CAOC) at Vicenza, Italy. The mission given to Dog, along with several other key officers from the air wing, was to learn what he could to help the carrier operate more efficiently, which he was doing. But he was worried—and with good reason—that he'd miss the carrier's first strike, which was launching the next evening.

"One of the handicaps I had was that the XO was at the CAOC and had missed the whole 'translant' [trans-Atlantic trip]," said Aucoin, "all the planning and speeches. . . . He kept calling me: 'Joey, you gotta get me back.' I said, 'I'm trying, I'm trying.'" The problem was, first, the carrier needed the information. The air war had started nearly two weeks before, and the air force and other allies had picked up tricks about how to operate in the war. Second, transportation, even if Joey could get the okay to bring him back, wasn't available immediately.

It looked bad for Dog. Aucoin was going to have to proceed without him.

It was a hushed, mostly wide-eyed group that looked back expectantly as their skipper began the meeting. Aucoin posed a question: what was it, did they think, that was going to keep them alive in combat during the next days and weeks?

"I got the usual responses—flag, family, patriotism. I've been shot at before, and I can tell you there are a lot of factors. But if you look at the literature, if you, for instance, read *All Quiet on the Western*

Front. . . . The family's there, of course. They're going to be on your mind. But when you get shot at and the screaming starts, your brain shrinks to the size of a pea. And what it is, is the guy sitting next to you, or your wingman over there. That is all you can keep focus on. That's all that is going to save you. . . . If you're not clear on it now, if you can't do what you've been trained to do, you're not going to get through."

There was the sobering possibility, he indicated, that some of them might not come back.

A lot of what Aucoin was saying to the Aces he'd heard himself from a commanding officer he'd greatly admired, Dave Frost, a revered Vietnam-era fighter pilot who went on to become an admiral. Frost had spoken to Aucoin's squadron shortly before they'd flown into Desert Storm. "It had helped. It helped a lot. He told us what had happened to him." Aucoin did the same. He told the Aces about his own fear over Iraq. "Just the amount of ordnance, hearing the shrill on the radios. . . . It's okay to be scared. . . . But you can't let it overtake you. . . . You can still function in those environments. You just have to compartmentalize. . . . Keep your mind on what you've been taught and what you've got to do."

Aucoin told them not to transmit fear over the radios. Showing fear could cause others to lose nerve. He told the "ground pounders," or nonflying officers, that from now on he didn't want aviators doing any paperwork. They must be free to concentrate on their jobs in the cockpit. He discussed the rules in the air, how important it was to determine that your target was, in fact, an enemy, and not a friendly, and that only strike leaders would make the crucial decisions. He outlined the kinds of systems failures that would warrant turning back, which basically were not many. Strike leaders would make that call as well, unless the pilot had no choice but to leave.

As he talked, Aucoin noticed the predominance of "puppy eyes" and "tenseness" in the room. They were listening with more attention than he'd seen in some time. "I didn't have to tell them to be quiet in the back of the room." The joking they usually had in such meetings was absent. Brurud remembers, "There were those with that look like, 'Come on, let's go do it. I've waited all my life.' And others who were in a little bit of disbelief like, 'I can't believe this is actually happening. We're actually going to go and bomb another country.' "

The meeting lasted over an hour. Aucoin wanted as much give-and-take as possible. "They needed to talk it out." Then he ended it with an invitation: "I told them, 'If you feel too scared . . . whether it's family, or spiritual, or you don't believe in the war, or something else is holding you back . . . if there is something I'm asking you to do that is above and beyond the call, please . . . you need to let me know. . . . Of course, nobody is going to raise their hands in a group. But you need to come see me, and we can work it out. We can always juggle the schedule. . . .' "

He left it at that. No pressure. No backlash. Come see him later in his stateroom. He didn't want any men opting out when lives depended on them. He'd take care of it, with no questions asked. And he understood. "It was a big thing they were about to do," he later recalled. Many of them were married and had children. He himself, a perennial bachelor most of his life, had his own concerns with his new family. Going into Desert Storm, he said, "I wasn't married. I didn't even have a girlfriend. I mean, I jumped in the airplane like, 'Yee Haw!' But this time. This time was different. I had a wife and a little boy. . . . It does put an extra stress in your life."

Three

Lt. Kurt Rhinehimer was one of the Aces' newly arrived nugget RIOs. The skipper's speech had made him nervous. The night of the meeting, he wrote in a journal he had decided to keep for his wife:

```
Yes, I'm scared. I think everyone is. This is a lot dif-
ferent than Iraq. In Iraq, the terrain is very flat with
nowhere [for the enemy] to hide. . . . In the FRY [former
Republic of Yugoslavia], SAMs [Surface to Air Missiles]
are everywhere. They [the Serbs] are a lot better and
smarter. I've trained for this for the past 3½ years
but I never really thought I'd be shot at.
```

The Naval Academy graduate had only been married for fourteen days when the *Roosevelt* left Norfolk, and he clearly was missing his new bride:

```
I look at our wedding pictures [taken] less than three
weeks ago. Who would have imagined that I'd be in combat
now? I think the biggest thing I'm scared of is not being
there for you in the future and not having kids. I think
it's better that we don't. I would hope that if anything
```

should ever happen to me that you would remarry if that's
what would make you happy.

But "Rhino," as his new squadron mates had christened him, wasn't
scheduled to fly on the first strike. The decision had been made that
the "A-Team," mostly senior, experienced officers and a few second-
cruise JOs, would fly in the first waves. Once the squadron leadership
knew what they were up against, had a handle on the combat, and felt
it appropriate, they would begin to schedule missions for the less experienced. Although Rhino was thought to be one of the top student
backseaters from his newly concluded F-14 training class, Aucoin and
Wog, who, as Ops O, made up the actual flight schedules, knew they
wouldn't be sending him into combat soon.

That wasn't the case with senior Lieutenant James Greg DeGruccio,
a thirty-one-year-old second-cruise JO who'd come to the Aces after a
year with the VF-213 Black Lions. "Gooch," as he was call-signed in
the squadron, had serious hours in the Tomcat for a JO, and was
scheduled to be one of the bombers in the first night strikes—only he
didn't know it.

As DeGruccio tells it, right after the AOM, Joey, his skipper, came
up to him in the ready room and said something like, " 'Hey, how are
you doing? Are you okay,' " to which Gooch replied: " 'I'm a little
anxious," but added that it was " 'No big deal,' " alluding to the decision to use only the most experienced men. " 'I'm probably not going
for the first couple of days.' " But Aucoin, he said, surprised him.
" 'No,' " he says the skipper told him. " 'You're going tomorrow.' "

In Aucoin's memory, Gooch came to see him in his stateroom later
in response to Aucoin's ready-room invitation. But both men say their
memories of what happened could be muddled. In any case, Gooch,
too, was worried. Joey "probably saw it on my face," he said. "My dad
[an air force pilot] was in Vietnam. . . . He lost a lot of friends there.
In the Gulf War . . . a number of people didn't come back. I look
around the ready room, and people . . . were not taking it as seriously
as they should. Maybe I was taking it too seriously. But I just wanted
to make sure that my house was in order and that I knew what I was
getting into."

Gooch, one of the more skilled pilots in the squadron, was on the
bubble. Stick-and-rudder abilities are important in a fighter pilot. And

he had them. He was also a student of tactics, procedures, and Tomcat systems, and prided himself on knowing the book on each, frequently arguing even the smallest points when challenged. As a maintenance division head, he was in charge, under Bru, of monitoring the recent switch to digital flight controls—an important position given the potential for problems there. But warrior spirit, the propensity to jump in a fight and lead it if need be, to move in harm's way even without an order, was traditionally the highest measure of a fighter pilot's élan. And it was Gooch's warrior spirit that was in question.

Gooch remembers replying to Aucoin's ready-room query thus: " 'Hey, I'm on board for the big win. Whatever you guys need from me, I'm there for you.' " But Aucoin says, "There was a certain hesitation on his part . . . enough instances that shaped my opinion that he was not really for this. . . . I don't know if I can accurately paint those instances . . . but there wasn't an eagerness to do this. [Gooch said,] 'If you need me, okay,' but I certainly sensed that he did not want to go."

The problem was that they didn't have anybody else. The carrier had two strikes scheduled for the following night. The Black Aces, one of eight squadrons of various types on the boat, had a prominent part in both, providing two of the many strike bombers, per strike, and several fighters per strike as protection for both packages. With Dog gone, Wog had run out of the seniors and JOs he'd marked as first team, and had scheduled Gooch as his own wingman/bomber because, in terms of JO seniority, he was next in line. "He had all the x's and o's checked . . . but is he going to perform when the chips are down? . . . I wasn't fully confident of that," said Wog. But, "We didn't really have another choice at that point."

So Gooch and his scheduled backseater, Lt. Doug "Thing" Thien, who was also his roommate and good friend, started preparing for their mission.

Lt. Jim "Dog" Bauser was in danger of getting shot down, becoming an international incident as a prisoner, or, worse, dying. It was spring 1987, in the dead of night, and he was high above a hostile country he won't name on a secret mission in an F-14 with a MiG closing on his tail and deadly fire in one engine. If he couldn't extinguish the fire, his Tomcat would blow up. If he didn't get to the ocean soon, he and his backseater, another young lieutenant, named Skippy Moore, would probably be shot down and paraded, injured or even dead, through the country's streets. And below them were antiaircraft batteries whose range he didn't want to fall into. But with the fire they were battling, that was a distinct possibility.

"I wouldn't call it scary because I don't really go, 'Ooooo, I'm afraid,' or anything like that," he recalled, talking about the compartmentalization he reverted to in such a volatile situation. "It's like I've got business to do. This has happened. Now how do you deal with it?"

The mission had started out as a routine night hop from a carrier somewhere in the Mediterranean. Then, to the surprise of Dog and Moore, the air-wing commander, or CAG, on whom they were flying wing, disclosed that they were going to divert for a little covert reconnaissance. The two young lieutenants were happy for the adventure. Flying at twenty-seven thousand feet, the two-ship was close to completing the mission when the enemy MiG was electronically spotted twenty miles on their nose dead ahead.

Uh oh, they'd been detected.

The Tomcats weren't looking to fight, which would have caused an international incident or worse, and wheeled 180 degrees to backtrack. The chase was on. Their pursuer (or pursuers), which they knew was at least one speedy MiG-23 Flogger, was getting closer to its missile-firing envelopes. They had to get away fast. It was then that Bauser and Moore got indications of the fire.

All they saw in the nightglow was smoke, but their instruments screamed danger. The problem was in the right engine, which meant they didn't have time to wait to see flames. An engine fire is a major emergency. And what they didn't know at the time was that the heat source—escaping engine air, hot enough to melt metal—was adjacent to a volatile fuel cell. "If you don't act fast, you'll lose the airplane," said Dog. He was already instituting memorized procedures to determine the problem's severity. "Throttle the affected engine idle . . . [f] fire [indicator] still on . . . shut fuel off . . . throttle affected engine . . . hit fire-extinguish button. . . ."

Now they were in real trouble.

Shutting down the engine had stopped the fire, but now they were unable to generate significant escape speed. "People think you can go half as fast with one engine," said Dog. "But engines are exponential." With one engine gone, the Tomcat, which normally can reach Mach 2 (approximately fifteen-hundred miles per hour at sea level, which is very fast for a fighter), can only generate about a quarter of that.

They were down to under four hundred knots and had lost maneuverability as well. They might have been able to get more speed by using their remaining afterburner, but such a burst of fire in the night would have given the MiG's heat-seeking missiles a perfect target. And the chasing MiG was now only twelve miles behind, having gained significantly on them when they made their turn. The plan was to reach the coast, where they didn't think the MiG would follow since its country's pilots didn't usually pursue over water.

But the coast was still thirty miles away.

The CAG gave them lead and became protector. But the route to the beach was over enemy antiaircraft batteries and surface-to-air missiles that could reach thirteen thousand feet. "So I don't want to go below that because I don't have the maneuverability to dodge a small MANPAD or SA-7 [shoulder-fired surface-to-air missile, also called a Stinger]," said Dog. "Maybe I could get away from one, but if they launch a bunch at me, I'm a sitting duck."

They were at approximately twenty-four thousand feet now, having lost altitude in their turn. Descending was good. Gravity would help them maintain the most speed. But they had to stay above the thirteen-thousand-foot floor, which would demand good piloting. At the speed they were going, approximately 375 to 400 knots, they figured they had three-to-four minutes' more flight time before they reached the beach. He and Moore calculated a rate of descent of approximately three thousand feet per minute.

Dog: "So I'm trying hard to fly a good airplane . . . to execute this descending out of there. . . . I don't want to screw it all away and suddenly be at ten thousand feet over this city and getting pelted. . . . And at the same time I'm checking around back at my six, looking for a missile firing. . . . It gets very quiet. . . . Who knows what this guy's going to do. He's just back there gaining on me, and he's getting up to where he can fire his missiles. . . . All of sudden, my RIO, who's also looking out back, pipes up, 'Hey Dog.' 'Yeah, Skippy?' 'This sucks. Let's do something else.' "

They broke up laughing ("like we really had an option")—and just as well, because they made it to the beach where the MiG, as they'd figured it would, turned back east.

So far so good.

But they weren't safe yet.

Now they had to make a night carrier landing—which medical tests during the Vietnam War showed can be more stressful than dodging SAMs or dogfighting—and they were going to have to do it with one engine gone.

Naval literature is full of allusions to demons and snakes inhabiting the night-landing cockpit. Because depth perception can be totally lost, the margin for error so slim, and violent death just a millisecond or hair-fine movement of the controls away, night carrier landing has been called one of the most harrowing and difficult coordination skills in the world.

Getting it right—meaning, basically, snagging a certain deck wire with a hook dangling from your aircraft—requires literally that a pilot put his head in an imaginary box, two-foot-by-two-foot, above the deck. If he does that, his plane will come to a jarring halt, and he will have survived what is actually a controlled crash onto the metal landing surface, which, at sea, is often pitching, sometimes sideways, sometimes up, sometimes both.

Without depth perception, which is often impossible in a black, starless night, or one whipped and churned by bad weather, vertigo—the sense that up is down and down is up—can mix with other illusions and cockpit demons to test any pilot's ability to carefully control speed, altitude, descent, and position with the precision and even delicacy that it takes literally to thread the eye of a needle. There *are* faint lights on the deck. But they are no more grounding on a dark night than distant pinholes in a faraway galaxy. Indeed, the experience has been described in terms of "hurtling into a black hole," "taking a turn in the barrel," "the night thing," and other images of claustrophobic terror.

In a more down-to-earth explanation, *Air&Space* magazine (May 1995) offered:

Imagine that you're in a car without headlights going 150 miles an hour down a narrow, dark road toward a one-car garage illuminated by a single light bulb. If you get

```
through the garage door, your car will stop automati-
cally. And the garage is moving around. That's what the
night landing is like.
```

But Dog and Moore were probably elated at having escaped a missile in the back, and, with some eighty-to-one-hundred miles to go before they'd reach the ship, they were beginning to deal with a new problem—fuel migration.

"The F-14 has a very complicated fuel system," said Dog. "Eight fuel cells in the airplane. You have them in the wings, externals, bladders inside, feed groups. Operating on a single engine, you're going to have a balance problem sooner or later. . . . So I was balancing our fuel from left systems to right systems, back and forth, pressurizing things and going through other procedures to keep [the fuel] from migrating."

It was a clear night, so the darkness wasn't such that he would be totally without perception. "No question it was going to be a challenge." But what he was worried about most was boltering—being waved off on his first pass and having to power forward and up for another. "Your wave off capability, it's not like you come to full power on both motors and fly off pretty as can be with a single engine." Without enough power, the plane might not generate enough lift, and as a result it might go into the water—a situation that is usually fatal. Threading the needle would be hard enough. Any last-moment realignments or corrections would take additional skill and precision because he'd have to compensate for the imbalance.

As they sped toward the carrier, he tested "the controllability of the airplane. What kind of corrections could I make? What was the throttle response? . . . What I should attempt to do and what I should not attempt to do. When will I get so far out of parameters that I can't land?"

What he found was that when he added power, the plane yawed to the right. And when he cut power, it came back to the left. "It also had a roll tendency . . . which increased the upward lift vector. . . . So I'm working to keep the power up . . . and constant as much as possible. . . . But it's something you train to. It's not like no one has never done this before. It's a big-time varsity thing, but you should be expected to pull it off."

From three miles in, they made their final turn, and he stopped checking things and started "flying that airplane to the best of my ability, to keep it on a glide path. . . . We have a [landing aid] like a commercial plane. A thing comes up on a display. It's sort of like crosshairs, and there's a little symbol for an airplane. And I've got to keep the plane on glide path, which is the rate of descent that will take me right into the carrier. . . . I've got to keep it on course. . . . I'm working very hard with the rudder-and-stick input to fight the airplane and keep it coming down [on the exact glide path]. I do not want to get very far out of parameters because I don't have the performance to bring it back in. I want to keep it as much as I can nice and true and everything and keep an approach to a good landing."

And when it came to that precise millisecond when he had to drop without mishap, put the big fifty-four-thousand-pound bird, as it were, almost on a matchbox, he did it. Nothing went wrong. He hooked a good wire on his first attempt. They were wrenched to a sudden halt with carrier deck in their wheels. No bolter. No accident. Whew! Drenched in flop sweat, he had brought it aboard.

But that was twelve years before and another aviator's life. No longer was he a young JO, loose and proud of such a commendable achievement. He was second in command, XO, of the Black Aces, a fighter squadron about to be launched into war. And since he happened to be stuck at Sigonella, Sicily, an Italian-owned base with a U.S. Navy air station on it, he was just trying hard to get a ride back to the *Roosevelt* so he could take his rightful place in the air wing's first strike.

Sigonella, at a historic crossroads near the boot of Italy, is a major Mediterranean base for U.S. and NATO military operations. But transportation to and from it depended on what was available. With the war going on, there wasn't too much. Bauser had actually been en route to the *Roosevelt* on a Sigonella helicopter, but it had developed mechanical problems and returned to base.

"It was getting close," he remembered. "I was getting ready to swim out to the ship. . . . We'd taken commercial air and rental cars to get to Sigonella, but then the helicopter went down. It was very frustrating."

He spent a day and a half there starting and stopping. Finally, he caught a COD, or carrier onboard delivery plane, that got him to the *Roosevelt* around noon on the day, April 6, that the night strike was to launch. But he still had a major hurdle before he could go on the strike. Regulations insist that a pilot who has not landed on a carrier in a week must do so to requalify. This was why his skipper, Joey, and Wog, the Ops O, had decided that even if Dog made it back, he probably wouldn't be able to go on the strike.

But Dog was having none of it.

"He came running in," remembers Wog. "The crews had already walked," meaning they'd already gone up on deck to man the day's flights. "He said, 'What do I have to do? I'm going tonight.' I said, 'CAG and Joey said you're not.' He said, 'Bullshit, put me in the air, I'm going.' "

Wog scratched Lt. Ken "Razor" Shick from a training flight with nugget "Rhino" Rineheimer in the backseat and penciled in Dog, who was already changing into his flight gear. In another move, he scratched "Gooch" DeGruccio from Tomcat 103 and moved his assistant operations officer, Lt. Comdr. Dave "Beaker" Lobdell, who had been scheduled to fly with him that night, into DeGruccio's seat and penciled Dog into Lobdell's. He knew that the XO would make his "qual" and that he and Dog would be flying together as lead plane on the second wave.

The 1999 Aces' first war strike was taking shape.

Four

USS *Roosevelt*, First Strike Imminent

On the night before the Black Aces went into combat, Lt. Brian "Meat" Fleisher, a second-cruise JO pilot who wouldn't be going in on the first strikes, wrote his wife, Laura:

> Everyone is pretty pumped up. I don't think anyone knows really how we are supposed to feel. The majority of us have never been in combat. I am sure that everyone has some apprehension. I know that I do. Some minutes I am really excited and think that it will be one of the most exciting things that I will ever do. At others I am really pretty scared. I might not make it back.

A week and a half prior, the Serbs had shot down with a SAM an air force F-117 Stealth fighter-bomber, thought to be the hardest combat aircraft in the U.S. inventory to hit. Fleisher, whose last name in German meant "meat"—hence his call sign—told his wife how he'd taped the zippers and hooks on his flight suit to make them "sound proof in case I find myself on the ground trying to evade," and how he'd stocked the suit's compartments with extra "water and camouflage stuff, just in case." He continued:

I have also been reading up on the threat. The Serbs present the hardest surface-to-air threat [Triple-A, SAMs], that we will face, much tougher than Iraq's. They are all Soviet trained and they have been watching us operate next door [in Bosnia] for the last several years so they know our tactics. . . . If a Stealth can get bagged, then so could I. . . . I have been seeing on CNN the last couple of days what the Serbs have been doing to those people over there. It really is unbelievable. We have to do something. No one else is going to . . . I know what we are doing is right. . . .

Lt. Clay "Squab" Williams, a second-cruise JO RIO who *would* be flying the first night, wrote his family:

There is an unpleasant topic that must be addressed. That is the unlikely event that I get shot down and become a prisoner of war. . . . Unfortunately [that] is a real possibility. . . . We do what we can to minimize the risks but. . . . Should that occur, what I require from all of you is that you say nothing.

I will explain. I have seen a newspaper article from sometime during the Gulf War with a headline that read, 'Military not releasing information on POWs' or something to that effect. Well there is a reason for [silence]. The article went on to detail aspects of one particular POW to include full name, hometown, wife's name, names of children and ages. . . . It concluded with a brief biography of his military career prior to getting shot down.

This is all bad. First, any—ANY—information that goes out to the media, whether it be newspaper, television, radio, world-wide web, or whatever, is immediately available to any captor nation via internet if not seen directly on CNN or some other news show. On the civilian side, anyone with ill will knows that this pilot's wife and children are home alone and exactly where that home is with husband/daddy out of the picture for the time be-

ing. On the military side, quite simply I don't want any
potential captor to know anything—ANYTHING—at all regarding me. Any of that information could be used
against me as a lever or to knock me off balance—
'Wouldn't you like to go home to Lisa and Taylor? Then
just tell me about whatever, and we'll get you home to
your little girl.'

Do you get the point? I cannot overemphasize the importance of this. There is simply no up side to talking
to the media. If the urge to get on TV is compelling,
then squash that urge. Understand that I will be wanting
to come home as much as you want me to come home but that
any tearful plea to my captors on CNN will most likely
not help. . . . Lisa [if this does happen] I imagine that
you will be in communications with military personnel
and/or state department types who, hopefully, will be
knowledgeable and will have my best interests at heart.
Be strong. . . .

What Williams *didn't* write home was that he personally knew Desert
Storm prisoners who had been tortured and beaten. "What stands out,"
he later said, "is that some . . . had electrodes put on their jaws, and
when hit with electricity, it would make them clench their jaw so
much that it would shatter teeth."

Letters like Williams's were typical of the mindsets of the squadron's
aviators on the eve of battle. Most, if not all, were apprehensive, some
more than others. A few were looking forward to the test, a kind of
final exam on what they had been practicing for so long and on their
own worthiness. Most found justification for going to war in the reports
of Serb murders and atrocities, although such justification was not
something they dwelled on, for there were "gray areas," said Skipper
Aucoin. Mostly, going to war was viewed by them as their job, what
they had been trained for and were duty bound to do. And to do it,
some of them were already hardening their attitudes, compartmental-
izing for the tough work ahead. For the veterans and those on the A-
Team especially, a get-your-house-in-order, let's-get-on-with-it mentality
was taking shape.

Still, for some, especially the younger aviators, the realization of what they were about to do didn't fully register until the strongbox in the ready room was, for the first time in the cruise, unlocked and they were handed, in exchange for their signature, a nine-millimeter Sig-Sauer pistol, two clips of live ammunition, encrypted codes for the RIOs who handled communications in the cockpit, and a "blood chit" for use as a last-ditch measure in case they were shot down and had no other bargaining chip with which to escape or survive.

The chit was a handkerchief-sized piece of paper made of durable material with an American flag depiction and a message in eight different languages, some of which were spoken in the Balkan region over which the air wing would be flying. The message said in essence that the bearer was an American and that if the recipient would help him either to escape or to get medical attention or both, he would be amply rewarded with gold or American currency. Lots of it. His choice. The chit would be ripped in half, and once the flyer was safe, all the bearer would have to do was appear with his half at an American installation, be it military or diplomatic.

It was the first time some of the younger Aces had ever seen the chits.

An earnest somberness was palpable on April 6 as the aviators rose late, just hours before the near-midnight first launch. Most of them had only gotten a few hours' sleep following nonstop planning in the hours before. They took the somberness with them as they left their staterooms, small and cramped as most of them were, and moved hastily, green flight suits stripped of identifying patches and scripts, through the crowded passageways to the rooms and other areas where most of the final preparations were being conducted.

Air combat "is intensely personal," notes Rear Adm. W. Winston Copeland, Jr., a Vietnam veteran and commander of the *Roosevelt* battle group at that time, which included the air wing and the carrier's attendant ships and submarines. "People react quite differently. Some get physically ill, some get irascible. Some become completely withdrawn. You don't communicate very well in that environment. You're getting ready to fly a mission that you might not come home from, and oftentimes all you hear is the sound of zippers, the boots on the deck. . . . It's tough to write those letters to be delivered *only* if you don't come back. . . . It's pretty personal."

But all around them, intruding on the stoic solemnity, the carrier was a cacophony of battle preparation—intermittent announcements over the public-address system, sailors and officers hurrying in the passageways, plus the mostly muffled, sometimes deafening, roars, bangs, and rumblings of the carrier's massive inner workings and open-air topside flight operations. The *Roosevelt*'s Airwing 8 included eight squadrons of six types of warplanes, some seventy aircraft in all, some of them secured or cautiously being moved or armed on its 1,092-foot-long top deck, others being worked on in the immense three-football-field-sized hangars below. Almost every squadron would have at least one plane, if not more, in the air after the first launch that evening.

In addition to VF-41, the air wing included the other F-14 squadron, the VF-14 "Tophatters," the Aces' so-called sister squadron. The name was now a bit of a misnomer because of the recent history of 41's embarrassment at having to use 14's airplanes on the previous cruise. Because of that situation, the two were more like rivals. The Tophatters were the oldest fighter squadron in the navy, having been formed in 1919. They too were flying the vintage A-model Tomcats. There were two F/A-18 Hornet squadrons, the VFA-15 Valions and the VFA-87 Golden Warriors. The Hornets were single-seat fighter-bombers, the navy's newest warplanes. They did not have the range of the F-14, or as strong a precision-bombing capability. But they had been designed for strike fighting as well as dogfighting and were nimbler and easier to service and, along with the Tomcats, would provide fighters and strikers in the bombing packages.

Important too was the lone EA-6B Prowler squadron, the VAQ-141 Shadowhawks, whose five-man, antenna-nosed jets would provide electronic countermeasures on the strikes against the enemy's antiaircraft radar and SAM guidance systems. Gone were the days of just spotting the enemy from on high and peeling off for a bomb run. Modern air war is an electronic video game of deadly proportions played in an arena of significant distances. It is waged with far-seeing radar, scopes with crucial, blinking data, pinpoint lasers, and supersonic guided missiles. But the bad guys aren't just virtual cartoons. They shoot back! And with deadly precision. Without the Prowlers, variations of the planes made famous in books like Stephen Coonts's *Flight of the Intruder* (the Prowler's first incarnation) and Sherman Baldwin's *Ironclaw,* the strikers, closest to the enemy's return fire, would have to rely on their own devices—awareness, aircraft maneuverability, and minimal electronic foils and warnings—which, when the battle heightens and goes "Star Wars," sometimes are not enough. It only takes a single undetected or undefended speeding missile to kill a U.S. pilot or aircrew. The Shadowhawks, named for an American Indian warrior reputed to have used magic against his enemies, jammed those missiles or shot their controllers. They, and the nonbombing fighters looking for enemy planes, were the striker's protectors.

Rounding out the air wing were a squadron of E2-C Hawkeye turbopropped planes and the VAW-124 Bear Aces, whose twin-engine aircraft had monster disks protruding from their backs. The distinctive disks housed part of the radar and scanning equipment that enabled the Hawkeyes to provide early warning of approaching enemy planes and to direct overall operations of the carrier's aircraft in hostile skies. A squadron of Seahawk helicopters, the HS-3 Tridents, provided sea-and-land rescue and antisubmarine capacity. The Seahawks were comforting to aviators, who knew that if they crashed into the ocean, where chances of survival from a heavy, fast-sinking jet and from often cold, churning waters are slim, they'd have the possibility of a quick rescue from the sky. Two more units, the VS-24 Scouts, and the VRC-40 Rawhides, provided reconnaissance and delivery to the ship. In addition, the Scouts, a squadron flying jet-powered S-3b Vikings, were the ship's inflight refuelers, a critical mission for fighters and bombers that gulped gas launching and were usually low on fuel returning to the carrier.

Airwing 8 was the carrier's air arm—a massive set of warplanes for almost any mission. Commanded by Capt. Dale "Sparky" Lyle, the CAG, it was the source of the carrier's power.

Approximately three hours before the first plane launched, the air wing held its mass briefing, a gathering of all the strike elements that had been meeting independently. Commander Aucoin, as the strike leader, conducted the briefing. It was in CVIC, the carrier's intelligence center (CV standing for carrier), which also had the largest briefing room on the ship. Bru remembers, "It was like one of those classic war briefs in the World War II movies." Rows of aviators filled the seats, nervous laughter breaking the tenseness until the brief began. Among those in front were Captain Lyle, a soft-spoken, thoughtful 1976 Auburn University graduate who had made his mark in attack aviation flying mostly Hornets, and Admiral Copeland, a plain-talking, unflappable fighter pilot who had the distinction of being a MiG-killer, a rare breed in 1999. That alone would have won him respect, for few modern pilots, no matter how good, ever get a chance to prove it in air-to-air combat.

Copeland had bagged a MiG-17 in 1972 toward the end of the Vietnam War. He didn't talk about it. In fact, it wasn't even in his official biography. But what everyone in his command did know was that his call sign was "Mad Dog," a moniker the press usually delighted in because of its implied ferocity. The truth was, however, that he hadn't gotten it for any meanness. Rather, he'd earned the name because, as a flight student, he'd mistakenly been cleared to practice maneuvers in a training jet as a significant storm approached. In the midst of the darkening fury, the mistake had been realized and Copeland had been recalled. "When I landed, all my classmates were waiting for me. They said, 'You're a mad dog.' I said, 'No, no, don't call me that. I didn't know [the storm] was coming.' They said, 'Nope.' "

He was a commander who gave his subordinates, including the CAG and VF-41 skipper Joey Aucoin, the freedom to carry out orders in the way they saw fit—as long as they kept him informed of what he ultimately would be held responsible for.

CVIC was packed, and Commander Aucoin was nervous. "I felt so grateful that I'd been picked to lead [in competition with some of the other CO strike leaders]," he recalled, "but everybody is looking at me"—the CAG, the admiral, the battle staff, everybody going on the strike. "They were packed in like sardines, and it was hot. I thought, 'Oh, God. . . .' But it went pretty well." Since the day prior, most of the strikers had attended their own smaller briefings. "They know a lot about [the strike] already. This was just to set the tone . . . to reassure the CAG and the admiral that I had my shit together."

He went right to the basics: It was to be a classic "Fallon-type" strike—Fallon being the big base in northern Nevada where 41's maintenance division had come together and done so well and where the navy taught bombing. They had all been to "Strike U" 's vast mountain and desert ranges practicing raids like this, although never in so large a force. This one would include over twenty airplanes and go right into the heart of a real enemy territory—Kosovo. Pristina was the province's largest city, a Serbian jewel, its history steeped in centuries of conflict. It had been the Serbian capital until the Balkan Christian armies were defeated by the Turks in 1389. The city was flanked by seven-to-ten-thousand-foot mountain ranges, farm lands, and dense forest, as was so much of Kosovo. The mountain ranges would present a constant hazard and obstacle. Pilots had to be quick to maneuver around them, and the lasers their planes used to guide smart bombs needed an unobscured, straight-on path to the target.

Ten miles north of Pristina was one of the region's largest oil refineries and fuel depots. To its east was an ammunition-storage facility. Those were their targets. The first wave, launching in the early evening, would hit the refinery. The second, launching around midnight, would attack the ammo dump. Large pictures on the CVIC stage showed both complexes. Joey would lead the first wave against the refinery. He remembers vividly the photos of its huge storage tanks and attendant buildings, conveyance pipes, and machinery. He pointed out key aspects for recognition. They would be approaching from the east, over Greece and Macedonia, at nearly thirty thousand feet. The high altitude was an attempt to avoid the enemy's defenses. The pictures would help the aircrews recognize the targets as they sought them on their target-acquisition screens.

Night was their ally. They had the new light-enhancing "cat's eye" night-vision goggles, small, cylindrical, opera-glass-type protuberances that dropped down from the top of their helmets like dark glasses on a baseball player's cap and gave them a buglike, robotic appearance. But they intensified ambient light. Night became day. Impressively so. Their target-finding display screens, like those in the new LANTIRN systems on the Tomcats, used more-sophisticated infrared technology to see up to twenty miles through the darkness and lock on their precision-guided munitions with accuracy that was described as "pinpoint."

He turned to the threats: " 'We're probably going to see some SA-6s tonight,' " he said he told the strikers about the deadliest Soviet-built SAM. " 'They are a very good missile, very maneuverable, very mobile. So you don't know where they are, and they are pretty prolific around Kosovo.' " Mindless killers in relentless pursuit. Intelligence estimated there were as many as sixty SAM sites of various types hidden throughout the province. It was a supersonic SA-6, code-named "Gainful" by NATO, that blew air force Captain Scott O'Grady's F-16 into pieces over Bosnia in 1995. "It was like getting rear-ended by a speeding eighteen-wheeler with an explosive warhead strapped to its hood," O'Grady later wrote in *Return with Honor*. Most of the Serb SAMs were less-agile SA-3s, deadly as well. It was an SA-3 that had downed the F-117 Stealth several weeks before. "I told the guys, 'You need to be looking on the ground for those smoke trails [hat the SAMs make]. That's what is going to kill you.' "

Antiaircraft artillery and MiG fighters were also threats. The "Triple-A," as antiaircraft artillery was euphemistically called, was mostly low-altitude, although there were reports of higher-reaching guns. Staying high and moving fast seemed the best defense. The Serbs had a handful of MiG-29s, two of which had already been shot down in the opening strikes of the war, and a bunch of older MiG-21s. While the MiG-29s were formidable day fighters, the Serbs hadn't been sending them up at night lately and didn't have much practice at night fighting. U.S. fighters also had better radar and air-to-air missiles of much greater range. The MiG-21s were even more poorly equipped. "The first night of the war they were a serious threat," said Joey. "But I told them, 'If you see an enemy plane, you are the luckiest guy in the world, because you'll kill it. Against our missiles, our radars, they don't stand a chance.' "

The problem would be if they didn't see the MiG.

The first wave would have a core of strikers: four Tomcats, two from each F-14 squadron, and two Hornets—six jets in all. Supporting the core strikers above and in front would be protective fighters (Hornets and Tomcats), several Prowlers, an E-2 away from the strike to monitor the skies, and tankers along the route to replenish everyone. Joey, as commander, with Bru piloting, would be in the lead striker, call sign "Fast Eagle One." Loose Cannon, with his roommate and friend, Lt. Cmdr. John "Alvin" Young, pilot, would be in the other core VF-41 Tomcat. The two VF-14 striker Tomcats would be led by Tophatter skipper Comdr. Ted "Slapshot" Carter, a RIO, and Lt. Comdr. Scott "Scooter" Moyer, his pilot and a former Blue Angel. The two Hornets had veterans in them as well. With fighters sweeping in front of them and fighter-protected Prowlers backing them up, the core six would be expected to get through any defenses the Serbs threw up at them and destroy their targets.

Later, the second wave, with a similar makeup, would hit the ammo dump.

Aucoin's plan for both strikes, complicated to a layman because of "so many moving parts" and the precise timing for a host of coordinated actions, was to the veteran strikers simple and direct. "Just go in there and suppress the SAMs," he recalled. "Follow the set routes. Bomb your specific targets. Follow the set routes out."

When he finished, CAG Lyle said a few words, and then the Aces' skipper asked Admiral Copeland if he had anything to add. The admiral rose. Brurud remembers, "He said, 'Gentlemen, you are all well prepared for this. You know exactly what to do. Just go ahead and do it.' He was deliberate and simple. It was very empowering."

Five

After the brief, Joey hurried to the ready room and got the laser codes he would need to guide smart bombs. Many of the bombs the striking jets would drop would be LGBs, or laser-guided bombs. The bombs had code-recognition devices attached to them. The lasers in the jets marked the targets. Once dropped, the LGBs would "look" for the codes and guide to the lasers displaying them. No code, or a wrong code, and the bomb wouldn't guide to the spot the laser was illuminating.

Codes obtained, the skipper "walked," the term carrier aviators use for going up on the flight deck to man their planes. "It was really very quick, and [there was] not much time to think about things." Unlike most going on the strike, he didn't take a pistol. "I said, 'Hey, if I had more room, I'd carry a pair of tennis shoes. If I get shot down, I don't want to be shooting people. I want to go climb a tree or dig a hole and then at night, run away.' . . . In some ways that might haunt me. But if I did get shot down and there's . . . one enemy soldier between me and freedom, I might have a hard time, but I've got my knife. . . . I'm gonna rely on just lying low, using my radio and my GPS [Global Positioning System] unit [which, with the aid of satellites, would tell him and rescuers exactly where he is] just to sneak out because I'm not gonna play gunman at the OK Corral. It's not going to work."

The night deck he emerged upon was a surreal scene of aviation

phantasmagoria—shades of heaven or hell, depending on the per-
ceiver's outlook. It was a clear night. Powerful sodium lights cast eerie il-
lumination on the dark and greasy deck, which was a beehive of shadowy
activity. Sleek and massive warplanes were being armed and fueled and
moved cautiously to stations carefully prepared to await an eventual her-
culean catapult shot. Their fierce silhouettes, occasionally showing the
glint of titanium or insignia, were accentuated by live bombs and missiles poking menacingly from beneath massive wings. Support aircraft
were already launching, the scream and thunder of their catapult shots
literally shaking the boat, and fire shooting from their exhausts like monster blowtorches momentarily lighting the night. Scattered everywhere
were color-coded attendants, young helmeted and goggled men and
women, some of them still in their teens, directing aircraft—waiting,
watching, signaling with exaggerated gestures and prolonged movements, their distinguishing colored jerseys and jackets dulled in the ticking semidarkness. One wrong move and they could be decapitated,
sucked into an engine and pureed, sliced and splattered by a propeller,
or incinerated by an exhaust. Or, worse, they could cause an explosive
conflagration among the airplanes that could be as devastating as any
terrorist attack any enemy could ever inflict.

But there was also a feeling of professionalism, even bonding, on
the deck. It was mixed with trepidation and good old American optimism. You could see it in the attention to detail, the abnormally large
number of well-wishing onlookers in the towering bridge and around
the deck, or in the occasional genuflection, pat on the fuselage, or last
look of an aviator before he mounted the ladder to his cockpit. Sometimes you caught it in the expectant faces the aviators encountered as
they made it to their planes. "Walking up, and it's loaded with bombs,"
recalled Joey, "and your plane captains are just grinning from ear to
ear. They are so pumped up. . . . They know you are going into combat, and they are just, 'Gosh, sir, wish you the best of luck, sir.' It was
their strike too. I'll always remember it."

Bru was already there. They were taking aircraft 101, its Black Aces
insignia, an ace of spades with 41 centered on it, with red-and-white
detail, gleaming on the jet's tail.

Together, they began preflighting the strike fighter.

•   •   •

Being the only black aviator in the *Black* Aces had its irony. But "Loose" Cannon, holder of that distinction, had no problem with it. As the only other combat veteran in the squadron (he had flown missions in Desert Storm), he was accepted as a very professional, albeit personally quiet, RIO, who, as a lieutenant commander, was also a member of the Aces' senior staff.

But there were cultural differences.

He preferred rhythm and blues, jazz and rap, to the various types of pop-rock music played constantly on the ready room's stereo, and he liked dance clubs rather than bars and beer, unlike most of the squadron's fraternity- or academy-bred aviators. He was married with children just like most of the Aces, and like them excelled in science and math. "I was the little, nerdy kid," the lean and now good-sized RIO recalled about his school days, "the brainiac of the class."

He was brought up in Washington, D.C. His dad was first a microbiologist and then a minister, and his mom drove a bus. He became interested in fighters and flying in high school but "didn't know anything about the military." Not until he went to Florida A & M University on an academic scholarship, hoping to become an electrical engineer, did he find a way to unite his interests. It was in ROTC, the student-military program that he joined and that got him in the navy. His vision wasn't sharp enough for him to become a pilot, so he settled for naval flight officer, or NFO, which led to his becoming a RIO.

Flight school in 1987 at Pensacola was "interesting. There weren't a whole lot of black aviators around." He was the only one who made it through the program, and it was pretty tough, not only because of the studies and flight skills involved, but because the aviation culture, predominantly white, was foreign to him. "I had to learn a lot of background as well as the flight stuff. I didn't fit in. When we went out, we went to different places. I never got called for study groups. They weren't withholding from me; I was just on my own, and as I got commissioned and continued on, the group I could identify with [other blacks] got even smaller."

The situation didn't really bother him, he said, because the path he was on, he began to realize, was pointing him in a new direction, forging a dream really. He'd begun to set his sights on becoming a senior naval officer, at least a captain, while his family had visions of him becoming an admiral—maybe the first black NFO admiral in the navy, although other blacks, more senior, could make it before him. He was inspired by the exploits of American black fighter pilots in World War II, the noted Red Tails of the Ninety-ninth Pursuit Squadron, part of the "Tuskegee Airmen." The Red Tails, a segregated unit, distinguished themselves by protecting American bomber crews as they flew into Germany against the Luftwaffe. And so he committed himself to the navy. Whatever happened, happened. He was going to see it through.

Having gotten his wings and completed another year and a half of advanced flight training, he was assigned to the VF-2 Bounty Hunters, an F-14 squadron stationed at NAS Miramar, near San Diego, California, which was known as Fightertown in those days before the navy moved the fighter squadrons to Oceana in the mid-1990s. "That was cool. They accepted me. I'd gotten through the schooling and other hurdles so I deserved to be there."

There were just a handful of black aviators at Miramar from 1989 to 1990. By 1991 he was flying in the Gulf War. "My perspective on life and death changed. It made me accept the inevitability of death. I don't have a death wish, but I'm not afraid of dying. . . . We were all together; we were all in a war. There were some friendships that became pretty close. . . . It didn't matter if you were black or white. That's not to say there weren't cultural difficulties. There was prejudice in the navy."

His "pet peeve," he said, was driving through the Miramar security gate and not being saluted by the guards. Thinking he was enlisted, they would just wave him through rather than check the sticker on his windshield that identified him as an officer. "Sometimes I'd count the number of times in a week and finally stop my car and lower the window. 'What color is the sticker on this car?' They'd notice and salute. I'd just drive away. It always got me."

But that was nearly a decade prior. He was now part of the squadron's leadership, influential enough that the shaved head he sported for cruise quickly became the squadron fashion, especially among the JOs. Loose, known for his reserve and quiet confidence, wasn't just a ranking officer. He'd been under fire, and that counted.

Now he was waiting to launch. He and his pilot, Lt. Comdr. John "Alvin" Young, who was his longtime friend and cruise roommate, were checking systems, waiting to move out to the catapult. Alvin, call-signed thus because of his flashing chipmunk grin, was an outgoing, ambitious "hinge." Lieutenant commanders like Young and Loose were called hinges by the JOs, the joke being that elevation to a managerial rank has the new senior officer undergoing a lobotomy, with the top half of his skull hinged for future brain restoration.

A naval academy graduate and former Delaware all-state athlete in baseball, football, and wrestling, Alvin, who chewed Skol tobacco, had met Loose at Miramar, where both were instructors in VF-124, the F-14 training squadron. He had joined the Aces about a year prior to this cruise because he saw, under Joey and Dog, who recruited him, a chance to advance fast. "I want to be a commanding officer," he said. "They were rebuilding, so you go where there's opportunity to be number one."

He would be competing with the other lieutenant commanders in the squadron, including Loose. At the end of the cruise, everyone from Joey to the senior JOs would be ranked against their peers. First-tour JOs wouldn't have to do much more than pass muster. They'd have to go on another cruise before they were seriously ranked. But the more seasoned aviators needed to finish high. How they did would determine where they went next. Number one would get them their pick of assignments. Middle of the pack or lower could get them Siberia, if that's where the navy needed them.

The strike was beginning to muster. "There's like twenty engines turning up," recalled Alvin. "Everybody's got their ear protection on. . . . It's an eerie feeling . . . a beautiful night . . . clear . . . the distant roar in your headset. You can see a billion stars in the Ionian Sea, and you're just sitting there going, 'Man, this is such a pretty night . . . I'd like to be here forever. . . .' "

Then it hit him.

"I've got these giant bombs on my belly . . . live weapons on my wings. . . . We're—no kidding—going to war."

Fear, monstrous and "overriding," began to envelop him. "It was strong . . . I'm gonna get shot. I could die tonight. I could be a POW tomorrow." The plane captain signaled him to begin the slow journey to the catapult. The big fighter, its engines whining up, moved cautiously from its side deck mooring and turned forward. "And there was fear of failure, which was outweighing anything else. I don't want to screw it up. I want to get to the target . . . release . . . guide my bombs."

The fear continued, but he didn't let on. Loose had no idea. "Just kept going through the checks and making sure everything's working okay: 'That's a check. That's a check. Yeah, good. That'll do. . . .' "

They neared the catapult, one of four on the carrier, a 310-foot-long forward section of deck that would give, in one awesome shot, the fully loaded and now nearly seventy-thousand-pound Tomcat the same kind of thrust a dash down a mile-long runway on land would give.

Four "cats" gave the carrier the ability to launch one plane every twenty seconds.

"All the time I'm very, very nervous. . . . God, this is not a normal hop. We're not gonna go out there and drop weapons on a dummy target. We're going out and gonna get shot at. We know it! We've already been told what's gonna happen. . . . And the fear of failure. How I'm gonna get to the target. How I'm gonna avoid the SAMs, just join up, get the gas, get on station. . . . It was a fear I never felt before. I was scared when I was in high school and I was going for the state championship in wrestling. But this was *absolute* fear. I'd never felt anything like it. . . ."

One of the yellow-clad aircraft handlers motioned them onto the catapult. A 10-foot-high metal fire wall rose behind, blocking them in. The big plane's wings, swept back for space at its mooring, were now fully extended, nearly 65 feet from tip to tip, which would give it more lift on the shot. The catapult shuttle line, a long slit in the deck, beckoned ahead. Attached to mammoth machinery below, the shuttle would sling-shot the plane down its 310-foot length. Nuclear-generated steam, the shuttle's power source, hissed and wafted from the slit, eerie in the nightglow. A handler knelt and attached the shuttle's holdback brace to a T-bar on the Tomcat's nose gear. When it was secure, another handler, monitoring the operation on the periphery, gave Alvin the signal to go full power. He did.

"I was just trying to do everything one step at a time."

Blue-white flame and thunder hosed from the Tomcat's exhausts, searing the fire wall and lighting the deck. The impending shot would rifle them from 0 to 175 knots in two-and-a-half seconds. The experience would be similar to the force experienced in a high-speed highway crash.

Alvin released the brakes. The big plane surged minutely forward and down, a monster racehorse bridled at the gate. They were poised and ready. "It was like a mini sporting even. . . . All I could think of were the guys on the flight deck, you know, patting me on the back, going, 'Go get 'em,' and . . . You just don't want to come back after twelve years of training and say, 'I couldn't do it. I didn't do it.' I mean what the hell did they pay me for? Just take my paycheck because I don't want it."

He gave a terse salute to the crewman on the periphery. It was now just a matter of seconds. The crewman, after a check that all things were right, turned into the night wind and in an exaggerated gesture crouched toward the deck, motioning forward. There was an ominous rumble, then a snap, as if a giant chain had suddenly broken. The Tomcat bulleted forward, a blur of monster gunmetal, trailing fire and earsplitting thunder. "A death machine," Joey calls it. Their faces distorted. Their eyeballs flattened. Steam hissed in their wake. They were off.

Once he'd cleared the catapult, Alvin's fear suddenly left him. Just like that. He can't explain it. It was probably analogous to the first hit in a football game, or the first few lines spoken on opening night. He just lost his pregame jitters. "I'm in the game. It's all business now."

But things weren't so good for their skipper-leader, Joey Aucoin, and his pilot, Bru.

Launched earlier, the crew leading the strike was having trouble with their IFF (Identification, Friend or Foe), a radar transponder that, using codes, "talked" to other airplanes, identifying them and telling them about itself. All American warplanes use IFF to avoid shooting each other. But the F-14As had old boxes, and they were constantly breaking down. The catapult shot, they later found out, had dislodged a wire. But, at the time, they didn't know what was wrong. Joey was livid at the thought of having to relinquish his command. He was trying to get permission to continue from the admiral, who, because it was the first strike, was actually on scene in the operations center.

Not only did Aucoin not want to give up this first chance in the war to distinguish himself, but he would be handing the command to Slapshot, his chief rival. All like-airplane squadrons have a healthy rivalry, especially when on the same base or ship. Like college fraternities, they have been known to steal or desecrate each other's symbols or trophies. And this rivalry had been exacerbated on the last cruise, when Joey and the Aces, for whom he was the executive officer at the time, had suffered the embarrassment of having to borrow VF-14's Tomcats because their own were down. It was a matter of pride. Using the Tophatters' jets meant the Tophatters could rightfully claim to be more ready. That humiliation had been the genesis of Aucoin's own rebuilding of the Aces, getting rid of deadheads and rejuvenating maintenance with recruiting and newer, better policies.

And anyway, Slapshot didn't need extra laurels.

Tall, good-looking, a recruiting poster in the flesh, Comdr. Ted Carter, a RIO like Aucoin, was a 1981 Annapolis graduate. He'd captained the academy's hockey team that year, hence his call sign, "Slapshot." Like Joey, he was a graduate of Top Gun, the Navy Fighter Weapons School, and he'd already won or helped win a string of awards either for himself or his squadrons, including Instructor of the Year in 1987, Pacific Fleet Tailhooker of the Year for 1988, and the "Battle E" for the best F-14 fighter squadron on the East Coast while Joey was occupied trying to upgrade the Aces. CAG Lyle, who would ultimately rate the squadron commanders, said he was pulling for Joey as they went to war because of the uphill battle Joey had waged with 41. But Slapshot, he said, "was one of my favorite heroes."

The admiral, along with CAG, said no to Joey's pleas. "Fast Eagle One"—the first two words denoting the Aces' tactical call sign—might get shot down by a friendly. Worse, the opposite could happen. They might shoot a friendly, an absolute nightmare for any U.S. aviator. Joey would have to relinquish command, and he and Bru would have to return. To Aucoin's credit, he'd already stipulated in his plan that if something like this happened, Carter was to take the lead. They may have been rivals, but there wasn't anybody on the strike better qualified than Slapshot.

Alvin and Loose heard their skipper talking to the carrier about the situation. But now they were having problems of their own.

One of the first things Loose, as the backseater, had to do once they got airborne was start checking systems. Because they'd not had the jets needed for training in work-up, he wasn't as practiced with the LANTIRN system as he wanted to be. Its FLIR (Forward-Looking Infrared Radar), the part that gave him a picture on his backseat screen, appeared not to be working, a problem that was perplexing him. What he did know was that their catapult shot had damaged the Tomcat's navigation system because it *definitely* wasn't working! Headings on Alvin's pilot display, for instance, were wandering when they should have remained fixed. His wet compass didn't work. They decided to use a little, palm-sized GPS (Global Positioning System) unit that one of the Aces, Lt. Merle "Brain" Perry, flying Prowler protection on the strike, had been able to obtain for the squadron just before it left. The portable unit, mounted on the right side of Loose's rear cockpit, could locate them by satellite and then plot their courses. Loose was familiar with the GPS, but Alvin had never used it, so Loose was going to have to navigate—a job usually handled by the pilot. In addition, he was checking the complicated, high-powered AWG-9 radar and getting it ready for use to find their first destination—the S3 tankers waiting for the entire twenty-or-so-plane package approximately one hundred miles ahead.

"Tanking always gets the adrenaline going because we need the gas after the cat [i.e., catapult] shot," said Loose. And night tanking is harder than day tanking. "You could say I had my hands full."

Things got worse.

"Normally, when your navigation system goes, you can just say, 'Head oh-six-oh,' or something, and he flies oh-six-oh heading, and you give him updates on how far it is. But with the headings off, I had to actually tell him, 'Okay, come right ten degrees, come left ten degrees.' . . . But because of wind or a little angle of bank, the nose would drift off that heading, so he'd end up flying in curved paths rather than straight paths."

It was frustrating for both. They started shouting at each other. "I'm yelling, 'Where is it? Where is the tanker!' He says, 'I don't know. I can't see it. Loose, you gotta help me out! Which way am I going!' 'You need to go this way.' 'I am going this way!' 'Well, you keep drifting that way!' . . . 'How's the LANTIRN?' 'Shut up! I'm trying to get it working.' "

With the aid of the radar and their night-vision goggles, they finally found the tankers and got two-to-three-thousand pounds of gas, and tensions eased. Replenished, they began an orbit, waiting for the spare. The spare, normal on most missions, was an extra Tomcat, armed and gassed, in case, like Bru and Aucoin, one of the strikers had trouble.

But after one orbit, the skipper, still waiting to land, radioed: "You guys are single. Go on." It meant that, for reasons unspecified, the spare wouldn't be launched, so that the core six bombers were now reduced to five, Alvin and Loose the only Aces among them.

Back on the carrier, Lt. Comdr. Steve "Wog" Carroll couldn't sleep. He'd left the brief for the second wave of the first night's strikes with the intention of resting before the near-midnight launch and then studying target pictures. "But I was wired. . . . I had such mixed feelings. . . . Is my time numbered on this earth? . . . What am I going to run into? Is my plane going to work? Am I going to buffoon this away and look like an idiot? . . . I'm very hard on myself when it comes to being able to do my job."

A Catholic, he decided to say a rosary. "I carry a pocket rosary with me." It had been given to him by Dog's sister, a nun. She'd sent one for each of them. He would be in Dog's backseat in an hour, the two of them leading a division of Tomcats when they took off. "I sat there and prayed a little bit." Then, looking at his family's picture, he thought about his wife, Donna, and their children: a daughter, Mary, four and a half; a son, Joe, two and a half.

The couple had recently gone through some bad times. Six years into their marriage, he'd had some peripheral professional problems that had caused great stress, and at home, "we'd had some personal problems. We weren't communicating. . . . It got pretty low . . . we were living in the same household, but it was, 'Uh, how are you doin'?' 'I'm doin' okay. You doin' okay?' 'I'm doin' okay.' That kind of stuff. And every little thing I'd do would just piss her off, and every little thing she'd do would just piss me off. . . . I can compartmentalize real well. I would leave and just put the family in a drawer and forget."

And being in the navy, he was gone a great deal. He was at sea, for instance, when little Joe was born with severe asthma and allergies. Donna was the only one there to take care of the infant's many hospitalizations. Helping rebuild the Aces had aggravated their problems. During work-ups, for instance, he had been gone for forty-two of the fifty-two weeks in that year. "Donna was basically a single mom with me coming home every couple of weeks and just disrupting her life." When her grandfather, who had raised her when she was a little girl, died, he had not been able to get off the ship to come home and take her to the South Carolina funeral. "With a sick child, she couldn't leave. My parents are seven hundred miles away." Since it wasn't his or her own father, the navy, despite interventions by Joey and Dog, had discouraged his attempts to leave, in effect stopping him. "My heart's being ripped out that I know my wife's lost someone very, very close to her, very dear to her, and I can't fly home from Puerto Rico to go be with her."

Lately, however, through a lot of "soul-searching," they'd turned it around. "I'd done some stupid things, and it took a lot for her to forgive me. But she did. . . . We'd finally come to an understanding that I needed to be more family oriented . . . put my job second." When the war, with its stepped-up demands, had intruded, she'd understood. It was his life. It was what he did. He'd missed Desert Storm, and this might be his last chance for combat, which was not only a crucible for self-testing but a career enhancer. "She's a strong woman, and when we left for cruise, she just said, 'Hey, go make me proud. Do what you need to do. I'll be here for you when you come home.' And the kids are sitting in the backseat crying, 'I don't want you to go, Daddy. Daddy, no. Don't go.' . . . It was tough."

He and Bru, now still orbiting the carrier with the skipper, had written their letters home, depositing them in their shared desk where the other knew where to find them in case they had to be mailed.

To Donna, he had written:

```
If you have opened this letter things have not gone the
way I planned. First of all I want you to know that you
are all I ever think of. Now know you have someone watch-
ing over you! I really do not know what to write but
there are tears in my eyes. I understand the emptiness
left in your heart now but time will heal the pain. Mary
and Joe need to be your focus and they will help you get
through these hard times. If I'm missing or captured
please know that your prayers will help me endure the
pain. If I have been confirmed dead let God into your
heart and let the healing process start. We have enjoyed
a lifetime of love and happiness that few people en-
joy. . . . You are a strong and beautiful person. . . .
```

Remember me in the best way you can. . . . God will call
me at my time. I'm sorry it was so early in our marriage. . . . I love you and [now] I can watch over you
and the kids. . . . All my love, Steven

To his daughter, he wrote:

I know you do not understand why I have written you this
letter now but I will not be able to be with you anymore.
I have died in a plane crash over Kosovo. I know you
don't even know where that is. But children like you
were being hurt by very bad people and I was trying to
help them. Pumpkin you are the best daughter a daddy
could ever ask for. . . . I will be watching you from
heaven. . . . Your dad loves you. . . .

He wrote nearly the same to little Joe.

After he dressed for the flight, it was time to go. He went to turn
out the light in the stateroom. "And I can remember looking at the
desk that had my letters . . . and looking at the pictures . . . and going,
'Well, I want to come back and see you guys, but I don't know if I'm
gonna. I just don't know.' And I kind of got a little lump in my throat
and walked out the door and went, 'Okay, it's now or never. I need to
be putting on my game face.'"

He flickered the switch. He had a job to do.

Six

The tanking for the first wave had occurred at approximately thirty thousand feet in the night sky somewhere near the boot of Italy. It was done piecemeal, first come, first serve. When Alvin and Loose got the order from Joey, their skipper, to go without the spare, they headed for the final leg of the pretarget trek, the rendezvous, the place where all elements of the strike mustered for the final assembly before they pushed to the target.

The rendezvous was needed because of the staggered situation of launching and tanking. There was a great deal of movement and timing built into the strike plan. In order for the participants to execute the plan according to its dictates, they needed to start from basically the same time and place.

Alvin and Loose now turned east, crossed the Adriatic Sea at perhaps its narrowest point, its mouth off the heel of the Italian boot, and then turned north to fly up into Albania toward the rendezvous spot. It was near and above the Macedonian city of Skopje, approximately two hundred miles from where they had tanked. By this time, Loose had the LANTIRN working. The problem, he had finally realized, was that it took time for the FLIR to "warm up," so to speak. In reality, its picture was based on measured heat, so its sensor actually had to cool down in order to sense varying contrasts of infrared and thus start delivering a picture to the screens. (Alvin had a smaller screen of the same green backlighted picture up front.) Now he had a lot of testing to do to make sure the LANTIRN, its main parts housed in a torpedo-like pod fastened beneath the Tomcat's right wing, was functioning properly. Although the radar was working fine, the navigation system was still down. They would have to continue using the little GPS unit, and with the LANTIRN needing the full systems check, "the overload," said Loose, "really started getting confusing."

Months later they would laugh at the ludicrousness of being in a sophisticated $40 million warplane but having to use an almost Radio Shack–quality gadget to navigate — one luckily procured by a JO lieutenant to boot. But it wasn't funny that night. In fact, they started yelling again when Loose, his brain-shrinking "pucker factor" increasing with the heightened overload, made a directional mistake.

The Prowlers and their protectors had a separate rendezvous area not far behind the bombers. Doing his LANTIRN checks, making sure all the soon-to-be-needed weapons delivery switches, some twenty-five in all, were in correct positions, and trying to study target pictures with a flashlight in the blacked-out cockpit, Loose, accidentally reading the wrong coordinates on a knee-board card he'd prepared, maneuvered them into the midst of the Prowlers.

"At that point, we really got mad at each other," he said. They weren't far from the bombers, who knew they were in the area. "There were people talking on both radios. I'm so overloaded, I actually turn one down, and they were trying to raise me, and [Alvin's] like, 'Loose, they're talking to you!' " Loose was too busy to respond. " 'I don't hear them.' " 'That's because they're talking to you over MY radio!' I'm like, 'Well, then, talk back to them for me!' "

Both of them, along with everything else they were doing, were trying hard to pinpoint the strikers.

Slapshot's VF-14 Tomcats had recently had some modifications done to their lights. When Loose looked out the cockpit and finally saw the unique configuration in the distance, he knew they'd finally arrived, and felt thankful. But what he understood from Alvin was that they were going to " 'abort.' I couldn't believe it. We're going home? 'But I can see him!,' " he yelled over the intercom. " 'He's right there!' Then I realized we were joining [with the jet]. What Alvin had really said was, 'Alvin's aboard' — not 'abort.' I had just misunderstood him. That took another ten years off my life."

But the hard part was still ahead—the run at the target, a gauntlet of Triple-A and SAMs stretching "in country" for the next fifty-to-sixty miles.

There were two other Black Aces Tomcats in the first wave of the strike package. Both were protecting Prowlers, and both were crewed by promising or ranking JOs whom Joey, as skipper, and the senior cadre, especially Wog, felt could be depended on to do the job—not that others couldn't. But these, including the select JOs on the next wave, were the few picked for the first team.

Surprisingly, Lt. Keith "Wrex" Harrison was one of those honored. What was surprising was that Wrex, a pilot who had gotten his call sign (along with a medal) as a student for landing a Tomcat using only the rudders when his stick jammed, wasn't one of Joey's favorites. Far from it. The tall, good-looking Texan and 1992 University of Virginia graduate had a reputation with the hinges for putting his own concerns above the squadron's. For instance, when there had been all the extra work during turnaround, Wrex was sometimes absent. For his part, he said he just took the time to be home with his wife and one-year-old son. But most of the other squadron members had wives and children too, and they had to stay late. An operator of sorts, with a tendency to pull talked-about pranks, he was also known to obfuscate when a straight answer was expected.

But no one could deny he was a heck of a pilot, good behind the boat, which was essential. "You can't fight again if you can't land," was the often-repeated dictum. And he was skillful at air-to-air tactics, which he believed "separated the men from the boys." Wrex had an easygoing, confident manner and was an excellent debriefer who knew what he was talking about and had the sought-after ability to impart that knowledge to others. He also had a fatalistic streak that bore on his job: "My wife . . . both of us, we're very . . . I almost said religious, but we're not fanatics . . . we're very rooted in our faith and very believing that there is a plan for everybody's life out there. And I've been flying so long [he started when he was fifteen] that I know that flying is the plan for my life, and that [the war] may have been why I am here . . . to protect people who needed to be protected and hopefully stop somebody from killing more people."

Death, he said, "doesn't really bother me that much. . . . We're going to make it through, or we're not going to make it through. Either way, this is where I'm supposed to be."

Wrex wanted to go to Top Gun after the cruise—a very hard assignment to get. He, like many of the other senior JO pilots, was due to move on to his next tour. But unlike most of the others, Joey had balked at preparing the way. Wrex, he said, "was on the borderline. . . . There's enough bad news about him that I could have just recommended him for the training command."

But as the war drew closer, Wrex's stock rose. Where some were cautious about going into combat, he stepped forward without hesitation. " 'Where do you want me? What do I need to do?' " Joey remembers him saying. In contrast to his absences during turnaround, he became highly visible. There was expectancy in Wrex's eyes, a heightened anticipation. He didn't see problems in the approaching storm, just opportunity. It was almost like he was looking forward to it. It was an attitude that the squadron leadership—Joey, Dog, Bru, and Wog—needed.

And Wrex had the skills.

So when they made up the roster, he was near the top for getting one of the nonstriker jobs.

"Joey wasn't very impressed with me when we started the cruise," he acknowledged. "This was my last shot."

In Wrex's backseat was Lt. Jim "Toadboy" Skarbek, a Baltimore RIO who had seen some shooting over Bosnia during his first cruise in 1993, although potshots and random targeting were not the kind of combat he was heading into now.

The other Aces Tomcat was crewed by Lt. Merle "Brain" Perry, pilot, and Lt. Doug "Money" Halter, RIO. Brain, an enterprising JO who liked to check stocks on the squadron's Internet-connected computers when he had the time, was the JO who had procured the portable GPS units, one of which Loose and Alvin were now using for navigation. Like Joey, he was a North Carolina native. They had that in common. And given Brain's squared-away, aloof manner, his concern for troops in his charge, which was another thing he had in common with his skipper, and his considerable abilities with the airplane, he was a favorite of Joey as well as some of the other seniors—a fact that caused mild irritation in some Aces who, rightly or wrongly, felt they were not so favored.

Brain was a landing signal officer, or LSO, one of the pilots who, standing on the platform at the stern of the carrier, guided and graded landings with direct communications to the pilots. LSOs, understandably, were supposed to be among the best pilots in the squadron, although that wasn't always the case since each squadron had to furnish several and sometimes there weren't enough good ones to fill the quota. But among 41's strengths *were* its pilots, and Brain was good enough to have already become a wing LSO, which meant he was qualified to wave any aircraft on the boat, a respected achievement.

Both Brain and Toadboy were engaged to be married when they got home — *if* they got home. Halter was a popular RIO in the squadron, a partier when they were on liberty who liked to play practical jokes on the other JOs and Pink Floyd, or what he called "Euro-trash dance music" (if he'd been able to buy it in port) over the ready-room stereo. He was one of the few single Aces.

Skopje, in Macedonia, was right outside Kosovo. Once the strike package mustered, its planes pushed across the border and into the dangerous enemy airspace. The five bombers moved out ahead, picking up speed, beginning to drop slightly in altitude, forming a wall of hellbound Hornets and Tomcats. Around them, the Prowlers and their fighter-protectors began fanning out and taking scripted positions, eventually moving to higher and outlying areas, where they would begin flying erratic, unpredictable patterns, the Prowlers jamming radars, including SAM guidance systems, and the fighters looking for enemy interceptors. Part of the plan was for them to play rope-a-dope, which meant trying to goad the Serb SAM operators to turn on their tracking radars. When they did, the Prowlers had an instant target for their high-speed antiradiation missiles, or HARMs. The bombers would continue to bore steadfastly in, jinking, trying to be as unpredictable as possible as they flew in to deliver their payloads.

Almost as soon as they crossed into Kosovo, antiaircraft fire began to arc. It was a deadly fireworks show that grew with every second.

Wrex remembers, "They knew we were coming, and as soon as we turned hot inbound, up came the high-altitude Triple-A. I thought to myself, 'Hey, they're not supposed to have this stuff. It's not supposed to come up this high. . . .' The fear hit me right then. . . . If ever there is a day that is going to be difficult, this is it. . . . But I felt more concern for the guys that were lower than me. . . . Those were the guys who were really flying into it."

Loose was looking at the same thing. And from that lower perspective.

He felt a disconcerting jolt of fear, something that surprised and alarmed him.

In Desert Storm, he said, the Iraqis weren't aiming. They just barraged the sky, hoping for a lucky hit. You only had to worry about the " 'golden BB' [a chance shot that finds its mark]. But these guys know where you are. They're better trained and equipped, and their aim is a lot better." He could tell that the bursts were below the Tomcat's altitude, "but what if they adjust?" The Prowlers were now shooting HARMs at the SAM sites, but, to Loose, the Triple-A shells that he could see vividly through his night-vision goggles seemed to be rapidly enlarging. "You've got to remember that when you see tracers, you're only seeing one in every six or seven bullets. There's a steady stream of lead and steel you can't see."

The fear heightened, and he knew he had to cope fast.

"At that point I was like, 'But I've done this. I've been here before.' . . . If you don't have the wherewithal to at least concentrate and try to do your job, then you put yourself and whoever is with you in jeopardy." He tried to shake it. "Okay, this is for the wife and kids." It didn't work. "Then I used another perspective. . . . I'd done this before. Nobody else [in the strike] had. . . . I had an advantage." He was a veteran, he chided himself; he was a leader. If *he* couldn't take it, who could? His composure started returning. "Basically, I'm talking myself into calm. This was just seconds. Then it was, 'Okay, take a deep breath. Back to your senses. Now let's find the target.' "

He brought his eyes back into the cockpit. He only had to look down for an unobstructed view. The night-vision goggles were not flush against his eyes. It was time for him to do his most important work: operating what could be called the world's most expensive and violent video game, the LANTIRN. Its FLIR screen, left-handed joystick, and many switches, mostly on the joystick, quickly became the focus of his concentration. Forget the Triple-A and SAMs coming up. It was Alvin's job to deal with those, and Alvin was a good pilot. His job now was to find the refinery and guide the ordnance.

He got to work.

This wasn't Nintendo he was about to operate, or the kind of easy system seen in the movies where the pilot pushes a button and the bad guy explodes. There were literally hundreds of mistakes that could be made. Joey describes working the LANTIRN system as "dynamic, like playing a football game, audiblizing at every turn, with a lot of preparation and groundwork needed to make it succeed." Switches have to be at correct settings, often in rapid-fire sequences, and the sequences themselves must be played quickly one after the other. They call such hand-and-finger movement, not to mention the required mental gymnastics, "playing the piccolo." One wrong note and you're the squadron goat — or worse. Smart bombs, by pinpointing the target, were supposed to minimize random violence. Hitting civilians was something no striker wanted to do.

Codes on bombs and in the system had to agree. Wrong code and the bomb would go stupid, hitting who knows what. And there were as many codes as there were weapons. Inserting them in combat was akin to dialing telephone numbers while doing somersaults on a trampoline.

Deciphering the FLIR's picture wasn't easy either. It was made of contrasting light and dark images and resembled an ultrasound in the doctor's office. It was grainy and imprecise and didn't show direction, often perplexing TV viewers of Gulf War footage or other publicly released laser-bomb footage. That was because there was little angle of approach indicated. The image, while showing slight movement, always appeared to be a picture taken from directly above, which was seldom the case. When that happened — when the plane actually flew directly over the target — the image instantly flipped 180 degrees, which could disorient the operator and possibly break the weapons lock. RIOs hated it on the occasions when the pilot did that, not only because they knew the problems it would cause, but because one of the benefits of the system was that it allowed the bomber to "stand off" when delivering, which was a safer approach.

The approach to the target when delivering a smart bomb was usually at an angle and to the side. It was seldom straight-on, as was usually the approach when dropping a "dumb," or nonguided, bomb.

Time was always an enemy because the target area couldn't be acquired with any clarity until they were approximately thirty miles away. By that time they were often barreling in, hell-bent for leather, approaching speeds of five-to-six-hundred miles per hour, and they usually had only a minute or so before they would have to drop. But patience and calm were required. The RIO was taught to use the large field-of-view setting first, in order to see recognizable landmarks like mountains and rivers in proximity to themselves, and then to switch to narrow view to find the specific target, which should be nearby. This technique of going from large picture to small was called "funnel naving." If he used the narrow view first and couldn't locate the target, there probably wouldn't be enough time left to redo the search. Given the distances involved, the narrow view was like looking through a straw; the wider view was like looking through a slightly bigger straw.

The RIO's job wasn't exactly like trying to find a needle in a haystack—but it was very difficult.

It took a lot of know-how, a lot of preparation.

And then there were the problems of lasering that didn't occur until after the bomb had been released.

Loose was in a pressure cooker.

"I remember at this time I'm in my own little world," he said. "I'm in tunnel vision, staring at the screen. I remember somebody talking about a SAM being launched [one of many]. I never see it because I never look outside the cockpit. . . . Features start appearing." But he didn't see any he recognized. A dread began rising. Had he screwed up? The clock was ticking. "I'm getting close to the target, and I know I'm in range." Where's the target? "I don't see it."

What he didn't know—what the entire strike package didn't know—was that a potentially disastrous error had been made before launch. In order to begin finding the target, its probable coordinates are dialed into the LANTIRN. The system then, when activated, goes to those coordinates and should show the target area. But someone in the early planning had made a mistake in copying the latitude and longitude. One number was wrong. Who was responsible is unknown. ("Those things are going to happen.") But it put them about a half mile to a mile off. Nobody in the prestrike planning had caught it. So the patch of landscape Loose was now looking at didn't have the refinery on it or any adjacent features.

But Loose and the other five strikers charging in didn't yet know about the error. They just knew that they couldn't find the target and that time was running out.

Loose now had about twenty seconds until he had to drop. A younger, less-experienced RIO might have started dotting the funnel all over the landscape, hoping to find something familiar. But Loose stuck with the textbook. "I'm going to sit on my hand. . . . Let the picture build and see what I do see, not worry about the fact that I don't see my target."

Up front, Alvin, dodging Triple-A and SAM calls, was worried too. He had the same picture on his smaller screen and deduced that there was an airfield on it, not a refinery. "I said, 'It ain't at the airfield'" he recalled. "'It's a half mile away from the airfield.'" Loose, listening to him, saw the runways too. "[Alvin's] pointing out things . . . and it gets my thought processes going."

He remembered that there was a railroad near the refinery and that it went by an airfield, too. With some educated scans, he found the railroad and started following it north. A triangular configuration began to materialize in the FLIR, then a storage tank, dark on the screen . . . and another . . . and another. . . .

"That's it! That's it!" screamed Alvin. "Don't lose it! Don't lose it!"

Loose says he was less emotional. "We haven't delivered anything yet."

They were approximately ten miles from the refinery, and ten seconds from drop. Loose really began playing the piccolo. Most of his switches were on the joystick, which had a little hood for a top. The hood, looking like a little hat or lamp shade, was his cursor, which moved the tiny crosshairs on the screen. He locked the crosshairs on his DMPI (Designated Mean Point of Impact), also called a "dimpy." It was square in the middle of the largest storage tank. Originally this was Joey and Bru's target. But since they weren't there, he and Alvin decided to take it.

"I'm moving the cursor with my left thumb," he explained. He was now within the small envelope in which the laser could be used. With other fingers, he activated it for the first time, raying it down briefly for a read on the tank, whose defenders in the area were now hurling up everything they could to stop him.

Then he shut it off.

From the read, called "laser ranging," the LANTIRN, using the Tomcat's inputted speed and its own built-in GPS, would hopefully calculate, with automatic corrections for wind and other variables, the precise time and place of release in the air needed to deliver squarely on the dimpy the jet's two-thousand-pound guided bombs (called GBU-16s).

All of this information, including the second-by-second countdown to the time and spot of drop, instantly appeared on both FLIR screens. Alvin would make the actual drop. But since the pilot's screen was small and he was occupied with flying the jet according to the new flashing dictates, Loose, still manipulating critical switches, including those that activated the jet's video camera to record the bombing—a requirement by CAG in order to prove hits—began announcing the seconds out loud:

"Ten . . . nine . . . eight . . . seven . . ."

Meanwhile, the other strikers kept looking for the refinery. Because of the lack of time and the complicated numbers involved, said Alvin, "it was too hard to radio them what we'd found. . . . The Tomcats [nearest to them] keep wanting to lean . . . to the bad coordinate, and we [because they were on their wing] had to keep leaning with them." But the two Hornets, which had now moved out in front, realized the mistake also and adjusted.

As the seconds ticked away, Loose and Alvin had to do more and more. It was important to have the jet in as precise a flight path as possible for the release. When Loose got to "zero," Alvin "pickled" and maneuvered sharply away. Although he had set the bombs not to detonate until they reached the storage tank, there was always the chance that they would explode prematurely. The maneuver was a safety precaution.

But the job wasn't done yet.

They had approximately forty seconds until the falling bombs reached the target, which was still some distance away, and the piloting of the jet and Loose's laser handling would determine their success.

For thirty seconds the bombs fell ballistic, gathering speed under their own momentum. He held back firing the laser. They were still too far from the target. Turning it on too fast would make the bombs go for the ray, and they'd lose the precious energy needed to propel them and penetrate. The Tomcat's release was designed to "sling" the bombs on a path that would put them as close to the target as possible even without the laser. Only when the ray and bombs were sufficiently close together would he switch it on.

He waited.

At ten seconds before impact, the bombs, sailing in, were close enough. He fired the beam. Each bomb acquired it easily and headed in with adequate energy.

Now Alvin had to make sure that he didn't somehow break the laser beam with one of the plane's parts, like a sudden dip of a wingtip or nose. Meanwhile, Loose had to manually keep the cursor motionless on the dimpy. Anything breaking the beam's straight line, even a cloud, would move the cursor and break the lock. The bombs would go stupid, most probably missing the target. The same thing would happen if Loose's thumb erred. The crosshairs would move, and the bombs would follow.

And he still had more "switchology" to perform.

He was glued to the screen, holding the cursor with one hand, working more switches with the other, when he saw the first bomb enter the FLIR screen. But it wasn't one of theirs. It was one of the Hornet's. It exploded in one of the refinery's nearby buildings, making only a moderate degree of puff and smoke. He saw another bomb from the second Hornet hit a second building and not explode. Probably a dud. Then his FLIR screen suddenly lost all imagery, as if someone had blowtorched it from underneath. Almost simultaneously, he heard a huge, but muffled, explosion and felt heat from the right side of the cockpit, the side between him and the refinery. The eerily lit cockpit was suddenly splashed with a blinding light.

"It was like a mini nuclear explosion," said Alvin, who also felt the heat. "It was like whoa, almost like going outside after being in a freezer all day. You had to turn your head . . . almost ruined our night vision [goggles] because of the brightness. . . . We had to turn them off."

To their right and out front, a huge fireball was billowing, rising thousands of feet into the air. Both bombs had made direct hits (although one would have done the job). The explosion of the main tank had ignited the others near it in a gargantuan chain reaction.

Up by their Prowler, Wrex and Toadboy saw the explosion too. "I'm looking at my little display in the cockpit to try and see the bombs come in," said Wrex, "and the first thing that actually catches my eye, more so than the things exploding on the screen [the Triple-A and SAM launches], was this huge flash. . . . I saw it out of the corner of my eye before I saw it on the display, and I was wearing goggles and had to look away. I thought, 'Wow! What was that?' I didn't know if I was hit or something. I didn't know what was going on."

Alvin said the explosion destroyed everything within a three-block radius. The fire would rage for a week, and aviators throughout the theater would use it as a directional beacon. The other Tomcats had not found the target—at least not until the fireball erupted, and by then it was too late. They were on their way out. No time for Loose and Alvin to celebrate either. They had to get out too. Alvin lit burners, spraying the already-inflamed engines with new high-octane gas, and the jet's exhaust shot flame fingers into the Balkan night. The Tomcat reared south and started a rapid egress.

But they were being stalked even in the midst of the conflagration.

Almost as soon as they got turned around, an SA-6 shot up toward them.

"I'm out of the cockpit now," said Loose, "and looking at it through my goggles." The night-vision distortion made it look like a Saturn 5 liftoff. He called out, "SAM! SAM!," and Alvin started evasive maneuvering. After about six seconds, the SAM appeared to go ballistic. "Keep in mind that the Prowlers are still up there, and they'll fire a HARM and kill [the SAM shooters] if they keep on tracking."

It was the first time they would see a tactic that would be increasingly used by the Serbs. The surface-to-air missile would guide on a jet just long enough to hopefully scare the pilot into departing the plane with violent evasive maneuvers. Departure—a sudden loss of controlled flight—would render the jet defenseless, and either the SAM or the Triple-A, which the jet would be falling toward, could finish it off. The evasive maneuvers alone could dive the jet low enough to put it within the Triple-A's range.

Alvin dove down, and the missile exploded above them. "We look below, and there's one-hundred-millimeter rounds being shot at us. I mean big old bullets," he said.

He'd taken the bait, although there wasn't much more he could do.

Up above, Brain and Money were seeing the same thing: "Egress was when the SAMs started coming up," said Brain. "The first are ballistic to bleed you down and get you in their envelope. Then the third, fourth, or fifth will be guided on somebody. . . . You need to keep your energy and altitude. . . . One came up and did a ninety-degree turn at us."

They dropped their chaff, which decoys the missile, and started dueling with it.

"They do maybe mach two," said Brain, "which is over two thousand miles per hour. I'm thinking about my energy state, what I can do with the jet. I don't want to move too soon because I'll bleed out before he does. So it's a waiting game . . . wait, wait, go down. . . . It's like the cheetah and gazelle. The gazelle doesn't run in a straight line. He ducks and reverses."

It was a violent game of tag played at supersonic speed. "You try and wear it out. The operators have a way of telling if the missile is running out of energy. They'll blow it up, even if it's not near you."

The missile tracked them for about five seconds, said Brain, then missed them and exploded.

As Loose and Alvin neared the Macedonian border, they were rocked by an antiaircraft shell that exploded beneath them. "I'm like, 'It didn't hit us,' " said Alvin, "but it got close enough to disturb the air underneath."

He tried to go faster, but he was already at maximum speed. Loose was urging him to jink more. But now gas was a problem. By using the burner, they had depleted their supply.

Luckily, the SAMs were receding into the distance.

They were going to make it.

After they had been in the air for nearly an hour, the deck was finally ready for Bru and Joey to land. "I knew Skipper didn't carry a gun," joked Bru. "I was just afraid he was going to ask me for mine." As maintenance chief, he was on the hot seat for their IFF breakdown. "First night of the war and my goddamn plane fails me," said Joey, now, in effect, a deposed strike leader. "I wanted to rip some heads off."

Meat Fleisher, a pilot and one of the second-cruise JOs not on the strike, had been listening on the radios. "I remember leaving the ready room when they were coming down. Everybody was kind of like, 'You don't want be here when the skipper arrives.' "

But Joey kept his feelings to himself.

"They'd worked too hard, and I just gotta, you know, I'm not going to feel good about it. And everybody's going to know it."

But not right then.

He deposited his flight gear, checked briefly in the ready room, and then went to his stateroom and stewed.

"Sure, I was mad. But the first wave was coming back."

But they wouldn't land until the second wave had launched.

Seven

The consensus leader of the JOs was Lt. Bill "Dewar" Dey (pronounced "dye" like the coloring), who was a straight-talking, highly respected pilot prone to confronting hinges when he thought them wrong, and who was also one of the best "sticks" in the squadron. He could really fly the airplane — and land it. Like Brain, he was a wing-qualified LSO. He was so good that CAG Lyle would eventually pick him to become one of only two air-wing LSOs representing him. "He had integrity," said Lyle, "a very honest individual . . . friendly, diplomatic . . . very good demeanor, one of the best LSOs at debriefing people [meaning he knew how to tell very competitive pilots what they did wrong without grating on their egos] . . . very professional in the air."

Dewar had a way of cutting through the chaff and arriving at a quick and sound decision. He didn't shrink from the tough choices and was humble about his own accomplishments. "I trusted his judgment," said CAG. "It's not a matter of who has the best eye [on the LSO platform]. It's who has the best judgment." He was "the guy we looked up to and followed," said Meat, one of Dewar's contemporaries, about the JOs. He'd tell it to you straight, added Toad. "He was a voice of sanity among us. If someone came up with an idea, the guy you wanted to convince was Dewar. If Dewar thought it was stupid, you'd better look for another idea."

Dewar also had a rambunctious, pranksterish side. It showed up mostly when he was on liberty, especially when he imbibed. Born in Hightstown, New Jersey, the son of a former New Jersey state trooper, Dewar, call-signed after the scotch whiskey, could handle himself. "He'd been around the block," said Joey. From the slight, but discernible, Jersey accent to the hint of challenge in his scrutinizing gaze, he had an unspoken toughness. "You didn't want to mess with him," said Lt. Tim "Mentul" Challingsworth, a RIO and one of the first-cruise JOs who looked up to the twenty-nine-year-old pilot. "He's got that scar on his chin, and you figure . . . tough guy." He also had a kind of smiling sarcasm that showed he wasn't worried. But in the air, added Mentul, he was "soft-spoken . . . made you feel confident . . . he was funny."

A type A personality, like so many fighter pilots, Dewar sought challenges. He was an athlete. In high school, he'd been a star soccer player, and he had played the sport for Annapolis until he'd graduated in 1992. And he was injury-prone. Once he and some of the other Aces climbed a mountain in Greece because he felt it could be scaled faster than Meat and Wrex and some of the others said it could. He was the only one to fall and end up bloodying his hand on a rock. No big deal. He had it stitched up, and they went on to wrestling matches. On another occasion, he got in a fight outside a bar in another port. Depending on who was telling the story, Dewar was either trying to break it up or was one of the outnumbered guys in the midst of it. But he ended up taking a two-by-four across the face, which gave him a bunch of stitches in the mouth and a shiner that he had to hide behind sunglasses when he reported back to the ship.

That was when his skipper, Joey, decided to step in.

"He'd press the boundaries in port," said Joey. "Sometimes piss off the Oh-fours [lieutenant commanders]. I would have to mediate, sort of cool it down. You don't want to quash a guy. You want him to mature. It's all a learning experience. I just told him, 'No more.' " And with the impending birth of his first child, a daughter named Kamryn, he'd been improving. His buddies in the squadron made a game of his rehabilitation. Wrex recounted: "We were in port a few nights, and I made a bet with him. Gooch and I said we'd buy him a night of drinks if he stayed under control." It grew into a joke. "Good Dewar" or "Evil Dewar"? Which would show up? Lately, it had been Good

Dewar. He'd even put his arm around a heckler during a confrontation in Key West, where the squadron had gone for training.

Wrex: "He and I and Doug ["Money"] Halter were out at a bar one night. Doug had just joined the squadron. Dew was wearing an LAPD [Los Angeles Police Department] T-shirt. These guys didn't like it and asked if Dew was in the LAPD. He decided to play along. . . . He was funny. . . . He would put his arm around people and get real close to them, into their face, and talk to them like he was their buddy. But you could see what he was doing. . . . We just laughed. . . . He knew we were there to back him up."

Dewar was happily married, a tough thing for a fighter pilot with the long absences and devotion to duty the profession demanded. Just the concentration, called "compartmentalization" by the aviators, needed in such a dangerous business often took husbands a million miles away from their spouses in terms of where their minds were when they came home at night. Unwinding, switching back to normal family life, was hard. Some of them couldn't do it. And then there were the additional problems, like the temptations of a being a near rock star because of movies like *Top Gun*, and being accessible at rowdy officer-club or liberty-port bars. (However, the days of excess were fewer now, as warplanes, ever more sophisticated, took longer to teach and master, and thus nuggets joining squadrons were older and more mature.) But Dewar, at least when interviewed in port, sloughed it all off with a shrug: "I'd rather be with my wife."

Dewar, with Squab Williams in his backseat, and Lt. Comdr. Dave "Beaker" Lobdell, crewed with Lt. Doug "Thing" Thien, were the only Aces besides Dog and Wog flying in the second wave.

Beaker, a tall, red-headed Waukegan, Illinois, native, whose call sign, he said, stemmed from his prominent nose, was a very experienced F-14 pilot who had joined the squadron after flying the F-117 Stealth for three years in an exchange program with the air force. A 1993 graduate of the navy's Top Gun school, he was somewhat frustrated at being a *junior* lieutenant commander. He aspired to more responsibility, eventually a squadron command of his own, but dutifully and quite capably took on the grunt hinge work, training JOs, supporting the senior lieutenant commanders who were department heads, while hoping to get lots of combat time in the war.

Since the 117 was a bomber and had an infrared heat-sensing targeting system like LANTIRN, he was, in effect, one of the squadron's bombing experts. Along with that job and other duties—for instance, being Wog's ops assistant in charge of training—he had taken it upon himself to try and motivate every JO to learn as much as possible about the systems he would need going into war. Because Beaker was a junior lieutenant commander, not that far removed from his former JO buddies, the lieutenants saw him as a kind of middleman to the senior hinges. Regarding him as still almost one of their own, they would come to him with gripes against management about which they were hesitant to approach Joey or Dog.

Thing, a quiet, introspective second-cruise RIO from Iowa farm country, known for his mastery of the Tomcat's sophisticated radar, had originally been scheduled to fly with Gooch, his good friend and cruise roommate, until Dog had returned and the assignments had been reshuffled. Later to be call-signed "Shamma," as in the 1950s rock 'n' roll refrain "shammalamadingdong," Thing had wanted to be a pilot since he was five years old. But less-than-perfect eyesight had relegated him to the backseat. On the last cruise, he'd seen a buddy, a Hornet driver, killed in a place in Oman that aviators called Starwars Canyon. (Navy training is frequently conducted in Oman.) The canyon is a deep, steep-walled gorge, a sort of mini Grand Canyon, that pilots like to fly in as a challenge to their skills. It meanders through mountains into the sea. Its scariest part is a horseshoe bend with a giant rock in the middle that leaves little space for a jet to negotiate.

"We saw the flash and the smoke come up from the canyon," Thing recalled. "Everybody knew where it was . . . the big rock. . . . He just went in there too fast." A plane needed to slow down and turn its wings vertically to get between the rock and the wall. "Another twenty feet and he would have made it. It made me realize stuff can go wrong. It actually made me question religion. God in heaven, is there really something after this? That guy was gone in an instant. What would that be like? You're here, and then bam. . . . They said they found enough of him to fill up a baggie. A Ziplock baggie and that was it. Just a big scorch mark on that ridge now. . . . It really teaches you are not invincible. . . . That was probably the third memorial service I'd been to where there was nobody to put in the casket."

Understandably, Thing was nervous about his first combat: "I was scared. We built these guys up to be ten feet tall, plus they'd just shot down that 117. No way in hell Tomcats are going to stay airborne out there." He'd written a good-bye letter to his wife. "Wrote a bunch. Planning was when it hit me. Everybody packing their survival gear . . . wondering what to take. Pistols. Blood chits. In my mind, I was just going over scenarios. If I get shot down, what am I going to do? . . . Generally, stay put. Soldiers will be soldiers. If you are on a mountain, go to the top. It will be hard for them to walk up there and get you. So stay where you are for awhile, then go to higher ground. . . ."

Squab, writing a journal about the war, had a pink-cheeked, portly look that belied his hard-nosed attitude and considerable abilities. A thirty-year-old second-cruise veteran who had special air-to-ground training, he could take charge or help when the situation in the air demanded. "If you want to buy a car, take Squab with you," said Gooch in describing him.

Born in Missouri and raised in Texas, Squab had lost his father when he was thirteen. Although an avid reader and good in science, he'd gone through high school with little ambition. "I was a tumbleweed." He didn't want to go to college, so his mother, raising a brood alone, sent him to military recruiters. He was an avid scuba diver, and the navy appealed to him. Once enlisted, he began to find purpose and rose rapidly, from hard-to-get-into nuclear-power school to an appointment to the naval academy. After exposure to jets one summer, Squab started thinking about aviation. Because of poor eyesight at the time, he became a naval flight officer (NFO), which ultimately led him to become a RIO and fly the Tomcat.

Dewar and Squab were assigned to protect a Prowler on the second wave. They took off before Beaker and Thing, who were flying wing to Dog and Wog.

Before launch, Dog had told the squadron's plane captains to tell their pilots, " 'Good Luck, go get 'em, and I'll see you when you get back.' I learned that from a guy by the name of Capt. Denny Ireland, a great American. . . . When he retired, he said, 'I'm going to share with you a couple of things that stick out about my career. . . . First, combat. I was so scared, and the plane captain strapped me in, shook my hand, and goes, "I'll see you when you get back." That gave me the confidence and faith to go on. I knew I'd come back. This guy expected me to, and I was okay.'"

Neither Dog nor Wog had ever seen two live two-thousand-pound laser bombs (GBU-10s) fixed beneath any Tomcat, let alone theirs, as was the case when they walked out on the darkened deck. "It was two thousand pounds of explosives that did the Oklahoma City bombing," said Dog. "We had twice that much. And we had two Sidewinders [heat-seeking, air-to-air missiles] and two Sparrows [radar-guided air-to-air missiles]. I just remember going, 'Man, we are loaded for bear. That's more than an entire squadron in World War Two.'"

Wog was so nervous preflighting that he needed help: "I do the walk around, and I remember asking Gunner [Lt. (jg) Andy Phillips, squadron ordnance officer, a nonaviator in charge of the squadron's weapons] to help me with the bomb preflight. My brain is going a million miles a minute. . . . The big thing I'm worried about is laser codes. What code is on the front of the bomb and what code to put in the airplane."

Entering the cockpit, he and Dog did something they'd never done before. They shook hands, a kind of last act of well-wishing and solidarity before going to war. It would became a preflight ritual for these two, who would frequently crew together, so much so that once when Dog would forget, Wog wouldn't let him climb in until Dog had shaken his hand and apologized.

Tanking was tough. Upwards of twenty aircraft were trying to get gas in the same relatively small airspace. In front of them were tankers waiting to be "milked." In order to swiftly move in for a turn, the jets had to stay close by. With their heavy bomb loads, the thirsty planes didn't maneuver as well as when they were light. "I'm surprised nobody ran into each other," said Thing. At first, Beaker couldn't find his assigned tanker, a Viking S-3, among those stacked in the midnight sky. And once he did, the coupling maneuver was tricky, more so with the heavy bomb load. He had to inch the Tomcat's male probe into the tanker's trailing, dimly lit basket, both of them traveling at the same high speed. Move too slowly and wind whipping the nose of the F-14 would move the basket away. Thrust too fast and the danger of collision heightened.

They eventually got coordinated high over water outside Albania.

Heading for the ammunition facility, they could see the distant fire from Alvin and Loose's direct hit. Wog had taken the advice of a Desert Storm veteran to wear extrawarm long johns in case he was shot down, and he was sweating profusely, even with the cockpit's strong air-conditioning. "I hate being hot," he said. "My adrenaline was frying me."

Starting to work the FLIR, he experienced the same confusion Loose had. He couldn't find the target. Unlike Loose, he started spotting his narrow viewfinder in different places, hoping to see something he recognized. "I'm doing what I'm not supposed to be doing. I'm sluing my soda straw, my FLIR, all over the place, trying to find my target too far away. Instead of sitting on my hands like I'm supposed to, I'm falling into the trap."

Just like with the first wave, there were problems with the strikers' distributed intelligence information. First, the pictures of the target supplied to them were not up-to-date. They did not show the target as it currently looked. Second, even if the pictures had been up-to-date, the target area had already been hit. The ammunition facility and its surrounding buildings had been partially destroyed by an earlier raid.

But, as before, the strikers didn't know this. They continued trying their hardest to find the target despite considerable ground fire by the alerted Serbs.

"SAMs were coming up," said Dog. "They looked like little rockets. I was surprised at how I could tell instantly which was a threat and which was not. Because there's a lot of airplanes out there. Are they shooting at little Jimmy Bauser or Jimmy Bauser's people? No. . . . Oh, now they are. You don't have training for that. I mean you do . . . but is that thing pulling lead on me . . . doing stern conversions [drawing a bead], or is it going after somebody else? . . . If you told me before the mission I would have that [ability], I never would have believed you."

Antiaircraft fire was also arcing. "It was like an upside-down Christmas tree. You could see it pointing at you. We were above it, but it was concerning because you really didn't know." So with Wog buried in the FLIR, he kept high and fast and dodged and jinked. It was like riding a roller coaster during an eight-point earthquake. The Serbs jammed their radios, trying to disrupt communication. "You could hear them coming in on our frequency. Sometimes it was music. One time it was 'The Girl from Ipanema.' Everybody was like, 'Okay. [Not bad.]' Sometimes it was static."

With fifteen miles to go, Wog still hadn't found the target. They were descending, driving in, and had perhaps fifteen seconds left before the LANTIRN would tell them to drop.

Since they had come over land, Wog had been using the FLIR to check navigation points—landmarks that, if they were flying their course correctly, should be beneath them. He also knew that near the target was a dam that had a river running from it that flowed near the target area. Remembering that the last navigation mark was near the dam, he found the man-made structure. And the river too! Now he knew where he was and where to go next: the river led to a wash in front of some trees beyond which should lay his target.

But he couldn't find the wash. "I'm just sluing my soda straw all over the place, going, 'Where is it? Why can't I find it!' . . . I finally go, 'Okay, stupid. Stop what you're doing.' I actually say on the tape, 'I'm sitting on my hands.' And the reason I can't find it is I'm sluing northwest when I should be going due north. It's little things like that." By waiting patiently, he allowed the image to get stronger in the FLIR, and he recognized where he was and saw what was wrong. He moved the straw slightly north, "and all of a sudden, I think, 'Oh, at seven miles, I have the target.' "

In fact, reviewing the tape later, he would realize that he had found the trees leading to the target the first time he'd FLIRed the area using the coordinates he'd been given. But in the brain-shrinking excitement of first combat, he hadn't let the image build enough to recognize it. Lesson learned. "If I had believed in the system right from the beginning, my heart wouldn't have been thumping."

While the main ammunition-storage shelter—their primary target—had already been leveled, one building was still intact. Wog put the crosshairs on it and began the countdown. The drop was good. They veered away, holding the laser. "I just kind of watched the time to impact count down," he said. "You see two two-thousand-pound bombs go into this building and just . . . secondaries come off . . . so there was something in there besides admin support stuff. . . . It obliterated that building, [what remained of] two buildings next to it, and part of a shed down the way. . . . It was like the weight of the world had just been lifted off my shoulders . . . I'd connected on my first time in combat . . . I was King Kong—until I slapped on my goggles and, you know, go to Dog, 'Good impact. Good impact.' And Dog goes, 'Let's get the fuck out of here.' "

Looking outside for the first time since they'd started the run, Wog, as they headed back, saw what Dog had been dodging. "Holy shit, they're shooting at us," he intoned over the inner com (ICS). Dog couldn't resist. "Where the hell have you been?"

Beaker and Thing weren't so talkative. Beaker was having a tough time staying on Dog's wing, which precluded his normal inclinations to coach a RIO, and Thing had mistakenly targeted the wrong area. Coming in, he had more trouble finding the target than he'd expected. A ridge separated the ammunition facility from a small town, perhaps a mile or mile and a half from the targeted facility. "I had kind of ignored a warning in the brief about which side of the ridge to concentrate on." The fact that the buildings he was looking for had already been leveled didn't help.

"It was very hard to pick out. . . . I sat there going, 'Okay, it [the ridge] is pointing in the wrong spot. It's up to me to figure out where everything is.' " He scrolled down a little. " 'Ah, there's a set of buildings that look like what I want to hit.' " He fixed the cursor and began the countdown, figuring that once the bombs were dropped, he'd find the ammunition complex and designate a better target. The only trouble was, he'd unknowingly targeted apartments, not government buildings, and they were probably filled with civilians.

Once they'd dropped their two two-thousand-pounders, he scrolled the area and found what he thought was probably the ammo-storage facility. He switched the cursor to it and waited for the bombs to arrive. Studying the FLIR image just before impact, he had a horrible realization: "I've seen this structure before."

It was a typical water-waste treatment plant.

"I go, 'Oh my God,' type of thing. 'That's not at all what I want to hit.' "

He slued the cursor off the target, and the bombs went stupid, exploding into the ridge.

It may have been a lucky moment for unsuspecting workers at the plant, but Beaker realized they'd missed their target and was furious. "He made a classic mistake," he later said about Thing. "My only concern [going into the war] was I wanted to do well. You've seen the movie *The Right Stuff*? The prayer they say is, 'Dear Lord, don't let me screw up.'. . . . I consider myself one of the best pilots, and I didn't want to screw up. . . . I wanted to get it done the first night. . . . I was very frustrated because I'd spent the entire afternoon planning the mission, and [Thing] didn't show up until the final brief. . . . At the debrief, after the strike, I asked him, 'What do you think you did wrong?' He goes, 'Well, I don't think I studied the photos enough.' I said, 'That's right. You didn't.'"

Thing basically agreed. He'd been scheduled to give Lupe Lopez, one of the squadron's nugget pilots, who were little more than "gofers" at this stage in the war, an airborne intercept lesson, so he'd been flying when the crucial preparations were made. "I should have been concentrating on more important stuff," he said. "It was a big, 'Hello, you're not as good as you think you are.' . . . I needed some redemption."

Although Dewar and Squab were as keyed up as any in the squadron, the strike's second wave was largely uneventful for them. From their perches high above and behind the strikers, they had a distant view of the primary action. Squab wrote in his diary:

```
Fast Eagle 106 had a King Kong radar and both the Phoenix
[long-range radar missile] and Sparrow tuned right away.
The jet was ready for an air-to-air kill. No enemy oppo-
sition encountered however. I did make 4 contact calls—
every one 75 nm [nautical miles] or greater off the nose.
All were reported friendly however. On the final leg to-
wards Pristina I did see one cluster of AAA. Looked just
like strobe lights going off.
```

(Dog later said that MiGs did rise that night but didn't come south to where they were. "The air force scared them off," he said.)

He also remembered the HARMs being shot both in front and behind him. "The HARM trucks [Hornets with that special job] were about ten miles in front of us," he later recounted in an interview. "You could see those things [the missiles] coming off. It was light enough [with the goggles] to see even the smoke trails after the

[HARMs from the Prowlers] went by." About a reported SA-6 launch, later revised to be a MANPAD (shoulder-fired rocket), he wrote: "We searched the skies and ground frantically for a missile coming up but saw nothing."

But Dog and Wog, exiting the target area and still much closer to the defenders, did see it.

Wog: "All of a sudden, I hear over our communications net, 'SAM launch! SAM launch!' And I'm going, 'Whoops, that's where we are.' I turn and look behind us and see these little curlicue things [smoke trails] start to come up, and with the goggles on you can't really tell whether they're ten feet [away] or twenty miles. I call it out, and we start dropping chaff, and we're climbing out. . . . I remember asking Dog, 'Can't you go any faster?' "

Dog was pushing the jet as fast as he could while still conserving gas. They still had a ways to go to the Macedonian border. They were high enough that they didn't think the SAM could reach them, but then they started flying over a tall mountain on which they'd been told were more SAM sites. "You know if you put a [SAM] system on a thirteen-thousand-foot-high mountain and the system can reach twenty thousand feet, then it can now shoot thirty-three thousand feet," said Wog.

And that was about the altitude they were at as they passed over.

But when Wog looked down, the SAM site was burning. "Thank God all the HARM they shot took it out."

As they made it out of Kosovo and into the relative safety of Macedonian airspace, Dog came up: "We did it, Wog! We did it!' . . . I was like, 'Yeah, but we still got to land.' "

By this time they had a problem determining how much fuel they had. One of the systems wasn't working, and they had to calculate by hand and memory. They decided they had enough to make the boat without trying to find the tanker, which might take another forty-five minutes. The first voice Wog heard when he contacted the ship was that of a female air-traffic controller he'd known years before. She'd been an unmarried nineteen-year-old civilian with a little baby, a neighbor's friend, and he'd helped her out by baby-sitting when she'd had to work. He'd only recently run into her on the ship, and they'd become reacquainted.

"So I knew her, and the first voice I hear . . . is her bringing us back. . . . It was kinda nice. She was worried, you could tell. . . . And the whole thing too of me being an officer, an oh-four, and her being a first-class petty officer. I mean we knew each other kind of like from a prior life . . . and I'm so happy that she's made good on herself, you know, chief . . . got all her quals, marching along. When I first met her, she was really a mixed-up kid. And now, you know, I could hear in her voice, she's concerned for us. . . . She kind of checked in, you know, 'One-oh-four?' . . . And like, you know, the whole tone of her voice changed. . . . 'Aaaah, okay, one-oh-four, here's your vectors.' . . . You can't really say, 'Hey Wog!' 'Hey Roz!' . . . But she was bringing us all back to the ship. . . ."

Back at the *Roosevelt's* ready room, Joey was beginning to feel better, not only because both targets had been leveled, but because *his* guys had done most of the leveling. (A few Hornets from the ship had hit targets on the second wave too.) Still in their flight suits, disheveled and sweaty, the returned 41 aircrews were showing their tapes, Alvin and Loose's tape being the main attraction.

"It was so exhilarating," said Razor Shick, a second-cruise pilot. "I'd been in on the planning. I would have done anything to have gone. I just wasn't chosen. They were talking about SAMs being launched. Triple-A. Getting locked up. I thought, 'We're here. We're doing it!' I was both envious and excited. . . ."

When Wog came in, he said he "tempered" his "exuberance. I know [Joey], and I knew that even though he's standing there with his good face on, if he was alone, he'd be just beating himself up." Dog looked "pissed," said Loose. "But then he gets that look in his eye." Dog said, "I was just feeling kind of goofy. Someone asked me how it went, and I go, 'Well, we did a little dance, made a little love, got down tonight.' " It was accompanied with a little dance to the popular refrain.

Unknown to the aviators, Admiral Copeland, worried about their safety, stayed up until they'd all come back. He then got some sleep before an early morning brief he was to give to General Clark, the NATO commander. Joey and the other strike leaders from the air wing's squadrons gave their debrief to CAG. Individual Aces had made mistakes, but, overall, the night's missions had boosted the squadron's confidence. They had done their part for Airwing 8. And without casualties. Their worries about aging jets, untested new systems, and ability to perform had proven largely unfounded — at least on the first day.

Book 2
FINDING A WAY

Eight

Brian "Bru" Brurud, then a lieutenant, knew he was possibly only seconds from death, but he thought he could fly the plane out. It was 1989 in the skies above Kingsville, Texas, and the big Oklahoman was in a violently gyrating TA-4 Skyhawk jet trainer that had stopped flying during a loop maneuver and was uncontrollably falling like a rock.

The flight had started routinely enough. Bru, who had gotten his wings only a few years before, was a young instructor at Kingsville Naval Air Station, where he taught undergraduate student aviators advanced dogfighting and bombing. It was time for his yearly checkout ride (required of all navy pilots to make sure they are still safe). So he and Jim "Dirt" Meyers, another instructor, had taken off to go through the required checklist, with Dirt in the backseat.

He had just pulled over the top of a fairly fast loop when the jet unexplainably started slowing and yawing to the right. A yaw is an uncontrollable sideways movement. It's like a car slipping on ice. It's hard to rein in. Pretty soon, the Skyhawk was nearly standing on its tail and out of airspeed. It flipped over and departed from controlled flight. Departure is an emergency. Normally, a plane, with the proper inputs from the pilot, will get its nose back into the wind and start flying again.

That hadn't happened.

Instead, applying the inputs, Bru said he got it upright, but the aging jet went into another yaw and a second violent departure. This time it hadn't flipped over. Instead, they were pancaking like a flat brick and violently yawing back and forth. The fall was causing extreme "negative Gs," a heightened version of what an auto racer feels taking a fast turn. The force was trying to pull them up out of their seats. If there's anything an aviator hates, it's negative G. Normally, when coming down from the top of a loop, the pilot inverts the plane so that the G forces pull him into the seat. This force, however, was lifting them up. A very bad feeling. And the departure had been so violent that it had loosened the bolts holding Dirt's seat down, and the negative Gs had penned him and the seat up against the canopy, where he couldn't move.

The mishap had begun at seventeen thousand feet, and they were rapidly descending. Bru still thought he could get the Skyhawk flying. But it departed more violently each time he gave it the prescribed inputs. Dirt, with more experience in the Skyhawk, knew something was irreparably wrong and wanted to eject. But scrunched up as he was, he couldn't get to the ejection handles. What neither knew was that a drop tank under the plane had jarred loose during one of the departures and damaged the tail. Subsequently, in the violent descent, the tail had ripped off. The jet would *never* respond to Bru's inputs. They were hurtling toward the Texas plain in a death spiral.

Bru: "He's a smaller guy than I am and was pushed up high enough where he couldn't reach the lower ejection handle. The upper ejection handle is now between his shoulder blades. So he's trying like crazy just to get us out of the plane, and I'm going, 'I know this is violent, but this thing should be recovering soon.' . . . I finally look over at the altitude, and I see we're whipping through nine or ten thousand feet, and at that point I'm going, 'Maybe we ought to get out of this thing.' "

About the same time, Dirt, with great effort, reached the ejection handle over his shoulder. They went out at about seven thousand feet. By that time, the plane had rolled over inverted again, and so they were blasted toward the ground.

It was an explosion Bru will never forget.

Bru: "I'm knocked half-silly. I don't lose consciousness, but it's dark and incredibly violent followed by incredible calm." He had no fear, he said. He thought he was dead. "People see bright lights and different things. I didn't see any of that stuff." But he felt his dead grandmother's presence. "I heard her talking to me. 'You're all right Brian,' she said." His dead aunt was there too. "It wasn't physical. Just a weird sort of presence deal."

Then he felt "incredible white pain" and realized the darkness was from his oxygen mask. It had been shoved up over his eyes in the ejection. He pulled it off and continued wondering whether he might be dead because he was in clouds and "it's all white outside." But then searing pain hit him, and "I knew I wasn't in heaven." He had a dislocated and broken shoulder. "It's sitting kind of midchest on me, and I've got a compression fracture in [two] vertebrae." Above him, his parachute had a hole in it where his ejection seat, which had gone out with him, had ripped through. He was descending much faster than he should have been, and his parachute, he knew, wasn't going to last.

While he was still high enough for severe injury, his parachute collapsed. A spiny yucca tree saved his life. Wearing heavy boots, he hit the six-inch trunk, breaking his fall. "Kinda shattered the tree and made a stump about three feet above the ground. . . . It hurt, but it probably saved my legs." He tried to get up but fell back. Looking skyward, he saw what he thought was the TA-4 coming down to crush him. "I felt like that Wicked Witch in *The Wizard of Oz*. I'm thinking, 'Which way do I roll so it will miss me?' " But his eyes were red with damage caused by the negative Gs. Most of the blood vessels had burst, and he wasn't seeing correctly. Instead of the plane, it was Dirt descending, a broken arm dangling.

A local rancher, sitting down to lunch, saw the mishap and rushed to the scene.

It took ten months before Bru had recovered from the injuries. But he spent the time productively. Among other things, he met his future wife, Susan. They'd grown up in the same town, Bartlesville, Oklahoma. But she had been younger, and he hadn't known her then. Her older brother, however, had been in Bru's Oklahoma State University fraternity, and when she heard about the accident, which was big news back in Bartlesville, she'd sent him a get-well card.

They were married in 1991.

Bru liked bombing as much as dogfighting and had orders to go fly the A-6 Intruder, the navy's two-seat attack jet at the time. "The old adage is right," he says. " 'Fighter pilots make movies. Bombers make history.'" But the accident made him leery of the Intruder's canopy, which could be dangerous during ejection for large men such as himself. There was an opening for an F-14 pilot, and he had taken it. In 1992, after a year of Tomcat training, he joined the Black Aces for the first time. That was when the Tomcat's role was first being enlarged to include more bombing. It originally had been designed as an air-to-air fighter—the result of lessons learned in the Vietnam War. But Desert Storm had shown that bombers were getting most of the action in modern war. The Intruder was old and was being phased out. The Hornet, the navy's new single-seat fighter-bomber, had range problems. Money for new planes was scarce because of downsizing and the political climate. Navy strategists realized that if they wanted to stay players in the game, they needed to do more with less. They decided that enlarging the Tomcat's role was the answer.

This was the climate that greeted Bru as he joined his first F-14 squadron, his first combat squadron. VT-21, the training squadron he'd come from, wasn't the same. Training squadrons don't go on cruises. The instructor jobs are mostly nine to five. Squadron members usually go home at night so there's little camaraderie. His commanding officer at the Aces was Comdr. Eric "Sodbuster" Benson, a RIO and a proponent of the new emphasis on bombing in the F-14 community. Sodbuster's wife was from Bartlesville. "Her parents' neighbor had a son I went to high school with," said Bru. "They called and told Sodbuster, 'We've got a hometown boy for you. You've got to get him.'" Bru and Sodbuster hit it off, and Bru became very proficient at bombing as well as dogfighting. "We bombed and fought everywhere, a true training opportunity unlike [any] I'd ever seen."

In 1993, representing the Black Aces in the Winter Mid-Atlantic Bombing Competition, Bru and his backseater, Lt. Mike Cecou, won first place. It was the first time an F-14 squadron crew had ever done so. The competition, a quarterly event, pitted A-6 Intruders, the navy's main bombers at the time, against Tomcats from Oceana. One aircrew from each squadron performed a simulated strike on a target at a remote location in North Carolina. The crews were judged on their planning, choice of weapons (called "weaponeering"), time to target, and bombing accuracy. It was only the first year Tomcats had participated in the competition, and the win showed that the aircraft was making real progress in the hoped-for transition. The same strengths that had made it a superior dogfighter were working for it as a bomber—speed, range, and payload capacity. That same year, as the civil war in the Balkans escalated, and the United States was being drawn into it, American peacekeeping officers in Bosnia had complained that navy jets didn't have airborne air controllers to spot and aid in hitting targets or the laser-guided bombs needed to support troops on the ground. Without either, American jets couldn't do pinpoint bombing and thus might hit the nearby ground troops or noncombatants. That had led to the F-14 getting the LANTIRN and to some of its crews getting a new kind of training—that of airborne controllers.

The *Roosevelt* happened to have been the carrier off Bosnia at the time, so the *Roosevelt*'s air wing, Airwing 8, and ultimately VF-41, one of the air wing's two fighter squadrons that were most likely to be in the thick of things, got the order to remedy the situation. Bru had recently completed some Marine Corps airborne controlling training and so had established a link for such training. And who better than the marines to teach airborne controlling? A marine aviator's primary mission is to support marine ground troops. Marine aviators knew how to do it. Forward air control, at least from an aviator's standpoint, involved finding enemy troops and weapons while in the air, usually at the direction of an aviator on the ground, and then destroying them without hitting his own troops—not an easy job given the altitude and speeds involved. Bru went back to the marines and took a six-week course from MAWTS (Marine Air Weapons and Tactics Squadron), which included training as a "FAC-A" (Forward Air Controller Airborne). The FAC-A did everything. No ground controller was involved. That training—among the first for today's navy pilots and RIOs—was to become very important in the days ahead over Kosovo.

Buoyed by the success of the first night's strikes, Joey Aucoin, as the Aces' commander, was inclined to let some of his JOs fly the next night's big mission. It was out of his hands anyway. Slapshot, skipper of the Tophatters, was leading the second-night strikes. Gooch and three other Aces were assigned to Slapshot's own four-plane division within the strike package. Joey would have been interfering if he'd tried to change aircrew members. "I wasn't going to be bumping anybody out of the seat," the 41 skipper said. Besides, he added, those Aces deserved a chance to prove themselves. In effect, it would be a test for the JOs. And Aucoin and Bru were going on another type of mission anyway.

The exact date is not certain, but it appears that on the morning after the first strike, April 7, CAG had gathered his strike leaders to-gether—Joey, Dog, Bru, Wog, Slapshot, some of Slapshot's top officers, the Hornet commanders, and their qualified strike leaders—and briefed them on a new direction that was coming ultimately from the NATO war chief himself, General Clark. In essence, the new direc-tion, still being formulated, stemmed from the following:

The immediate goal of the Kosovo War was to stop Serbian mas-sacres of ethnic Albanians. The killing was occurring in Kosovo Prov-ince, and, so far, with the war going into its third week, NATO's strategy of primarily bombing nonvital (in terms of crippling effect) "fixed" or "stationary targets" in and around the Serbian capital of Belgrade—bridges, military barracks, weapon-and-fuel-storage facili-ties—had not stopped the slaughter. (From the beginning, the air force had wanted to hit the more important Serbian infrastructure—power grids, communications hubs, heating and cooling—believing that the destruction would be more punishing. But NATO feared political re-percussions.) Now, in view of the failure to stop the slaughter, there was increasing talk among the warrunners about going after the Serbs' "fielded forces"—their troops, tanks, and mobile artillery in Kosovo proper. The air force, with generally more aerial assets than the navy, was concentrating on the larger targets in the north, although navy Tomahawk missiles, fired from surface ships, had done considerable damage. Naval air, now that it was there, was being sent to Kosovo, which was closer to the carrier and had fewer major fixed targets. CAG told his officers that it appeared their days of hitting large, stationary targets were numbered and that they had better start thinking about how to find and destroy the elusive, mobile Serbian Army—the ones actually doing the killing.

After Bru had completed his MAWTS training in the early 1990s, he'd gone to NAS Fallon, Nevada, as an instructor to teach what he'd learned about controlling bombing from the air to other navy fighter aircrews. As a result of the expanding instruction, both VF-41 and VF-14 had three FAC-A-trained Tomcat aircrews each by the time the

Kosovo War had started. The new Black Aces FAC-A crews were Gooch and Thing, Dewar and Squab, and Wrex and Toad. But there wasn't much enthusiasm in CAG's meeting for the new direction. Bru's was the only positive voice. Captain Lyle, the CAG, himself had reservations. Like him, his strike leaders, as well as the new FAC-A graduates, wanted to continue flying the large Alpha-type strikes against fixed targets for which they had trained hard at places such as Fallon as an air wing and with which they felt most comfortable. They did not see how, given the easy-to-hide-in Kosovo terrain and the NATO-imposed altitude floor of twenty thousand feet, below which they were not allowed to fly, they would be able to even *find* the smaller, mostly mobile targets, let alone bomb them. At twenty thousand feet (imposed to minimize NATO air losses), a tank, even in the LANTIRN scope with the FLIR's considerable magnification abilities, is little more than a spot. A soldier would be imperceptible.

Even if seen, such targets could run and hide.

But CAG had been directed to explore the mission. In other words, it was his problem to solve. He therefore tasked Bru, because of his experience, to fly with his skipper, Joey, that night in what was technically called a SCAR (Strike Coordinated Armed Reconnaissance) mission but was listed on the squadron's April 7 daily flight log as a "QB," probably because of its preliminary nature. The two letters stood for quarterback: go out and find the Serbs' fielded forces and then "quarterback" their destruction with bombers that would be put at the QB's disposal.

As there was no NATO invasion, they would have no help from the ground.

That was the unique problem: nobody down there to help them.

They had to do it themselves.

The air force was doing some SCAR already but obviously with little success. The A-10 Warthogs trying to find the Serb forces were great killing machines but were hampered by the altitude restrictions and lacked sophisticated detection and bomb-targeting-and-guidance gear like LANTIRN. Both navy and air force planes had performed SCAR back during Desert Storm. Areas of the Iraqi desert had been sectioned off into "kill boxes," and Allied planes had hunted in them, unaided from the ground, bombing or strafing any enemy they could find. But the desert was flat. There were few places to hide, the weather was always good, and the Iraqis didn't have the weapons or antiaircraft threat in the desert that the Serbs had in the mountains. Nor did they have the hiding places. Kosovo had the SA-6s and SA-10s, and was stormy, mountainous, covered with trees, and pocked with caves, villages, and similar-looking farms, any one of which could conceal men, tanks, and SAM launchers.

Everybody in the room knew that finding and destroying the Serb fielded forces, if it could be done at all, was going to be both hard and dangerous. Most of them, given the altitude restrictions and their preference for fixed targets, thought it would be impossible.

Tophatter skipper Slapshot's mission that night, the main strike of several from the air wing, was to destroy some large underground fuel tanks on the outskirts of Pristina, the city around which the previous night's strikes had been sent. The storage tanks were deep in the ground, massive, and reinforced with concrete. To do the job, large, GBU-24 Penetrators had been selected — "cow bombs," as Joey called them. They were two-thousand-pound bunker-busters with moveable fins, special drop characteristics, and a front casing that enabled them to bore through five feet of concrete before detonation. It would be the first time any VF-41 aircrews had ever "lased" the monsters; that is, directed them to the target with the laser they could generate with their LANTIRN.

The core bombers in the strike would be two Tomcats from VF-14, including Slapshot's, piloted by Scooter; and two Black Aces' Tomcats: one piloted by Beaker, still smarting from the night before, with Toadboy as his RIO, and the other by Gooch, with Money, a first-cruise JO, in his backseat.

Gooch was a little discombobulated. Because he'd gotten bumped from the previous night's strike, he said he hadn't been able to prepare much for this one. "I just got with [Money, who had been on the planning team], and we looked quickly over target-acquisition stuff and the plan." Money remembers: "Gooch was really nervous. . . . I was the legal officer at the time, and he basically wrote out this big will and last letter to his wife. . . . He was very anxious about it, and that was getting me pretty anxious . . . I was maybe just, 'Uh, I don't know if I want to say in denial,' or just maybe too stupid to realize what we were going into, but I felt really good about it."

Beaker, now preparing for his second strike of the war, was nervous too — but for a different reason. Because of what had happened on the strike the night before, and because Toad had other duty during the premission planning sessions, the lieutenant commander said he "made a point to specifically take him all the imagery so he could study. . . . I said, 'I want you to know this imagery cold. . . . ' I was not going to go through the same thing again." Toad had calmed him. "He sat there and studied it, and he actually said he was fairly comfortable," Beaker recalled. "I was also comfortable switchology-wise because he was supposedly [one of our] LANTIRN experts," as Beaker himself was.

The mission briefed near midnight and launched early in the morning of April 8, at approximately 2:30 A.M. The weather was good, the night dark. Everything went relatively smoothly as they flew roughly the same route as that of the previous night's strikes — north from "Big Stick," the code name for where the carrier was operating, to a point off the boot heel of Italy where they tanked. Then east across the narrow entrance to the Adriatic to "feet dry" over Albania and into the Balkans, where the force of some twenty planes marshaled above Macedonia for the last time.

Earlier in the day, said Beaker, the Battle Group had gotten word from NATO that mustering over Macedonia would no longer be allowed. The problem was politics. Macedonia still had relations with Serbia. "We could flow through but not marshall," he said. But they'd already planned the mission, so "we acted like we didn't know that."

When it came time to push, the Tomcats lit out four abreast, dropping gradually from an approximately twenty-five-thousand-foot altitude as they sped toward the target.

In an evasive tactic, they weaved back and forth, doing a kind of bombing ballet so as not to give any ground targeters an easily plotted optical shot. Because it was early morning, ambient light from the approaching sunrise, not visible to the naked eye, was glaring in their night-vision goggles, and both Gooch and Beaker had to make adjustments in order to see. But in a surprise, they received very little ground fire, which Beaker attributed to the early hour. Gooch said his most threatening moment was when a Prowler-fired HARM streaked above his canopy and dived down, startling him until he realized what it was.

The RIOs, meanwhile, were focusing on their backseat LANTIRN scopes, eight-inch-by-eight-inch screens near their laps with black-and-white pictures being etched by heat or the lack of heat on the terrain below.

Both were making classic beginners' mistakes.

"You're crushing me making me think about this again," recalled Money. "But it was purely my inexperience. . . . I could not find the target. . . . I got very jumpy and antsy coming inbound, and I started moving the LANTIRN pod all over the place. . . . Rather than just sitting on my hands and letting the target picture form in front of me, I was sluing all around."

Beaker, looking at the same infrared picture on the smaller LAN-TIRN screen he had up front, discovered that Toad was doing the same thing.

"I look down in the cockpit, and Toadboy is sitting there surfing around," he said. "Just like Thing did the night before. I said, 'What are you doing? Just go to the target! Go to the target!' He says, 'Well, I'm just making sure I'm in the area.' . . . One of the mistakes that the guys were making is . . . they start getting impatient around twenty miles and start moving the cursor around checking out the scenery. . . . You are not going to recognize anything [close to the target] until about ten or twelve miles. . . . You cue the system to where the target is, and then you just wait."

Ten miles out, however, Money thought he found the target dimpy, a ventilation shaft sticking up through the ground.

"I talked myself into it," he said. "I saw a few tree lines and a road that looked a lot like what I was looking for. . . . Gooch and I had a quick conversation. . . . His scope was smaller than mine, and he was busy weaving. . . . We decided in the heat of battle that this was it and that we were going to drop."

Gooch was so busy that he neglected to see a seven-degree steering error in the LANTIRN-provided bomb-delivery course that he was sup-posed to fly. Money, too, should have seen the error. The correct course was being displayed on both their screens. Because of the error, even if Money had designated the right target, the bomb would have been released on a trajectory that would have delivered it over a mile away from where it should have been. The plane had to be pointed in the exact direction.

But they weren't aware of either problem.

They dropped and waited.

The cow bomb needed a precise and lengthy flight path in order to work its destruction: a high angle that would produce a steep, almost straight-down descent. The trajectory would give the hard-headed bomb penetration velocity. Because of that flight profile, the lasing time was longer than with smaller bombs—about sixty seconds.

Gooch banked away, and Money started lasing. They waited and waited, turning back toward home.

Nothing happened.

They waited sixty seconds, and still nothing happened.

Nearby, Beaker was getting more frustrated with Toad. "I said, 'You got it [the target]?' . . . He said, 'Yeah, I got it. I got it.' I said, 'Switches all set?' He said, 'Switches all set.' I figure, 'Okay, give me a count-down.' " But the pilot heard nothing from the backseat. "Dead quiet." Beaker said that he glanced at the range and that it didn't look right. "He wasn't counting down and giving me any backup." They were running out of time. "I went ahead and pickled."

Toad turned on the laser, and they executed the breakaway maneuver.

"We waited and waited . . . for what seemed like forever," said Beaker. Toad kept the laser on the entire time, but the bomb never entered the LANTIRN's field of view. They saw no detonation anywhere and didn't know what had happened, although Beaker believed that Toad had probably made some wrong inputs.

Gooch and Money experienced the same thing, as did Slapshot and his wingman. "We never saw anything after time of impact," said Money. Gooch was already heading home, some twenty miles ahead of Beaker. He and Money were both so excited to reach the safe skies over Albania that they broke into a song they'd learned from a 1980s hit television show.

"He and I were both big *Cheers* fans," said Money. "I don't know if you remember the show where Coach and Sam were . . . taking a geography class . . . and had to make up songs to remember all the different countries. The song they sang in the show was for Albania. . . . It goes, 'Al-ban-ia, Al-ban-ia. You border on the Adriatic. You are mostly moun-tain-ous. And your chief export is chrome!' . . . So flying on the egress over the ICS, we're both chanting that song to each other. 'Al-ban-ia. Al-ban-ia . . ."

But when the euphoria subsided, they began to deal with the failure.

Money: "In the jet we had the ability to rewind and watch the tape. Once we were over water heading back to the ship, you know, we had a good twenty minutes' downtime. I'm just looking and playing with [the tape], and that was the point—whenever we watched it together, I think it was maybe the second time through, we realized, 'Look at that. Seven degrees of steering error.' "

The only thing uplifting about the rest of the ride was that the sun was up when they reached the carrier so they didn't have to make a night trap.

Nine

Even before the meeting with CAG, Bru, who had gotten word of what was coming, said he had told Joey, " 'Whether you realize it or not, you probably do, but we're supposed to be able to do this sort of thing [SCAR].' . . . I had laid it all out to him, showed him what it entailed." The problem was that few in the navy ever practiced the mission. There was little call for it. The United States usually had controllers on the ground. FAC-As like Bru were the only naval aviators doing airborne reconnaissance, identification of targets, and coordination of attacks from the air. Joey himself was not a FAC-A. His background was air-to-air. Even the navy's 1990s shift to emphasizing bombing had been a learning experience for Joey. Although he was reacting as a skipper to CAG's request in going on the first SCAR mission, his professional thinking on April 7 was still mainly about the big, fixed strikes. He had no problem with literally taking a backseat to Bru's leadership as an airborne searcher and destroyer.

He and Bru had launched late in the afternoon with Dewar and Squab, both newly trained FAC-As, on their wing. The two JOs, hand-picked the night before, were the pair they thought would be the best FAC-As to spell them should they need to be relieved sometime during the mission. And in the meantime, they could be counted on to be good wingmen.

The plan was to give the two-jet section strike packages for use as bombers. The strike packages, medium-sized with four-to-six jets each, would be made up of the air wing's Hornets. They would arrive at different times and be nearby in order for the FAC-As to have at least one package available to them at all times. They'd also always have secondary targets assigned in case the FAC-As couldn't find any for them to bomb at the FAC-A location. The FAC-As would be protected by a Prowler, as were the strike packages. If they found a target, they'd quarterback the strikers in. If they didn't, the strikers would go on to their secondary, fixed targets.

The Tomcats went first to Skopje in Macedonia, the holding point that was now, for political reasons, forbidden to large strike forces. Kosovo, about the size of New York State is shaped like an erratically bordered diamond. It's thick in the middle and tapers at both ends. They were just opposite the southeastern slope of the diamond, on its eastern side. It was just before sunset. SA-6s had been reported in the area. When their Prowler arrived, they moved over the border. According to Squab's diary, they had "late tipper information about a troop/tank concentration south of Urosevac," a village perhaps twenty miles below Pristina. Using the LANTIRN's FLIR as a spyglass, they saw some heat images near the border that drew their interest. They were too high to identify the images, and even if they could, they were not allowed by NATO to strike that close to Macedonia. But Bru felt the sighting was worth reporting.

He told Joey to radio it in to an airborne relay that could send it back to a higher headquarters. Joey balked. " 'What good is it going to be?' " Bru says Joey replied. "Since we couldn't strike, he felt it was perishable information. . . . I told him, 'We've got unmanned aerial vehicles [UAVs] around here flying, and maybe they'll send one to go down and take a look.' . . . He said, 'Oh, well, that makes sense.' . . . Unless you're a FAC-A, you don't understand why to do that [report it]. Even when you are a FAC, you have to play that command-and-control fiddle to push information so you can get information."

In fact, said Bru, they later found out that those controlling the UAVs did send one of the little remote-controlled, flying cameras to the area and identified what they had seen as "some [Serb] army dudes and APCs [armored personnel carriers]."

The sun went down, and further searching yielded nothing. "The weather wasn't that good," recalled Joey, "so we're going in and out."

The FLIR couldn't see through clouds so they were circling holes in the layers at about twenty-five thousand feet, trying to FLIR through them. "You don't have any visual reference of the horizon. You are in the dark, looking at a screen, doing these left-hand circles." The plane was turning clockwise. He was sluing counterclockwise. It was two opposite rhythms. "It's, 'Boy, this is going to . . . I'm glad I've done this for years and years because somebody doing it for the first time, it can be unsettling for the stomach.' "

Without any targets to hit, their first strike package left and subsequently returned to the carrier after being challenged for mustering over Macedonia before pushing to their secondaries. Bru and Joey decided to go for their midcycle tanking. The two Tomcats had spent approximately two hours searching with only on-the-job training for Joey to show for their efforts. They tanked and next went to the Albanian side of the Kosovo diamond (opposite where they had been at Skopje) to wait for their next Prowler at the border across from Dakovika, one of the larger Kosovo towns.

While they were waiting, they saw sporadic antiaircraft fire erupt from the ground but were too high to be hit. A theater-controlling E-2 Hawkeye surveillance plane, housing an Airborne Command and Control Center, or "ABTripleC," tried to direct them to some suspect vehicles it had received information on from an unmanned aerial vehicle in the area. CAG Lyle, would later call what happened a "command-and-control nightmare. [The Hawkeye] wasn't sure where the targets were, we had no cueing . . . it was just a mess." But Joey and Bru, using the infrared picture in their FLIR scopes, finally spotted the vehicles moving down a road in what Squab, in his diary, labeled a "convoy."

Bru: "And we're like, 'Holy cow, we need to get in there.' " Their Prowler had just started tanking. The executive officer of the Prowler squadron, VAO-141, was one of the four-seat Prowler's crew. His call sign was "Otter." "We made a call to him and said, 'Hey, how much longer you gonna be?' . . . He looked over at the pilot and said, 'Hey, they need us over there.' " The pilot hesitated because they hadn't finished. Bru said Otter flipped. " 'I don't care how much gas we got, pull out and get in the fight!' He was a maniac."

With Dewar and Squab circling cover above, Joey and Bru were able to discern that one of the vehicles was "really big, and the other was a little bit smaller." They were trudging down a road, oblivious to the eyes above. The Tomcats followed the vehicles for miles, said Joey. Bru thought their spacing was a formation for minimizing bomb damage. "If one gets hit, it doesn't frag the other." He suspected they were a tank and an APC (later confirmed), but the "acuity" of the FLIR "wasn't as great as a picture." It only registered heat. "We couldn't find an artillery tube or anything to confirm."

To protect civilians, they had to be sure.

Bru had heard that P-3 spy planes in theater had special cameras on them that might be able to make a determination. He called the Command and Control Center in the Hawkeye, which, after considerable confusion, put them in touch with a P-3 some 250 miles north, probably up near Belgrade.

Bru: "The first thing they said was they couldn't come down because they needed fighter protection. And we go, 'Well, we've only got about thirty-five fighters out here. Won't that work?' They said, 'By golly, it will.'"

But the lumbering propjet, which would become infamous for the China Sea shootdown by a Chinese jet in April 2001, was forty-five minutes away. With it only about ten minutes away, the second group of strikers, waiting for it, got so low on gas they had to leave. And the Prowler, already low because it had been yanked from the tanker, also had to exit.

They were out of luck. Even if they could identify the vehicles, they had lost their protection and bombers.

They told the P-3 to go back home.

Back on the carrier, Bru and Joey had a long debrief. It was a tough sell to CAG but, as was his style, he listened patiently. All and all, argued Bru, they hadn't done so bad. A few more minutes of gas in the strikers' tanks and they might have gotten their first kill. But the details, he admitted as he was being bombarded with questions about them by staff questioners, were a problem — the altitude restrictions, the lack of timely intelligence, the weather, the rules of engagement, the command-and-control nightmare.

At one point, recalled CAG, "I said, 'I just don't think under the architecture we have, we can do this mission.'" But he was also mindful of growing problems with the fixed strikes—the turn back at Macedonia, the assignment of targets to his aviators that had already been struck, continued forecasts of bad weather—"a mess of things going on that day and the previous day."

And he was impressed with Bru's "enthusiasm."

Joey, said CAG, "was more reserved. He said, 'I can't do this from twenty-five-thousand like they want.'" But "'if we could get down to twenty thousand feet. In fact, if we could get down to eighteen thousand feet, I think we can do this.' I said, 'Well, it's against the rules.' But Joey basically said, 'Well, Bru is awfully enthusiastic. It's kinda his baby. He's been working with it an awfully long time. . . . I think if we can modify some rules . . . we might be able to do this.'"

Bru's conviction, said CAG, gave him an "inkling" that maybe Joey was right.

He told Bru, in effect, to draw up a plan.

The upbeat spirit of the previous night was probably gone from the Black Aces ready room as the dawn returnees from the Pristina strike tried to figure out what had happened. Stragglers from the mission turned back from Macedonia, if any were still there, certainly would not have been upbeat. Other JOs, including Brain, Thing, and Razor, had been on that mission and had missed their chance to push into hostile Kosovo. Most of them were probably trying to get some sleep in their staterooms, happy to be alive but hoping for another try. Lt. (jg) Ed "Moto" Mayle, listed as the SDO (squadron duty officer) that morning, meaning he was behind the squadron's barlike duty desk area taking care of routine business, was a nugget. He was probably wide-eyed at this early stage and would have taken his cues from the more experienced aviators like Beaker, who was getting angrier by the minute.

Gooch and Money already knew what had happened to their cow bomb. They had blown it. They both felt bad. "It was my low point," recalled Money.

It had taken several ready-room tape replays for Beaker and Toad to determine that Toad had not in fact put the cursor on the correct target. "He was on a little circle with something in the middle, but what it turned out to be was a tree of some sort," said Beaker.

Someone else in the room had showed him a second mistake on their tape, one that he'd not been able to find himself.

"I could see Gooch's error," said Beaker. And the hinge had little trouble pointing out the problem on the VF-14 wingman's tape. "Nowhere near where they needed to be," he said about his sister squadron's crew. "But I couldn't figure out my tape until a VF-14 guy came over and helped and we ascertained that, hey, we didn't have any good laser ranging."

The penetrator needed extra input from its droppers. Because of a software glitch, the LANTIRN's automatic calculation of range to the target at the time of drop was wrong. The RIO was required to do a manual laser range prior to release and then adjust several of the LANTIRN's automatic figures with other manual calculations.

Toad had not done that. And Beaker hadn't caught it.

"What happened was he messed up his switchology and he didn't update our system to get laser ranging prior to release," said Beaker. "So the system was working just off passive ranging, and it was about a half mile different than what the actual ranging was. . . . So we actually released the weapon about two thousand feet inside of its minimum range."

Being successful with the penetrator was like hitting a three-pointer from way beyond the circle. The shot was hard and demanded a high, arcing route. There was almost no room for error if the ball was to drop inside the very small parameters of the hoop. While other bombs the squadron was using were less demanding and had larger envelopes for success, thus allowing for minor deviations in calculating airspeed, altitude, and course heading, the bunker-buster was unforgiving. Its envelope was small and tight. And if all inputs were not precise, it was squandered.

Beaker: "For a variety of reasons everybody is releasing outside of the envelope, and as a result we have four GBU-24s at sixty thousand dollars each, a quarter-million dollars thrown out the window and landing somewhere in the Serbian countryside. Didn't know if they went off or not."

It was not a happy ready room.

It had been a long post-OB mission debrief, especially for Bru, who was glad to get out and weary when he left. "We've had our meeting down in CAG's spaces," he recalled, "and a lot of the skippers are going 'Well, gee, I just don't think we can do it.' And Joey is being the leader that he is and going, 'Well, I think we can do it.' And all up and down the passageway . . . I'm getting these sidebars with a couple of different XOs just going, 'Bru, it sounds all right, but I just don't think we can do it.' I was just fed up."

Aucoin went to his stateroom, and Bru walked into the ready room. He remembers Gooch, Squab, and Dewar still being there. Gooch, tired and disappointed about the Pristina mission, was also contrary about the OB. "Gooch told me, he goes, 'I don't see how we're gonna do it. I just don't see it.' "

Gooch remembers, "What I expressed to him was . . . that the LAN-TIRN system wasn't capable of doing what he wanted it to do from the altitude he was talking about. . . . The original plan that he told me, to go high, very high and supersonic to avoid the threats and still be able to ID tanks"—in effect, what Joey and Bru had done that evening—"I said, 'That's not going to work.' . . ."

Bru remembers, "I just, I kinda lost it. . . . What he was saying was right. But it wasn't solving the problem. And that was the difficulty I was having. I mean our guidance had been given. And in probably the rarest opportunity in aviation history . . . because rarely has there been the employment of air power that was being asked to be done. No ground forces. And the objective was, 'We want you to go out and engage a ground army without a ground army of your own and effect a resolution.' And I understood that, or I thought I did, when the whole thing started out. And I was going, 'My God, this is pretty unique.' And I kind of relished the thought of it, actually." And then to be hearing the same nay-saying, he said, in his *own* ready room, "I was kind of a little bit frustrated . . . and vented that towards Gooch."

Squab remembers that he was "already familiar with Bru's gift for passionate arguments," having served under him as a maintenance-division officer. But coming back from that first night, he agreed with Gooch. "We can't do this mission. It's too hard," he says he told Bru, to which he said Bru immediately shot back, "Bullshit!' "

It's not clear who Bru was talking to next, but he acknowledges, "I just blew up. I mean, I'm like, 'What in the fuck do you mean we can't do this! How many times have we done it?' 'Well, once.' I go, 'You know, that's not enough. That's not enough to make a decision.'

And I'm going, 'Goddamit, here's a chance to do something that we've trained our entire career for, and then the answer is [that] we can't do it? That's utter bullshit! . . . How have we always done this stuff throughout history anyway? We find a way! So stop sitting there saying we can't. That's too easy. Start thinking how we can!' . . . I just remember I needed a release, and the only way to do it was in my own ready room. . . . Those poor guys had to sit there and listen."

Apparently he got through because, he says, "they just started nodding their heads and going, 'All right.' "

Dewar, he said, just watched.

While the Aces on the Pristina raid had identified their errors in employing the GBU-24, VF-14 crew members were not so sure. "I knew that when I left CVIC that morning, Slapshot was saying, 'Hey, there's something wrong with the bombs,' " recalled Money. "Maybe the fins didn't open, whatever. Of course I knew that wasn't the case for me, but I was a first-tour lieutenant, and he was a skipper and strike leader, and I was on his strike, and I had let him down. I'm obviously not going to speak up at that point."

The other Aces involved apparently were of the same mind.

By the time Joey was in the mix, which was probably mid-morning, he was hearing conflicting views: Beaker, Gooch, Money, and Toad knew they couldn't blame the penetrator. But CAG, said Joey, "was thinking about sending out a message saying that these bombs are defective." CAG, as he should, was listening to his strike leader, Slapshot, who apparently was not convinced that he and his pilot had made an error.

CAG: "My first input to the admiral was that we failed and that we don't know why. . . . We had gone back through the loading procedures meticulously at that point and could not find a single mistake. . . . We couldn't validate a switchology problem." He was mindful that his aircrews had never dropped the penetrator before and that others using it against Iraq during Operation Desert Fox in 1998 had reported problems. "My second input [to the admiral] was that we think we could have a serious problem with the weapons themselves."

When Joey told CAG what his flyers were saying, CAG asked Joey to review all the tapes. The easy thing would have been to defer to

VF-14 and the probable airlifting in of an expert on the bomb, an option CAG was considering. Joey wasn't doing himself any favors by trying to confirm that his aircrews had erred. But he spent considerable time going over the tapes, including Slapshot's. Maybe there was a degree of pleasure in hunting for his rival's mistake. But it was a two-edged sword.

Joey: "I sat down and went through the tapes for a couple of hours. . . . It turns out all four had mistakes. . . . It wasn't the bomb . . . it was the guys." Slapshot's jet, he said, was off in heading a couple of degrees. He went back to CAG, and the two of them went through the tapes together.

CAG: Joey "came and fessed up. 'Hey, we blew it. . . . The reason we missed was aircrew error on all four of them . . . and this is what we did wrong.' . . . The third time I went to [the admiral] I had to say, 'Okay, now we know the truth. The good news is we don't need any help from the outside. The bad news is that we gooned it,' and [I] explained why. The admiral took it pretty well, I thought."

But the failure changed Joey's thinking, which was constantly being shaped by the whirlwind of combat.

"After we got through the first couple of strikes," he said, "I had wanted to spread [the missions] out so that everybody flew [on a big strike] . . . stress the teamwork part of it. . . . But then, the outcome of [Pristina] was, I decided, in my squadron anyway, we're going to continue going with our best guys. I'm sorry, we can't do a team approach here. There were things more important than making everybody feel happy. This is making everybody survive. . . . I said, 'Guys, you show me you're capable of doing this. Then you can step up to the A-Team. This isn't on-the-job training anymore.' "

Ten

"During the fifty-five days of [the *Roosevelt's* involvement in] Allied Force, there was 50 percent or worse cloud cover 70 percent" of the time, wrote Tophatter skipper Ted "Slapshot" Carter in a postwar article (winter 1999) in *Wings of Gold*, the Association of Naval Aviation magazine. The statement highlights how weather, specifically bad weather, was perhaps the Serbs' chief weapon during the Kosovo War. Clouds obscured the enemy, hiding targets from planes and satellites and allowing troop and vehicle movements to go unnoticed. Most important, the lasers the Allies were using didn't penetrate clouds and were hampered by rain, snow, and sleet. Although wispy or small or both, clouds, rain, hail, and sleet were nevertheless made up of solid matter. And when the laser hit the solid, it reflected back just as if it had hit a concrete wall. The laser didn't discriminate. The result was that the obstruction broke the lock on the designated target. The bomb the laser was guiding went stupid. Bad weather and the quick changes in temperatures it could cause could also diffuse the infrared, temperature-generated picture on the LANTIRN scope, further degrading the aircraft's ability to bomb. Crews couldn't hit what they couldn't see and didn't want to target what they were not sure of.

In addition, lightning striking an aircraft could sometimes short electrical equipment, leaving the plane without essential navigation, identification, and even communication capacity. And without such essential equipment a plane's crew was nearly helpless in a dark storm, where usually there was no horizon to indicate what direction was up or down. Worse, lightning could start an onboard fire. Hail, which was a component of storms, especially in their upper regions, could literally destroy a jet. Golf-ball-sized or larger, it could rip holes in the aircraft's skin like antiaircraft fire or break an engine if injested. At the least, bad weather, because of the decreased visibility, increased the chances of midair collision and added danger to the already-dangerous tasks of tanking and landing—not to mention just plain flying.

Jets flew by forcing their wings into the wind. The wind, pushing on the underwing surface, lifted the plane. The wind going over the curved top of the wing created a suction that also lifted the jet. When the wind became unruly, as it did in bad weather, it could interfere with the aerodynamics. Gusts could toss the aircraft so that the wings weren't grabbing the wind. The plane would start falling. The condition was called "stall." Stalls in which the plane was not only falling but also spinning were usually unrecoverable. Severe downdrafts and updrafts could cause sudden, violent differences in a plane's altitude, dropping it drastically, which could cause a crash if the plane was near the ground or a mountaintop, of which there were plenty in Kosovo.

Icing, also a hazard in storms, especially in the storm's colder upper regions, could clog or break crucial outside sensors and decrease or eliminate the needed airflow over the wings and other crucial surfaces. "Clear" ice often couldn't be seen until it was too late. Spring was a volatile time for weather in and around Kosovo. The changes in seasons brought violent winds and quick reversals in temperatures, which, in turn, could cause sudden weather changes, especially in the velocity of winds. And these conditions were also around, or in near proximity to, the carrier. The result of all this was that the Roosevelt's bombers during the war were often emasculated by bad weather.

The next two days in the Roosevelt's first week of war—April 8 and April 9—saw almost all combat flights from the carrier canceled because of storms and clouds. "The weather sucks," Squab wrote in his diary April 9, "so today becomes a day to catch up on sleep and paperwork." Also on April 9, Bru presented his SCAR plan to Captain Lyle, the CAG. In preparation, he'd called a marine buddy, MiGs

Roberts, an F/A-18 pilot on the *Enterprise* in the Persian Gulf, the carrier the *Roosevelt* had originally been scheduled to relieve. Roberts was an expert on spotting and hitting targets from the air and had been one of the marines who had helped teach Bru earlier. "I was using him as a sanity check for what I was going to propose. He was in agreement."

Bru's plan, although full of flying and weapons details, was really very simple. Two sections of FAC-A-trained Tomcat crews per day would launch for separate two-to-three-hour hunting missions. The first section would be relieved by the second so that there would be continuity. The section returning could update the section arriving. They'd start with southern Kosovo, where the killing was concentrated. He drew a line marking the area. It stretched from Dakovica in the west to Urosevic in the east. They'd use "whatever means available" to identify the target, which meant UAVs [unmanned aerial vehicles], binoculars, LANTIRN, other aircraft in the area, and secret sources. They'd need stacked strikers for when they found targets and Prowlers for defense. Minimum altitude and Rules of Engagement (ROE) were still questions. For instance, it would be nice, said Bru, if they could go lower than the current floor. And if they got clearance to hit one target, could they go ahead and hit another nearby?

Bru: "This was an intimate little meeting. It was me and Joey, CAG, CAG's Ops officer, the sister squadron skipper [Slapshot], and his XO, Commander [Sam 'Slammer'] Richardson [the handsome Tophatter who was to be featured live on NBC's *Today Show* after he flew cohost Matt Lauer onto the *Roosevelt*]. Slammer was an old Top Gun guy and pretty critical of whether we could hit those mobile targets." Everybody there, except for CAG, who mainly listened, and Joey, was critical. There were also rumblings about the air force taking the better targets, meaning bigger and easier-to-hit targets, and leaving the scraps for the navy. Whether that was true or not was another matter. The two services, because of interservice rivalry, were sometimes at odds. The nub of the problem was that there were more large targets north of Kosovo, which was the territory war planners had given the air force to bomb. The navy had been given the south. The assigning of territory had been done before the *Roosevelt* had arrived and involved the ranges of various warplanes, so there wasn't much that could be done about it. But the strikers, even CAG, still wanted to hit what they'd practiced to hit in Nevada, which were the larger targets. None of those listening to Bru were happy. CAG later said, "I initially thought it [hunting for fielded forces] was a misuse of our assets . . . but we do what we're told."

Apparently Bru's plan was taken under advisement. SCAR, and whether to commit to it, were still being debated, both on the ship and at higher levels. Bru said he left the meeting feeling everyone was "onboard" but "reluctantly." It was an uneasy exit, given his feelings for the mission. But he had little time to worry about it. Two big strikes were ordered for the night of April 10, and Joey was to lead one. Bru, scheduled to be his pilot, was heavily involved in the planning, which was commencing the same day as the meeting.

They were going back to Pristina, to another ammunition-storage area. Anxiety levels for both men were high, said Bru. This was their first big mission since their jet's failure four nights prior. They didn't want another equipment malfunction. The recent QB had not gone as they'd hoped. There were myriad mission details to decide, and the weather loomed as a constant problem, threatening to cause the strike to be canceled before they launched, or even en route. Joey said operations planners were telling him, "Hey, you're probably not going to go on this." There was a feeling at the time, said Bru, that "hey, this thing's gonna be over any day. So maybe we'd missed our opportunity?"

Both of them were frustrated.

As usual, the air order had come from the CAOC in Vincenza, via the admiral and then via CAG. "We sat down and looked at what the targets were," said Bru, "what they wanted taken out, and then came up with the numbers of airplanes, the ordnance on those airplanes, and then what support assets we needed to help us out, the amount of gas, all that sort of stuff."

They decided on four Tomcats as the core of the strike package, two each from the air wing's two Tomcat squadrons. Each of the four Tomcats would carry GBU-10s, or two-thousand-pound laser-guided bombs. Because the aim points on the targets were small, Joey, as leader of the strike, felt the best sensor with which to find the dimpies was the LANTIRN on the F-14, as opposed to the Hornet's Nite Hawk FLIR, which didn't have as much magnification. So none of the air wing's Hornets were going to be strikers. They didn't have to worry about collateral damage to nonmilitary targets because the storage facility was in the countryside, basically on the side of a mountain. They thought four jets for the core, a minimum amount for such a strike, could do the job because it only took one hit to set off all the ammunition.

Two Hornets as fighter escort, two Prowlers, each with a Tomcat escort, three S-3s for tanking, and two E-2s as controllers made up the rest of the package. "There's always a trade-off," said Bru. "You want to eliminate something with the utmost efficiency. . . . You want to save your ammunition [which was scarce] for something that may be of higher priority . . . plus you don't want to put more people at risk than you have to."

To fly their wing, Joey and Bru chose Wrex, who apparently was doing well with his "last chance" to impress the skipper, and Mentul Challingsworth, who got his call sign from the first part of his last name ("challenged"), not from any deficiencies or manias (although the "u" was ribbingly inserted to imply an inability to spell). Squadron mates said the husky RIO looked a little like Wog, so they started calling him "Son of Wog," and called Wog "Father of Mentul," and then shortened the two to SOW and FOW—call sign absurdum. None of the names bothered the good-natured, unassuming lieutenant. He was on the rise, having flown his first combat mission on April 7. But that was an HVAAP (High Value Airborne Asset Protection), a CAP (Combat Air Patrol) mission for a Prowler, high and away from the center action. In Wrex's backseat, he was going to be down in the thick of things and get a chance to drop a bomb, which, next to bagging a MiG, was RIO Valhalla, especially to one who had never done it before.

When time came to launch, the night sky surrounding the carrier was clear. But Kosovo, and the route to it, were being raked by storms. No one wanted to cancel. The storms aided the enemy, whose atrocities were being trumpeted by the press. They decided to go. "We had to transit some really bad weather to get up there," said Bru, "and thank goodness we had the night-vision goggles. I remember looking over at the Prowlers that were trying to weave back and forth through the clouds and kind of giving them a heads up on where clouds were . . . they didn't have night-vision goggles. They still don't, and I remember feeling how, you know, those poor bastards are flying blind out here and there was lightning and stuff going on all over the place. What a mess."

Next to them, in the backseat of the Tomcat shadowing their wing, Mentul was getting "a little nervous. It's my first combat. . . . The day we were planning for it, you don't have time to think about it. . . . But off the ship, flying towards it, you've done all your switches, and you're just sitting there. Okay, this is it. . . . You start really thinking . . . 'Is there anyone more prepared to go to war than me? Well, yeah. But the only ones that are, are the people I'm flying with because there's no other country in the world more trained than we are. . . .' And that made me feel pretty good—that and the fact that I'm flying with Wrex. . . . He's very good at keeping you calm in the cockpit. Going into battle, he's one of the guys to be with. He's real calm. He listens to what you say."

They went through checklists. From the front cockpit, Wrex looked down at one of the monitors on his dash as Mentul, using the LAN-TIRN joystick to his left and rear, dialed in the bomb laser codes they'd been given before they left. They both had the codes written down, probably on knee-board pads. The two crewmen's codes coincided. Then Wrex flipped up the guard cover on his master arm switch and moved the toggle to "on." Electricity surged to all their weapons switches. Any weapons switch or button they activated would now ready the particular weapon for drop or launch. In this case, since they were going on a bombing run, it was drop. "Trigger lights hot," Wrex said. Mentul verified, and Wrex moved the toggle back to off and put the guard back over it. It was only a check they were doing. They didn't want to arm for real until shortly before they were actually ready to drop. But they now were satisfied everything was working correctly. "We told some jokes about the brief," said Mentul. "The normal stuff in the cockpit."

Anything to pass the time.

Around each one of them was an array of panels, gauges, switches, dials, and buttons. Some of them had "warning" on them. Wrex had a "heads-up" display on the windshield that gave him various readings, headings, and other information he needed in order to fly the jet, shoot missiles, or drop bombs. The fact that it was on his windshield meant that he didn't have to bring his eyes into the cockpit to see what was going on. Mentul could view the same information—but not the view outside—on the large green-glowing scope he had in front of him above his knees. The scope was a square approximately eight inches by eight inches, larger than the one Wrex had in front, and could be used to view radar and other databases. Their seats gave them enough legroom to stretch out and reach pedals on the floor. Wrex controlled the jet's rudders with his pedals; Mentul controlled the radio and intercom with his.

It was a no-hands-needed system.

No longer allowed to muster over Macedonia, the strike package rendezvoused at twenty thousand feet above Albania, west of Skopje and closer to the Adriatic than on previous nights. Ahead of them, 120 miles to the north, backdropping their target, which was closer, was a scary and dangerous sight: a broiling, undulating cloud stack, layered in whispy tiers, towering as high as they were. It was crackling with lightning and underlit by the still-soaring petroleum fires from the first night's strikes. Bru: "It looked like something on TV from Desert Storm with the oil wells burning. . . . What made it really eerie was the overcast layer. . . . It was bright orange," which made it look "like you were going into a big room . . . a big cauldron."

A devil's cauldron.

It was clear the package had lost any protection the night's darkness might have provided. Going in, they would be lit up like players in a giant amphitheater. There were open patches in the clouds. But for how long? If they couldn't see the target, they couldn't lase. Worse, a carpet of clouds beneath them—should that be the case—meant they wouldn't see SAMs coming up.

"You gotta see the ground," said Joey, both for bombing and protection.

It was decision time.

"We had to push or go home," said Bru. "Joey asked me what I thought." If he went in and something went wrong, he could lose his command.

They asked the Hornet leader above them if he thought he could keep sight of the four Tomcats in the weather. It was his job to protect them.

He said he could.

Bru: "I said, 'Well, what if we just push in and see? If it gets worse, we'll abort.' "

Joey: "I just made a decision . . . I mean I probably pressed them to the limit . . . if you asked anybody on that strike, they thought it was going to be an abort . . . but then it was another bust. . . . I looked at it. . . . It's workable . . . I said, 'Bru, lets try this.' "

The package pushed, the core beginning a calculated descent. They didn't make a wall this time. The two Aces' Tomcats sped out in front. The Tophatter F-14s dropped in trail. The four were in a "box," creating more options.

The Hornets stayed above, their radars searching. They would attack any MiGs and be extra eyes for the target-concentrating strikers.

Almost immediately, the package began to see Triple-A, or antiaircraft artillery. But it was far below. It was the first hostile fire Bru had ever seen. "It wasn't all that spectacular," he said. But as they got lower and it got closer, the bursts began to "distract" him. "I looked outside, saw a flash, so I'd turn the other way. . . . When you're leading these things, your real concern isn't the preservation of yourself; it's more everybody around you. And if you do it right, you put a plan together that gives them all a sanctuary. And part of that is maintaining situational awareness for everybody."

In other words, he was trying to keep all four from getting hit.

The strike plan called for approaching the target at an angle and then turning in at the normal begin-targeting point for a straight-on run. But while dodging Triple-A and looking for open patches in the weather, they couldn't do that. As a consequence, Joey didn't get the twenty miles ahead of the target needed to find his dimpy and fix the cursor. He started about ten miles from the target—mere seconds—and didn't recognize it when he had it. When he finally realized his error, they were nearly on top of the ammunition facility and out of their bomb's parameters.

"I'm looking, looking, and I don't get it until we're in too close," he said.

Bru: "It all goes back to the training and practice. . . . A forward-looking infrared picture [FLIR] and a photograph don't always look the same. [The FLIR picture is] similar to looking at negatives . . . the colors can be off . . . it's white or black depending on the heat differential. . . . I always say it's a good thing [the war] lasted a couple of months because everybody in the air wing had to screw it up three times in order to get really good. . . . What that basically identified was training limitations that we had as a result of inadequate funding, resourcing, what have you."

Wrex and Mentul, following their leader, didn't drop either.

But the two Tophatters in trail did.

"They were like seven or eight miles back," said Joey. "They had enough time, like a minute or so, to designate. So they were able to get their bombs off."

Bru: "I was disappointed for an instant. You know, 'Aw shit, we missed our basket to drop in.' But that's part of the planning. . . . Until you've proven yourself, you bring extra assets along because you know that if you send out four, two of them are gonna hit. If you send out eight, four are gonna hit. . . . So the target got serviced properly, and that's when the rodeo started."

Turning around and egressing back south, they were attacked by SAMs.

"There was stuff all over the place," said Joey. Bru said it started as they approached Urosevac, perhaps fifteen miles from the ammunition facility. "You could see the lights of the city . . . we were going to fly right over the top of it [when] here comes the first surface-to-air missile I've ever seen . . . It looks just like a Saturn rocket in my night-vision goggles. It comes up, and it's backlit by the lights of the city . . . then turns and points at us."

He guessed it was "six-to-eight miles away," and he said that as he looked at it, time stood still. "It seemed like forever before I did anything. I was like almost in disbelief, going, 'Wow, that's really a missile coming up,' and my radar early-warning gear is screaming at me, meaning I'm targeted. It makes a high warble noise, really obnoxious. And then you've got a display . . . a strobe that tells you what direction the thing's coming from."

Listening to the tapes later, he said it was only "a second or two" before he called the SAM launch. But it had seemed much longer. "It just really got your blood pumping." He started evasive maneuvers aimed at destroying the missile's energy when one of the Prowlers shot a HARM. "It smacks the base of the thing, and [the launcher on the ground] just blows up . . . kind of a Christmas tree explosion. . . . The

SAM just kind of starts wandering willy-nilly and goes stupid."

Simultaneously, at least four other SAMs were shot up at other jets in the strike package. Bru and Joey think they were ballistic rather than guided, but the threat caused the other strikers to "bail out every which way . . . kind of looked like an 'exploding cantaloupe' I think is the term . . . planes just doing whatever they could to defeat either the radar guiding it or the missile itself."

Nobody was hit. More HARMs were shot and sites destroyed. And although he remembered it as a time of "screaming and yelling [,] . . . you play back the tape, and you're going, 'Wow, you know, given the circumstances, everybody was kind of pretty well held together.' . . . They were a little more deliberate [on the radios], but it wasn't like anybody had been castrated or changed gender quality. . . ."

They got away "through airspeed and route," said Joey. By then most in the package were extremely low on gas, having used full burners during most of the egress, and facing them once they reached the Adriatic, hiding any tankers, was the same system of thunderstorms they'd had to negotiate after launch.

They climbed to try and find a way through, but there was none.

They flew in.

"Lightning's going off and all this sort of stuff," said Bru. "Everybody's low on gas. . . . We've got to have gas to land."

Air force tankers were too far away. They called the ship, which sent out some S-3s, and these met them in the chaos. Now they had to perform the precise mating maneuvers demanded in tanking, and Bru got the scourge of no-horizon night flying—vertigo.

"You could be upside down or sideways. It's hard to tell without a horizon. And then you've got this leaning thing going on where you feel like you're in a turn and you're wanting to right yourself while you're trying to get in the basket. . . . I told the skipper, I said, 'I feel like I'm in a left-hand turn all the time.' And he goes, 'Okay.' And so over a period of time, he'd tell me, 'Okay, your wing's level, your wing's level.' And he continually reinforces, and you condition yourself to not listen to your body."

Vertigo, the result of false sensory impressions to the brain from delicate inner-ear canals, can cause severe disorientation. In flight, the sufferer thinks he's in a different altitude than he really is and has to fight his wrong inclinations. And as if that weren't enough, they were so low on gas, and the weather was so bad at the divert bases — Sigonella, Sicily, and Brindisi, Italy — that if they couldn't tank, they probably couldn't make it to those bases and would have to ditch.

"You've got to take the goggles off because they don't give you depth perception. So you go from being able to see this whole airplane to just seeing the lights, which are pretty small.... You're like, 'Oh, great.' So you just kind of slowly and controlled get on up in there, and this slow and controlled is in conflict with, 'I need to get gas in my airplane right now.' ... And you're thinking, in the back of your mind you are inventorying everyone else's fuel state and [asking], 'Is there somebody worse off than me?' — which there was ... and then the weather ... and the divert ... [and the vertigo], and you've got some anxiety going on."

So much so that he began experiencing time compression again. "Seconds seemed like hours." With Joey's help, he finally, after repeated tries, threaded the needle. They were fifty miles from the carrier. Joey's recollection is that they made it back on the first pass. Bru's is that they were waved off and had to tank again. "Just as painful as the other one.... You can't see. You've got a little bit of vertigo going on." And because they were much closer to the water, with planes stacked above and below them, the danger and anxiety were even worse. "You're looking at your instruments; you're looking outside. You're inside; you're outside. You feel like you're standing on your head.... You're cross-checking where the water is because you could be watching somebody, and in just a few seconds, if you don't cross-check, you could descend five hundred or one thousand feet.... You're both kind of playing the who-can-sound-cooler-in-a-stressful-situation game because the last thing you want is to come in and have somebody say, 'What were you doing up there? Did I hear you crying out there?' "

Whatever the truth of their return, lost in a blur of bad-weather memories, Mentul remembers how exhilarating it was to finally be back on deck: "I'm thinking my bombs are still on my jet. I failed. I did not do what I was sent out to do." And then, "We got on deck, and the skipper has this big smile on his face, and he gave me a high five, and he says, 'Good to be alive, isn't it?' ... And I didn't feel so bad. He didn't hit his either. At least I knew I wasn't a total failure. It was a lot harder than we thought it was ... and the skipper, being the great guy he is, said, 'Look, you did everything you could. Just be happy you are alive with what happened out there.' So I said, 'Okay.' . . . It was pretty intense."

Joey remembered the high fives: It was "a pretty scary night . . . pretty colorful . . . I felt, 'Shoot, I wish I'd gotten my bombs on there.' Then I went, 'Wait a minute. I led a successful strike. If we had the normal run in, I would have had enough time.' . . . I mean, there's a lot of pressure to get the bombs off and all. But I felt real proud . . . we took out the target and got everybody back safely . . . the weather . . . we were shot up quite a bit. . . . It was pretty ballsy. . . . Guys feel proud about it, and then it'll be another day."

They walked off the deck, a lifetime of drama and tension for some behind them to be nearly forgotten with the next day's mission — killer storm, first-combat jitters, decisions that could ruin careers, murderous antiaircraft fire, precision bombing with its split-second, brain-busting calculation and decision, disappointment, rockets fired up to blast them, more killer storm, and vertigo and tanking, dangerous even in calm skies.

They shrugged it off.

They were men of action, not reflection.

During another strike mission on April 10, Dewar and Squab were involved in what appears to have been the squadron's first encounter with Serbian MiGs. Flying close escort in the daylight hours for some Hornets going after a highway bridge, they received warnings that there were MiG-21 fighters orbiting above Podgorica, Montenegro's largest city and home of one of the Serbs' largest outlying airfields. For political reasons, Podgorica and the airfield were off-limits to strikers. But if the enemy jets flew into adjoining Kosovo, they were not.

"We are on top of the weather at about twenty-seven thousand feet, and the MiGs are down at one thousand feet, through many layers of weather," wrote Squab in his diary. "We never get a good radar track, and we can't get below the weather to VID [visually identify the MiGs as an enemy plane, a requirement before shooting] — not a good idea over Podgorica with its numerous SAM sites."

The airfield, maybe twenty miles from where the strikers were, was reputedly ringed with the missiles.

The Hornets went down to twenty thousand feet, but they still couldn't get a radar "print." The strike was aborted for weather, so the entire package decided to perform a CAP, "trying to get good radar on these MiGs so we can shoot them down." Eventually, "We have three sections of fighters orbiting, just waiting for these MiG-21s to do something. They never do. . . . That was certainly the best opportunity we have had for a [long-range] Phoenix [air-to-air-missile] kill yet."

Most of the Aces' senior JOs flew on the night of April 10. There were two other missions scheduled to leave the carrier after midnight, and the squadron was taxed to put at least a second cruise veteran into each of the front seats of the Tomcats assigned and have veteran-led crews as backup spares in Tomcats in case any of the scheduled crews developed mechanical problems and were not able to proceed.

A strike being led by Hornet skipper Comdr. Ken "Stalk" Thompson had Beaker and Lt. Eric "Pappy" Anduze, a Puerto Rican–born naval academy graduate, piloting HVAAP missions, the "asset" in this case being a Prowler. Beaker, who was now making his RIOs draw the target for him in prestrike briefs, had young Moto in his backseat for what appears to have been the nugget RIOs first outing of the war. Toad was crewed with Anduze. Brain with Money, and Meat, finally getting a shot, with rookie Rhino in his backseat, were scheduled to man one of the Kosovo CAP stations set up in Albania and Macedonia. The CAPs, manned round-the-clock, strikes or no, were there to intercept Serbian planes at all times.

All three missions had spares. Gooch and Thing were the spare for Bru and Joey when they took off at around 11 P.M. Since nobody went down, they left their jet, got something to eat in the officers' mess, and then climbed into another waiting spare for the HVAAP, euphemistically called "have-a-pee," which was leaving around 3 or 4 A.M.

In a clear validation of the need for spares, Beaker and Moto developed a fuel leak on deck and couldn't launch. So Gooch and Thing took their place. In the meantime, Bru and Joey had returned from their mission and were several hours into a long debrief when they heard that one of their jets was coming back prematurely. Having already experienced their own problems in the bad weather and cognizant that an early return meant something was wrong, they ran down to air operations to find out what was wrong. What they heard would anger both squadron leaders.

Gooch and Thing had taken off with the normal complement of air-to-air missiles: one long-range Phoenix, one short-range Sparrow, and two heat-seeking Sidewinders, used mainly for close-in dogfighting.

The Phoenix and Sparrow were radar missiles.

They also had guns.

Bru: "The skipper got on the radio and asked them, 'What's the matter with your jet?' Thing was talking from the backseat, which is normal. He said, 'Well, we're at tactical joker on our missiles.' " "Tactical joker," said Bru, is code for "a predefined minimum number of weapons you need on your airplane to complete the mission. . . . The feeling amongst a few of us was that [since] the air threat . . . does not have anywhere near the air-to-air proficiency [we] do . . . night-vision goggles and heat-seeking missiles should allow you enough of an armament system to go on ahead and complete the mission. And that's my perception of what Joey's feelings were when he finally said, 'Well, what does work?' " The answer: " 'Well, our radar missiles won't tune,' " meaning they weren't showing readiness to be fired in preliminary testing. "And that's when Joey said, 'And for that, you're running away?' "

Bru said there was silence on the radio, and then Joey slammed down the receiver.

Neither Joey, Gooch, nor Thing recall the precise exchange. But Joey agrees, "I was pissed. . . . He aborts the mission . . . and I'm like, 'You're telling me he aborted because he didn't have a Sparrow missile? . . . You gotta be shittin' me.' . . . We were like, 'Come on, there's enough Allied fighters out there that if we have a problem, all we have to do is just, if we're getting targeted, we've got the fastest plane out there. We can run away and then have one of our wingmen or some other plane target them. But don't abort the mission. We're a bomber squadron. We're out here to kill targets. . . .' "

Gooch remembers: "We launch, and we have no operating radar missiles. . . . We may not even have had a sidewinder that worked. So we're basically a piece of metal up there. . . . We could not protect the Prowler at night with no missiles. . . . Now what ended up happening, the skipper called up, and I think he was worried [because there wasn't a spare to spell us] on deck, and he wanted us to go on the mission. . . . I think he was a little upset and wondering why we didn't go, [but] I don't know that he really knew the extent of our system degrade, because if he really knew that we had no weapons, I can't believe that he'd really want us to go."

Thing remembers: "We didn't have a single missile that worked. . . . I think we had a downgrade with the sidewinder. . . . We had nothing but a gun on board. The question was, 'Hey, we do not have a combat-capable jet.' We made the decision that we should not go. Flying back, the skipper, well, he almost called our courage out. . . . I still remember the tone of voice. . . . I thought, 'Oh boy, we're going to hear about this.' "

After the war, and in view of the conflicting information, Dog commented on the incident: "I'm very well briefed on this. . . . [They] basically could not fire radar missiles. . . . But he could fire a sidewinder. . . . He made the wrong call. . . . It [was] kinda Gooch's philosophy. Just survive. . . . Our job is not to live. It's to make other people die. . . ."

Gooch was a stickler for the rules, a squadron training officer who could recite chapter and verse from the tactics and how-to manuals. By the letter of the law, according to Bru and the others, Gooch was right. You don't go into battle without a full complement of missiles. But, added Bru, "The initial impression was, 'Okay, he's using the rules as an excuse to come home.' "

The squadron leadership wanted more.

Bru, in meetings on the carrier, was on a roller coaster as to how the air wing was going to fight—continue with the large air strikes, or start the smaller hunter-killer missions?

He says that sometime around the 10th, as the bad weather raged, CAG came to him and said, " 'All right, we're not doing any more of this mobile target stuff. We're just gonna hit fixed targets.' "

The order, he said, was the result of consultations between CAG and targeting officers at the CAOC at Aviano. "They're going, 'Hey, were not having any luck at [finding the fielded forces]. We're not even sure we can do it.' . . . And I remember guys coming up and going, 'Hey, sorry Bru, you gotta be bummed.' I said, 'I could care less. . . . We've got a mission. Let's just go do it [instead] of sitting around whining because we're having a hard time at it.' . . . I mean, that irritated me a bit."

But then, four hours later, he said, CAG called all his strike leaders and skippers into his office and reversed the guidance. "He goes, 'All right, here's what it is. It's not fixed targets. That's over. Our mission is to hit fielded forces. End of story. . . . Now how are we going to do it?' " The same objections heard at previous meetings were voiced. We can't do it. It hasn't worked so far. The altitude restrictions make it impossible. "He finally sat back and goes, 'I'm not asking you. I'm telling you. This is what we're doing. All right? So figure it out.' "

It was a vindication of sorts for both Bru and Joey, who had been the only ones supporting the mission—Bru more than Joey. After the meeting, Joey and Bru, despite the consternation they knew it would cause in the squadron from FAC-As and others who would want to fly on the missions, decided they would take all the initial SCAR missions. Because of the opposition being voiced, it would be the only way, they felt, to make sure that the job got done. If they didn't do it, they asked, who would? The naysayers? They didn't believe it. And it was important that the mission get done. CAG was obviously responding to higher authority. The navy had been tasked, and if it couldn't find and destroy the Serbian fielded forces, then what good was it? The air force was taking care of all the larger strategic targets. NATO didn't need the navy for those.

"Bru was very emphatic about, 'Hey, we're going to get fired if we don't figure this out,' " said Squab.

One versatile Black Ace, an aviator with the skills, intelligence, and talent to make it not only as a carrier fighter pilot, but as a country singer, actor, or even nuclear engineer, was Razor Shick. The thirty-year-old, Hanover, Pennsylvania, native was a ruggedly handsome, personable high school scholar and athlete who had won the school's chess tournament, starred in school musicals, and graduated first in his class.

"I don't think I was the smartest," he recalls. "I just tried harder. . . . I wanted to be best at everything"—a trait common to good fighter pilots. They call it type A personality—aggressive, competitive, driven to succeed. He was also "a blue-collar guy. Nobody in my family went to college. My dad still works on machines, busts his butt. That's why I work so well with the troops."

He was set to go to college on a scholarship and wanted to be a doctor. But an unexpected pregnancy caused him to marry at sixteen, and he ended up bagging groceries in Hanover at thirty dollars a week. The marriage disintegrated. He was divorced at eighteen. Hanover, a small town, had become stifling to him by then. Although he had a little daughter, he had to escape. He enlisted in the navy after being promised, on the basis of test scores, a slot as an electronic technician on a nuclear ship. "Two months later, I finished boot camp and hated the navy. I hated the saluting. I hated everything about it . . . clean floors . . . clean heads. And I'm thinking, 'Now I have six years of this.'"

A poster-boy young ensign had come to the boot camp and addressed the new sailors about what the navy could mean to them. "He was really cocky. I'm just sitting there going, 'Wow! I want to do what he's doing.'" When he got to nuclear-power school, he met with a career councilor and began a series of tests and interviews that got him admission into advanced nuclear school and eventually an ROTC (Reserve Officers Training Course) scholarship to Penn State. He graduated with a degree in nuclear engineering and was commissioned an ensign. He had a new lease on life. His attempts to reconcile with his daughter, he says, were quashed by his former wife.

He had planned to serve on a nuclear submarine. "I just wanted to go back in the navy and make money. But once I saw that going to flight school was an option, I thought, 'This is exciting.' I started going to programs. . . . At the time I asked to go to [flight school], they were cutting back, which was great for my ego because there were only about twenty-five of us accepted."

He survived an even-tighter cut to get jets.

"We were all good. I didn't think I'd do as well as everyone else. I was very quiet. Didn't talk about what kind of grades I got." The low point was when he received a "down" on an instrument landing. It could have ended his career. "I have to put a hood on. Can't look outside. I went too low." The instructor, who also happened to be the commodore of the school, took control. It was "the sickest feeling I've ever had. Failure was . . ."

His words trailed off.

But he rebounded and made yet another cut: he got Tomcats.

"You're used to being trained by pilots. And now you have NFOs [naval flight officers who, in this case, were backseaters]. He's not a pilot. He's an instructor. Really doesn't know what's going on in the front seat. They think they know. . . . Plus the F-14 community eats their young. The older generation there smelled blood in the water. Look out. You got a call sign, and it was very hard-core. If you wanted to be on that team, you had to pay the piper. It was not a whole lot of fun. . . . Everybody was so intense. . . . Jerks, really. Maybe I was a little oversensitive . . . because throughout my training I had never done poorly. And then to have a nonpilot tell me I'm doing poorly. . . . But it all worked out, and I got through it."

He had come into the squadron the same time that Dewar, Thing, and Wrex did.

"You're not accepted initially. No book saying this is what you have to do. You are kind of feeling your way. Everybody has a different personality. But the squadron has a personality promulgated by the skipper. But you don't know this when you first check in. You just have to figure it out. I thought the way to be accepted was to do well. And so I did. . . . But to be accepted you need to go through experiences with the squadron. You need to go on cruise. Until you actually do a cruise, you're still a nugget and not treated as an equal. And that's why I go back to [how the F-14 community eats their] young. It doesn't matter how you do. Or how good you are until you've been there, done that. . . . Until then, you're an outsider."

He was an insider now, newly remarried, one of the senior, second-tour JOs, a squadron LSO, along with Dewar and Brain. And he was the squadron's air-to-air training officer. "ACM [air combat maneuvering] is all about the peaks of balls and brains because you need to know how to fight the airplane very well, and you can't be afraid of putting the airplane through its paces. You need to know how to use your energy [speed] as well. It takes efficiency. . . . Getting into a dogfight is real combat. That's what you hope to do."

He preferred an "energy" fight: see what the bogie is doing, then try and entice him to bleed energy while conserving your own. "Make him think you're bleeding too, but keep your nose slightly down. . . .

Once he challenges, spring up. He can't go with you. He doesn't have the energy, and you shoot him on the way down."

Rope-a-dope.

Already assured by Joey of getting a postwar assignment as a pilot in an adversary squadron against Top Gun classes, Razor wasn't in a make-or-break situation on the cruise. But "there's a lot of politics in the squadron. You have to assert yourself and maintain a presence, kind of step out of the crowd . . . who is doing what jobs and how well they're doing it is always an underlying theme. . . . But you can be LSO [landing signal officer, the pilot who directs landings on the back of carriers] and training officer and still have no credibility because everyone gets to know you." A phony gets sniffed out. "We live together. We know each other even better than our wives almost know us."

Titles and ranks don't earn respect. The character of the person, revealed in the confining, dangerous situation, does. As Dog says: "You want to get know someone? Go to war with them."

If there was a knock on Razor, it was that he had a thin skin. Squadron mates remember when he accidentally set fire to his motorcycle and the fire spread to his house. They began calling him "Sparky." Razor didn't see the humor. He demanded they stop, which only fueled the ribbing. But in the ready room and on shore he was known as a comedian and showman. He had natural mimicking talents that would send his buddies into hysterics. He was a golfer, as most of them were. And in a postwar bar in Palma de Majorca, Spain, he would bring the house down with his rendition of the Garth Brooks country song "Friends in Low Places." Even the surprised band that he'd coaxed to accompany him was visibly impressed.

In port, during the fun time in the suite of rooms the squadron rented and called "admin," he was the only Ace in the room to take up Dog's challenge of a wrestling match. Dog was bigger than Razor, more muscled, and had that wild look in his eyes. Razor lost. But he won respect. Razor was his own man. He was someone you went to with a problem. He had no hidden agendas. He was a great backer of Joey and Dog because he was like them—straightforward, concerned for his men, good without flourish. "I love what we do," he said about the special circumstance of going to war with a fighter squadron—the excitement, the adventure. "It's never going to happen like this again for me. . . . You're constantly evolving . . . feelings start to grow, and this excitement starts to happen . . . places you are sent . . . things you go through and how you are built up and brought down or brought down and built up . . . you don't realize how close . . . you all start to become."

But he didn't see himself making a career in the navy because flying is what he really cares about, and, ultimately, careerists fly a desk. "I'll fly for the airlines. . . . I'm a realist and . . . there's a lot of ugliness in the navy. And even though there's magic in a squadron, there's a price. The price of being gone. . . . You lose your hair, or it turns gray. . . . You age twice as fast during those three or four years that you're on a ship. . . . At least I did. . . . It's very easy to get very depressed, to get very aggravated easily, to start heated arguments about nothing just because you've got all this pent-up depression. . . . You grow fast. But you age fast."

It was a disappointment to Razor that he wasn't chosen to fly on the first strikes, on April 6. He was in the second-wave spare but wasn't launched. He sucked it up and diligently helped with the planning, sat there and watched the others fly off, and was envious and relieved when they returned. He got his chance on the second night with Thing in the backseat. But that was the night NATO started saying strikers couldn't muster over Macedonia and they had to return without dropping their bombs. Bad weather had helped stymie him after that.

Now he was finally getting another chance. It was early evening April 11. He and Squab were one of the wings in a division led by Slapshot. Their target originally, wrote Squab in his diary, was a radio tower "on a ridge line in the middle of nowhere . . . VERY difficult to find with no cueing [coordinates] whatsoever. . . . The imagery we have is terrible and, oh by the way, everything is now covered with snow and will look markedly different than the pictures show."

But that was their target. They studied hard. Squab was "fairly confident" he could find the tower if the LANTIRN worked well. Then they were informed just before final brief that air force B-2 stealth bombers were assigned the same target and had launched twenty hours earlier. It was frustrating knowing they had no control over such errors. They did what they were told. They switched to a bridge that Squab was familiar with. He and Dewar had been scheduled to bomb it the night before until weather canceled the mission. He'd studied it well.

They launched and flew to the tanker, which was at thirty thousand feet. The air is very thin at that altitude, and they were heavy with bombs, which made the coupling all the harder. They were worried about the weather, said Razor. An earlier strike had already been aborted because of cloud cover. "Will we be able to see the ground?" The weather was cloudy at the tanker, but they could see the lights on the boot of Italy, and the skies looked clearer in the direction of Kosovo.

They tanked. So far, so good.

They took off for the rendezvous. Suddenly there was a loud "pop," followed by a flame-out in their left engine. It stalled. "It felt like one of our thousand-pound bombs had come off," wrote Squab. They were at thirty thousand feet with only one engine working. "That high, with two big bombs and the missiles, the jet doesn't fly very well." Now it was flying horribly.

They fell back from their leader. It took Razor three attempts to finally relight the engine. "I thought, 'We'll deal with it when we get back,'" he said. They scooted forward to where they should be.

Ten minutes went by. The strike package reached the rendezvous. The weather over Kosovo looked good. They were two minutes from push when they heard another pop, accompanied by a second flame-out. Squab looked to his left and saw "glowing things streaming out behind us." What he didn't know was that the engine's starter had exploded and that the streamers were pieces of molten cast iron from the blast that had ripped a hole in the side of the engine not visible to them.

The engine was unstartable, but Razor didn't know that. He kept trying to relight it, losing altitude, falling away from the others "because I can't stay up at thirty thousand feet on one engine. I told Squab, 'Hey, we're done.'" Their strike was over. Now they had to worry about getting home on one engine, or worse, having more trouble and possibly going down over enemy territory. The more they fell, the closer they got to the Serbs' Triple-A. And being heavy with only one engine for power was not a good scenario for outsmarting SAMs.

Razor: "Getting shot down was not something I looked forward to. And I remember seriously when they started talking about the SAM threat and they went through all the SA-6s, SA-3s, SA-2s and the retired Russian operators who were going to run these things. I was like, 'Wow, these guys are really good. Somebody is going to get shot down.' . . . So the way I prepared was to say it wasn't going to happen to me. Too many others out there."

And he was right.

They got out over water, and the problem became how they were going to get back on the carrier. "It's nighttime, and a daytime single-engine landing is not easy," wrote Squab. "Now throw into the mix the live ordnance that we are carrying." The carrier was going to be very skittish.

They were 120 miles from the *Roosevelt*. Razor called air operations and eventually got Joey.

"First he says—he's trying to pump me up—'When you come back to the ship, really watch your rate of descent. Don't want to go into the water. Need to be up on your power the whole time. Don't get too much rate of descent because you're not going to be able to stop it. Make sure you go full power in case you bolter on that one engine. Make sure you have good blower.' So he's giving me all kinds of good advice as if I'm coming back to the ship. And I said, 'Roger that, sir.' And I said to Squab, 'He wants us to come back to the damn boat!' Black night. No moon. One engine. All these weapons. I did not want to go back to the boat."

Joey told him to start coming in, and he'd get back. The skipper went to the admiral. "He's coming back with an emergency. . . . There are all kinds of variables, and you gotta weigh those. . . . Does he still have all his bombs? . . . How are his flight-control characteristics? . . . What's the wind over the deck? . . . I think [we finally decided] because he was single-engine, it was night, and he was real heavy."

Joey radioed back for them to go to NAS Sigonella, approximately three hundred miles away. Brindisi was much closer, and Razor wanted to go there. But the idea was nixed because they wanted the Tomcat at an American base so that it and its weapons would be guarded.

After about an hour and a half of slow flying, they limped into Sigonella at about 2:30 A.M.

"We had to make an arrested landing," wrote Squab. They couldn't park until "the arresting-gear folks could get the cable off of our tail-hook." They were ushered to an isolated spot at the end of the runway because the base didn't want "live ordnance next to any of the refueling tankers that carry a couple hundred thousand pounds of jet fuel. . . .

Live ordnance anywhere is treated with healthy respect, but at Sig . . . they kind of freaked."

A Tomcat repair crew was going to be sent over from the carrier the next day so they went to the BOQ (Bachelor's Officers Quarters) and were told there was no room for them on the entire base.

Neither could believe it. "We're in a conflict," said Razor. "I'm in a jet that's part of that conflict. I'm in an emergency, and they don't have room for me. The fact is they did. But we weren't considered VIPs. I'm telling them this isn't right. We just came from bad-guy country, and we're going to have to sleep on the couch!"

And he still hadn't dropped a bomb.

Squab: "We had to sleep on a couch in the BOQ lounge in our flight suits with all our flight gear beside us, including loaded nine millimeters." But in an innovation of modern warfare, "I found an AT&T phone and called Lisa and talked to her for awhile."

That and e-mails on the carrier had to be firsts.

The next morning they had to supervise the moving of the Tomcat because a huge C-5 cargo transport couldn't taxi by it on the runway. When the maintenance crew from the *Roosevelt* arrived, it was determined that it would be another day or so before the Tomcat was fixed. They had to put in a new motor.

With a fresh change of flight suits and time on their hands, Razor, Squab, and the crew of the COD (carrier onboard delivery) plane, which had brought the team and clothes, went out to dinner and drinks. "Backing up," wrote Squab, "on last cruise we hit Irish bars in every port and drank a lot of Guinness beer. For those of you who have not had Guinness in Europe, it tastes nothing like what arrives in the U.S. It is actually quite good. So since Razor and I had some Guinness, it became official that we were on cruise."

But he was "still a virgin," lamented Razor.

He still hadn't been tested in combat—something every good fighter pilot wants.

Eleven

For the next few days, the squadron, along with all the carrier's other planes, battled the weather, which largely restricted the number and size of strikes. On April 12, the beginning of the carrier's second week on station, Bru and Joey flew their second SCAR mission. Following the first mission several days back, Bru was even more convinced that they could succeed. But he was now acutely aware of what they were up against. And while "biting my tongue" at the continuing naysayers, he had begun telling CVIC, the carrier's intelligence center, that the FAC-A crews had to have cueing in the form of pictures or at least coordinates to start with. Just flying around looking, while not to be stopped, wasn't going to cut it.

But CVIC couldn't help him. The best they could provide were satellite pictures that were often old and out-of-date. The system of getting those pictures and even coordinates, when they were available, was inherently flawed for FAC-A purposes. Anything spotted by satellites or noncarrier sources like air force UAVs or pilots in the field took a lengthy and circuitous route to reach the carrier. From point of origin, the intelligence would be sent to a higher command, often in London, then to NATO for coordination and action and then, should NATO deem it appropriate, to the carrier. The route invariably took days if not weeks. This was the way NATO wanted it. Under the current system, the carrier just didn't have any timely intelligence on an elusive, hiding, moving target, and the bureaucracy that could change that had other priorities.

Joey and Bru's second SCAR mission was another exercise in exasperation. "We went up and tried and tried and tried," said Bru, "but we just couldn't get through the weather, couldn't see the ground." They spent three and half hours trying, mostly in the darkness, mostly in fear of the demons below the cloud layers that could send them tumbling out of the sky. "I still had the hair standing up on the back of my neck," said Bru. They were loitering, flying in circular patterns, hesitant—exactly what a pilot does not want to be when lightning-fast SAMs can strike in an obscured flash.

"The frustration was mounting," said Bru. And if Bru was building angst, Joey was worse. When they got in the cockpit, rank and position went out the window. Bru was the experienced vet at what they were doing; Joey, although skipper, was the novice. And there was a lot to learn. This wasn't what Joey was expert at—trying to keep sight of a wily bogey, using his innate talent of projection to see where the bogey might go and help his pilot kill it. It wasn't the hunkered concentration of finding and dropping on a fixed target clearly delineated by prestrike pictures and coordinates. It was a whole new method of doing things. He had to use the LANTIRN to find something about which he had no useful information. Where do you look? What do you look at? If it wasn't driving down the road with its lights on, it was as hard to spot as any phantom. He had a package of bombers waiting impatiently for his call, and he had to keep them coordinated as to position and time. That demanded a lot of "com," or radio communication, something Joey liked to keep to a minimum on normal strikes in order to have the airways open for important traffic.

"It was frustrating," he acknowledges. "We were trolling, and the weather was lousy. . . . It was like, 'Holy cow Bru, this is going to be. . . .' It takes awhile to get used to."

But an idea was taking shape: VF-41 was one of only eleven navy Tomcat squadrons (and the only one in the Kosovo theater) wired for TARPS (Tactical Airborne Reconnaissance Pod System), which was a way of getting intelligence pictures. TARPS missions were exclusively to take battlefield-damage and reconnaissance photographs. The heart of TARPS was a seventeen-foot, 1,850-pound gray tube with cameras in it slung under the aircraft. The pod protected the cameras from the elements and vibrations and from jet droppings like oil and fuel. The cameras took optical and infrared photos and had lenses for wide fields of view. On certain days, a Black Ace F-14 would shoot near Kosovo, usually staying over water, making far-reaching pictures to be sent back to higher headquarters. Bru and Joey began seeing the potential of using the TARPS cameras to find the Serbs' fielded forces. Up-to-date pictures were what they needed. But higher headquarters controlled the flights and had other agendas, among them BDA (bomb damage assessment), which was needed in the planning of future strikes.

In addition, TARPS missions were very dangerous. Crews sometimes flew them lower than other missions in order to get better pictures. This could put the TARPS airplanes within the lethal ranges of the enemy Triple-A and SAMS, which was why higher headquarters didn't like them going over land. TARPS missions made NATO and Sixth Fleet, the battle group's higher headquarters, very nervous. A major priority for each was not having its planes shot down, not only because of their concern for crew members, but also so that the enemy could not make political gains from it.

Joey and Bru knew that it was going to be tough to get TARPS missions flown for their benefit. But sometime during this second week in the war, they decided to try. It was an answer to one of their fundamental problems: getting fresh, as-close-to-real-time intelligence about the Serbian Army as they could.

They went to CAG with the idea.

From the first day the *Roosevelt* took up a secret position in the Ionian Sea off Kosovo, battle-group commanders and Airwing 8's aircrews wanted to destroy Serbian military bases. Plans had been made to attack major Serb airfields and naval bases in Montenegro, the Serb state closest, and thus most threatening, to the carrier. Admiral Copeland wanted to attack Tivat on the Adriatic, where it was believed the Serbs had at least one submarine. But political constraints imposed by NATO kept such plans on the shelves. "Had we included those targets," NATO commander General Clark told the Senate Armed Services Committee on October 21, 1999, "we might have contributed to the destabilization of Mr. Djukanovic. . . . He's the president of Montenegro, and he's trying to take that country in a direction of Westernization. . . . This was known at the time, and it was one of [our] higher strategic aims. And so there was a constant trade-off between the risk to our forces . . . making us want to attack, versus the risk to Djukanovic."

The policy had angered many of the war fighters in both the navy and the air force. Any military strategist knows that one of the keys to victory is to destroy the enemy's war machine. You don't attack a bully with taps to the arms. You go full force for the head, the main target, and keep hitting as hard as you can until he goes down. But that was not the way the Kosovo War was being fought. There were sanctuaries and restricted targets and rules of engagement that limited the blows. It reminded some of the Vietnam War, where force was constantly restrained and the enemy benefited from every lapse, increasing the dangers to the war fighters.

"We were a little bit frustrated as an air wing," said Dog. "What we wanted to do was go and wipe out the bases . . . take the threat aircraft issue away. . . . 'Why am I risking life, limb, and tooth to go after this [nonmilitary target] when I've got something that's a real threat to me?' . . . I think a lot of people lost their belly for what was going on. . . . I'm only speculating, but it was hard for us to figure out what they wanted us to do. . . . We had very clear ideas on what needed to be done. You want to neutralize the situation."

But the political climate changed suddenly, albeit briefly, on April 15.

On that morning, General Clark learned in a video teleconference that twenty-four U.S. Apache helicopters and their crews that he'd brought to Albania in his mounting efforts to stop the killing in Kosovo were threatened by activity at Podgorica's Golubovci Airfield. The airfield, the same that Squab had seen MiGs over, was only thirty miles from the Albanian border, noted Vice Adm. Daniel J. Murphy Jr., commander of the Sixth Fleet, which included the *Roosevelt*. Testifying before the Senate Armed Services Committee on October 13 and 14, 1999, the admiral said, "The Serbs had moved a significant number of air-to-ground aircraft . . . into that airfield. When we detected that move, General Clark . . . said, 'I have to have that airfield taken out now. We cannot afford a strike, even an ineffective strike, against Task Force Hawk [the code name for the Apaches].' "

Included in the conference was U.S. Air Force lieutenant general

Michael C. Short, head of the war's air operations. "He [General Clark] turned to General Short and said, 'Can you do it?' " General Short said no. It was too little notice. The air force needed three days between the time the target was designated and the time they hit it. The navy, however, was used to mounting strikes more quickly. "General Short said, 'The navy can do it.' . . . He [Clark] turned to me and said, 'Dan, can you do it?' And I said, 'Yeah, we can do it. . . .' "

Murphy didn't really know if the *Roosevelt* could handle such a daunting task — knock out a major airfield, with all the planning, weapons, and plane-equipping and refitting that would be needed — and do it before the next dawn. It was going to be a monster undertaking. But he wasn't going to say no.

Navy pride was on the line.

Nor was Admiral Copeland or CAG going to say no when they got their calls. "There was clearly a sense of urgency," said CAG. "My impression was, it was all politically driven to some degree. Maybe there was some concern . . . they were going to lose approval at some point as someone lost the stomach for it or [for] whatever reason."

The ship began planning the raid.

CAG was pressed for time. He had to report to the CAOC within an hour about the feasibility of the mission, he said. He needed a mission commander immediately. Normally, he had a system of rotation in which various strike leaders would get the chance to lead strikes daily. On this day, Dog was the rotated-in strike leader and was planning a makeup raid for the bad April 7 Pristina mission. But CAG's need was unroutine. "If this had been a normal situation," he said, "I probably would have gone down to where Dog was planning, and we would have gone from there."

But he didn't.

Close to where he got the news about Podgorica, he ran into Joey and several other key strike staff. Joey had already planned an earlier Podgorica strike that had been shelved. He said CAG reminded him of that. "I don't know whether he'd heard about it and just positioned himself or what?" said CAG. "Any good commander will do that. To be honest, I don't remember [the previous planning] having anything to do with it. I just needed somebody fast."

He didn't hesitate. "I asked Joey to take it."

Joey said he was helping Dog with the Pristina mission when he ran into CAG around 10 A.M. Infused with urgency, he went back and informed Dog he was going to be the strike leader that day. Dog wasn't happy. Because it was his turn in the rotation, the XO felt *he* should be leading the newly ordered strike. In the haste that was now taking over, Joey may not have adequately explained what had happened. He indicates that since he was appointed by CAG, he felt duty-bound to take it. The apparent misunderstanding would become a bone of contention between the two good friends later. But his job right then, said Dog, was to support his skipper. He held his protest. "I'm a big man," he said. "I can take it." Joey was not aware of Dog's feelings.

The good thing, added Dog, was that the strike, because it was so hastily ordered, was not going to be on the air tasking order, which was written days in advance. Dog, like many in the air wing, was convinced that the enemy "had our basic air plan of when we were flying and when we weren't." He believed this, he said, "because when the air wing wasn't flying, they'd take off [in] their Super Galebs, their air-to-ground attack planes, and go whoop up [in Kosovo]. And then as soon as we got airborne, they'd run like hell and hide."

Because the air tasking order issued each day had to be approved by all NATO members, spies or those at least sympathetic to the Serbs, he believed, were passing the order on.

In any case, Joey was now the Podgorica strike leader.

Podgorica's airfield, on the outskirts of the city formerly known as Titograd, was a fortress. It sat at the base of a mountain. Its runways and aprons had MiG-21s, the little Galebs—two-seat, two-engine bombers that resembled navy trainers—and possibly other aircraft. There were an SA-6 school at one end, four large hangar buildings near its center, and fuel-and-ammunition-storage facilities. It was guarded by SAM batteries, some with target-tracking radars. But the crown jewel of the base was a huge underground hangar encased in reinforced cement and dug into a mountain. It was approximately one-half mile long and curved in the middle, with giant cast-iron and steel doors at both ends and small shafts for ventilation visible on the hilly mountainside. The planes that had recently been moved to the field, mostly Galebs, had been parked nose to tail in the underground hangar. It was believed that there could be as many as thirty-five in the mountain vault, along with stores of fuel and ammunition. An army of technicians and workers attended the planes and stores inside.

Initially, mission planning appears to have begun with everyone assuming that the air wing would strike late in the night, using darkness as a cover. "We had the goggles," said Admiral Copeland, which was a definite advantage. But the more Joey thought about the timing, he said, the more he didn't like it. "Traditionally, what happens there, when the sun goes down, with the mountains and all, you have a temperature drop . . . not only do you have clouds, but there's a fog that rolls in." The fog had been hampering them constantly, and when he received the forecast, fog was again predicted for the evening.

"The admiral had actually come up to me and said, 'You know, you're cleared to do [whatever you want].'" He decided to up the time on target (TOT) to sundown, mere hours away. "This was already, you know, a shot in the dark. And to move it up to daylight meant that the flight deck would be rushed even more."

Not to mention everything else.

"We had to launch earlier, walk earlier, brief earlier," recalled Bru.

They were going to need a miracle.

As strike leader, Joey not only had to worry about his own squadron, but also about all the other needed elements from the various air-wing squadrons that would comprise the total strike package, which would be the largest the carrier had fielded so far in the war.

"We pressed," he said. "The biggest part for me was getting the priorities down and getting people assigned to do their jobs and putting it all together."

As CAG wanted, Joey created, with Dog and Bru's help, a simple, time-tested plan. "You gotta be careful about how much you deviate from regular procedures in a crisis," said CAG, "because that might be the very thing that trips you up . . . Stick with the way you operate normally . . . maybe demand more of your people."

Only the A-Team would drop, or fly other important positions. They'd throw every available plane into the package. They'd over-ordnance the jets on the theory that more blasting power would be better than less. The core strikers would use GBU-24 "bunker-busters" to attack the mountain tunnel, the primary target. They'd hit it at both entrances and also try to put penetrators through the ventilation shafts. The Hornets would be loaded up with cluster bombs for attacking planes and people on the base. If they hit something soft, like grass, the clusters would bounce up and explode, spreading their lethal cargo like a fan. If they hit something hard, like a plane, they'd detonate right there. Because the various targets at the base were relatively close together and lots of airplanes over the field at the same time could cause midair collisions, they decided to send four waves from two different axes, one after the other. Each wave would have a different objective, swooping in at the precise time the prior wave exited. The result would be sustained pounding for over fifteen minutes. Joey left the details to the others.

"I didn't have time 'cause I was constantly going to CAG, the admiral, strike ops, proposing things, getting the go-aheads. 'Yes, you can go in the daytime. Yes, you can use this route.' And then going back to my planners saying, 'Okay, yes, you can do this; yes, you can do that.' . . . And just doing this without screaming . . . just walking around, you know, trying to show some kind of confidence and not hurrying."

It was important, he said, that they all felt that he believed in the plan, that he had faith they could succeed.

Of course, in his own mind, there were doubts.

They'd still not dropped a successful penetrator bomb. The weather was a constant worry. And beyond the loss of time that his decision to strike at dusk had caused, twilight was a bad time to bomb. It was the time that many targets went from detectable-hot to cool. Since the LANTIRN sensors depended on contrasting heat and cold, finding and defining targets would be harder. In addition, twilight meant more glare and reflection from the horizon.

But once the mission was assigned, preparation commenced as if the aviators were called to douse a five-alarm fire.

"If you want to know the truth of the matter," said CAG, "it was absolute chaos that day."

Bru remembers drawing up the plan on a five-by-eight-inch piece of paper, putting it up on the blackboard for Joey's brief, and making pencil copies for everyone else. There wasn't time for normal computer computations. For instance, he needed to know the distance between the point from which they were going to push and the target. This was in order to coordinate the Prowler's HARM shooting with the attack. But when he asked one of the squadron's Top Gun graduates, specially trained in such minutiae, to give him the answer, the "expert" couldn't do it without the computer, which, at the time, was being used. Wrex finally figured it by using one of the little GPS units Brain had gotten the squadron.

The ship had been in the midst of normal cyclic operations, launching and recovering small missions like TARPs and training flights and readying for the Pristina makeup, when the new mission changed everything. Pristina "was a large strike but not on the magnitude of this," said Joey. Podgorica "required a different ammunition load-out. These things normally take three days to get ready. You gotta put in your order, you gotta put in your weapons load, and the weapons guys have got to dig this stuff out of the magazines . . . seven floors down and then arm, and then build up these bombs. The GBU-24 takes quite a long time to build . . . put the seeker head on. Put the fins on . . . and do all the safety checks and make sure the thing is ready to go."

Dog remembered: "So we had airplanes all over the flight deck, and we've got to bring some up from below. And we're moving them around to get them situated for launch. That in and of itself is a big job, not to mention that we have bombs to load. And a lot of the airplanes park tail over the water, you know, to make room. So their ass is hanging overboard, but you gotta move them forward so you can load the bombs and then move them back again. Then you gotta, you know, develop a launch-sequence plan. Who's going first and coordinating that through the tankers and then a tanker plan. And then, of course, there's the tactics of actually how we're gonna do this hop and how we're going to predetermine the HARM coming down. I mean, there's more to it than most people realize."

CAG said he personally went to every squadron skipper and department head who would be involved to brief them about what he wanted so there would be no confusion. "I was vitally concerned that in the rush to get things done they would hear lots of things that were right and lots of things that were wrong." He wanted to make sure each had the exact same game plan. "I can remember briefing my gunner [air-wing ordnance officer] on the flight deck, and I thought he was going to throw up on my shoes when he saw [what I wanted—and how fast]. It was the most awful look I've ever seen in my life, like, 'I can't believe you're asking me to do this.' . . . I told him, 'Why don't you start breathing again, and let's get on with business. . . .'"

Squab, who apparently missed the early scurrying (perhaps because of a late HVAAP mission the night before), wrote in his diary that he went to the ready room about 1 P.M. expecting to hear a SCAR mission brief from Bru, only to find out "the air plan has been entirely rewritten to strike Podgorica airfield with everything we can throw at it." He was penciled in to fly in one of the bombers in Wrex's backseat. "This is a no-shit Alpha strike [the biggest]," he noted. Alvin, picked to carry one of the GBU-24s with Loose as his RIO, likened activity in the ready room to "sixty cooks in the kitchen." Everybody in the squadron, whether on the strike or not, was involved in the preparation. Dog, also in the core package, with Wog in his backseat, said, "Everybody's running around saying, 'I gotta do this, and I gotta do that.' And people are coming in and going, 'You know, that's fucked-up because of this and that.' . . . And I said, 'Joey, you gotta get control of this thing.'"

And he did.

Joey: "I had green shirts [safety observers] doing red shirts' [maintenance and catapult workers'] work; brown shirts [crew chiefs] doing green shirts' work." Everybody on the flight deck was doing double and triple duty. "It was just a whole time compression and then making sure that with the limited time we didn't get bogged down in the details." As Joey's XO, Dog had his hands full implementing everything Joey wanted done. He and Wog were also dropping a penetrator, but, scurrying as he was, he couldn't put in the target preparation he wanted. "So I sat Wog down, and I go, 'Wog, you're on your own on this one, buddy.' I'm just too damn busy. And he goes, 'Yeah, I'll get us to the target.'"

Wog himself was heavily involved in the weaponeering.

Despite the chaos, the mission took shape. When it came time for Joey to give the brief, it was uncharacteristically just that—brief. Maybe fifteen minutes. They had to walk by midafternoon. "Instead of having power-point slides, it was just a couple of vu-graphs," he remembers. "Most of it was just me talking off the cuff. . . . We just didn't have enough time." CAG agreed. "There was nothing productive I could add. . . . One guy's gonna have to lead it. I don't have time to countermand anything. If he doesn't have it right, then it's just not going to be right."

As Joey was still wrapping things up with the planners, CAG was on deck checking the weapons loading. It was getting close to launch time, and 50 percent of the aircraft were still not completely fitted with their ordnance, not to mention the fact that there was still the threat of the mission being called off at the last minute. Decisions had to be made. Go on time with what they had and maybe be undermanned or underweaponed, or wait, move the launch time back, and chance ruining the timing built into the plan.

Timing was crucial. Put tankers in the air, for instance, without strikers to get the gas and all important synchronization starts deteriorating.

"My gut feeling," said CAG, "was that we should launch on time. . . . There may be [some jets] that are going to get off later. . . . But by my count, my calculations, the main pieces will be there . . . I went down to find Joey. He hadn't even been up there yet. . . . I said, 'You know what, I think we're going to make it.' . . . I don't know if it was just confidence because he's the guy in charge, and optimism is the way to go here. . . . But his answer was, 'I *know* we can make it.' "

On deck, rain had begun to fall, which, by itself, wouldn't hurt flight operations. "It was a crappy day," recalls Gooch, who had not been tapped for the mission but was involved in the weapons selection. "It was gloomy, overcast." The deck had more airplanes on it than he'd seen in practically his whole career—approximately fifty-five, some in the process of being moved below, most with their engines roaring and their attendants scurrying. The launch ballet was in high frenzy—tankers, Prowlers, Hornets, Tomcats, all dangerously readying, aiming for the launch. "It was pretty unbelievable," said Joey, " 'cause I saw the CAG and the admiral walking around [a rarity for a launch] just watching guys build up bombs and putting them on the flight deck, and they gave me a thumbs-up. I couldn't believe this was happening. It was really like going to war with the Russians."

The launch began, some forty planes moving to the catapults, straining, roaring. "It went surprisingly smooth," said Dog. As the last jet lifted from the deck and zoomed up to join the others, an eerie silence filled the wake. "I'd never seen it empty like that," said Gooch. Nor had the others. "It was strange," said Mentul, "like a ghost town." Admiral Copeland said CAG turned to him. "He said, 'Admiral, you know it's a good thing nobody told them they can't do the impossible' "—echoes of James A. Michener's "Where do we get such men?"—but said from the heart. Acknowledging it later, CAG added, "Yeah, sometimes it's because they don't know they can't, that they can."

At least that's what he and the admiral were hoping.

Up in the sky, Joey had a single purpose. "There's an E-3 AWACS [air force Airborne Warning and Control System aircraft] blabbering on the radio to an F-16 . . . some rinky-dink question, and here we got forty planes getting ready to do a major strike." He wanted the airways clear for important communication. "I just yelled at him. . . . 'If you don't have anything good to say . . . shut up.' . . . It was very forceful. . . . I think it set the tone because everybody heard it. I know the admiral was listening on the radios back home."

Podgorica was perhaps thirty miles inland from the coast, directly across the Adriatic from the ankle of the Italian boot. The huge air armada flew almost due north, its formation in the stormy skies looking like clouds of roaring iron. The farther they went, the worse the weather got. "We were going in and out of the clouds," said Joey, "and that's one of the hardest things . . . going up to the tanker, getting gas, and then going to the rendezvous points. . . . We were looking up north, and it was just solid clouds. Goddammit, it's going to happen again. You know, we've done everything we can, and now the damn weather. . . . It was looking doubtful."

But they'd come this far, and he wasn't about to turn back. They pressed on, tanked in very rough conditions, and made their rendezvous. Wog: "I remember being in the rendezvous stack, just sitting there going, 'Wow, this is amazing.' " So many airplanes. "We were in the first wave . . . a five-plane of F-14s."

It was the Black Aces contingent, their ace-of-spades tail insignia leading the pack: In addition to Alvin and Loose, those carrying a single GBU-24 penetrator included Bru and Joey, Dog and Wog, and Beaker and Toad. All four were going after the main target, the mountain tunnel. Wrex and Squab were with them, too, but had two smaller GBU-10 bombs (thousand-pounders) and were assigned to destroy the field's control tower. The only other Aces in the package were Dewar and Lt. (jg) John "Slugz" Kelly, a nugget RIO and former enlisted man who was impressing the hinges with his coolness and savvy. They were assigned a distant CAP.

The rest of the planes were piloted or crewed by members of other squadrons, including Slapshot leading a second wave against the buried hangar.

As they pushed, Joey got word of MiGs in the vicinity. "The E-3 came up and said—I forget the code word—but there were two MiG-21s orbiting south of the field. . . . I vectored two fighters onto them. . . . They asked me if I was gonna delay, and I said no." The MiGs kept holding. "To tell you the truth," said Joey, "we were closer to them than the [vectored fighters]. I said, 'It doesn't matter, we're gonna run over them. If they're in the way, we'll shoot them down.' "

As they were about to push, Bru realized that the distance Wrex had computed on his GPS unit was wrong. "It was twelve miles off," he said. If he pushed at the time he had on his knee-card, they'd arrive over the target too fast. The HARMs, the successive waves of planes, would all be out of sync. "It cracks me up," he laughed, "that some of the smartest people in our squadron rely on technology, delay all that time, and still get it wrong."

They were approximately seventy-two seconds ahead of schedule. They pushed but did "S-turns" over the water to burn off the seconds. The different packages exited for their different runs from the two axes. Joey's "heavy" division (so designated because they were carrying the biggest bombs) turned so that they could ingress out of the west, which put the setting sun behind them.

As they encountered land and got closer to Podgorica, Triple-A started coming up. "Now they know we're coming," said Joey.

The first of at least twelve SAMs was launched, and the Prowlers began firing HARMs, which streaked by the incoming first wave, leaving contrails in the already-cloudy sky. But Joey was only vaguely aware of it. By then, he'd begun working the FLIR in wide field of view, trying to pick up cues to the target. He wasn't seeing anything because of the cloud cover. "There's so much shit going on, but I'm relying on, you know, a lot of experience, and I know I need to act calm and all that, so nothing's fazing me. We're just going on in there. And I'm feeling kind of down because the weather's so bad. . . . You can't see anything. . . . And the sun's getting ready to set [behind them]. The glare [off the clouds] is pretty bad . . . the fog is starting to come in. . . ."

Suddenly, when they were approximately twenty-to-twenty-five miles from the target, the clouds moved from over the airfield, and their FLIRs gave them a clear picture. "Unbelievable," said Joey, "because up until that point it's like solid cloud cover. We go through this last set of clouds, and then right there, it's like, 'Oh, my gosh, I can see the mountain . . . the airfield.' . . . I thought to myself, 'God, we may have a chance.' "

In his exuberance, he broke silence and broadcasted a low-key "target area clear. Target area clear." Wog had seen the same thing. "I can remember going, 'Okay, I'm not going to screw this up,' 'cause we'd screwed up every GBU-24 drop up to this point."

Following his fiasco with the penetrator a few days earlier, Beaker had checked by phone from the carrier with some air force buddies he'd served with as an exchange officer who routinely dropped the bunker-buster from their F-15E and F-117 jets. He had learned that a certain dialed-in setting for the bomb the navy flyers had used was probably wrong. The air force had trouble with it too. When the air force had switched to a new setting, they had gotten much better results.

Now Joey's A-Team was using the new setting. They were also very mindful of the aircraft-steering errors that had been made at Pristina and the fact that they had to manually correct the range from the target the LANTIRN was showing. And to make sure the bomb would stay within its very narrow working envelope, they'd decided to release it at the exact distance from the target, given their speed and altitude, that allowed it the greatest margin of error for success.

Each would go for the absolute perfect shot—not just the approximate envelope as had been used at Pristina.

If they weren't perfect, they'd still have a little margin.

The division roared closer. More SAMs came up. Most were shoulder-fired and ballistic, harder to see but with shorter range. The Triple-A increased. They were still above it. The cockpit audio of Dog and Wog's video of the run gives a terse account of the speedy approach:

Wog (approximately twenty miles out): "Okay, I got the fuse [of the bomb] armed. . . . [to Dog] Need to drop down a little lower."

They had started at roughly thirty thousand feet and were passing down through twenty thousand feet.

Dog: "Nineteen miles."

Wog: "I'm looking . . . clearing in clouds. . . . There's the road."

Dog: "Don't see any SAMs . . . yet. . . . Steering looks good."

Wog: "Fifteen miles."

Top: Bru (left) and Joey on a good day. Photo courtesy of Joey Aucoin.

Left: Bombs on deck of the *Roosevelt.* Photo courtesy of Marcus Lopez.

Below: Black Ace Tomcat at rendezvous with tanker. Bad weather or darkness made refueling very dangerous. Photo courtesy of Marcus Lopez.

Top: XO Jim "Dog" Bauser in flight gear. Photo courtesy of Jim Bauser.

Left: LCDR Steve "Wog" Carroll following his and Frank Silebi's escape from an SA-6 "sambush." It's easy to smile when the fear subsides. Photo courtesy of Steve Carroll.

Below: A Back Ace Tomcat launches. Photo courtesy of Joey Aucoin.

Top: Second cruise JOS, from left: Lt. Clay "Squab" Williams, Lt. Bill "Dewar" Dye, Lt. Eric "Pappy" Anduze. Tragically, Dye, a JO leader, died in an F-14 crash, following the squadron's return from Kosovo. Photo courtesy of Clay Williams.

Right: Nugget James Corlett. First cruise is always rough. Going to war makes it doubly so. Photo courtesy of Robert Wilcox.

Below: Pilot Lupe and backseater Slugz in the air. Photo courtesy of Marcus Lopez.

The squadron's aviators on their way to war:
Shaved heads, started by "loose" Cannon (sixth from left in front), were the
predominant fashion. Photo courtesy of Marcus Lopez.

Right: Aces over Kosovo. Photo courtesy of Joey Aucoin.

Top: A Tomcat banking, its underside bristling. Photo courtesy of Marcus Lopez.

Left: Lt. Doug "Thing" Thien on liberty after Kosovo. Photo courtesy of Robert Wilcox.

Below: Bru and Joey walking to their jet. Photo courtesy of Joey Aucoin.

Top: The CO and his wife Cassandra, the organizer of the wives when the squadron is at sea. Photo courtesy of Joey Aucoin.

Left: Rookies Slugz (left) and Lupe. Photo courtesy of Marcus Lopez.

Below: Swing wings extended, a Tomcat rises over the carrier. Photo courtesy of Joey Aucoin.

Alvin (left) and Dog celebrate a successful mission. Photo courtesy of Jim Bauser.

Dog: "Concur . . . looking . . ."

Wog: "Thirteen miles. I can see it [the underground tunnel] going around. . . . There's the other road coming in [leading to the tunnel]. . . . A big Y."

Dog (in reference to Bru and Joey's forward airplane): "Okay, I'm sneaking in behind them a little bit."

Wog: "Ten miles."

Dog: "Okay, coming west."

At nine miles, Wog began rapidly calling off every mile, including fractions of the miles, until they reached the exact distance from the target at which they knew they had to release in order to give the bomb its best chance to guide. "Drop! Drop! Drop!" said Wog with emphasis.

Just ahead of them, Joey and Bru had already made their release.

Joey: "We drop this thing, and it's like 'ka-dunk!' I mean this is a big cow bomb coming out. And then my wingmen, Dog and Wog, drop theirs. You see this big thing come off . . . it sort of goes with you for awhile . . . it's got big fins, and it hangs up there, sort of like having a little wingman right beside you."

They maneuvered away, as did Dog and Wog.

Alvin and Loose and Beaker and Toad made their drops.

Each RIO began lasing. The bomb's need for speed and more arcing delivery demanded they start the lasing quickly. Joey kept the FLIR in wide field of view as he lased because "it was still kind of hazy. Wait until about halfway time of flight and go to narrow field of view, and I can see the access road going right up to the bunker door." He put his cursor right on it. "There's talk on the radio about stuff going on, but I don't listen. The only thing that's in my mind is to put that bomb through the door."

The division had been very close to the target at the time of the drops. Now they began passing it. Joey's FLIR picture, he knew, was going to shift a full 180 degrees. He might lose his lock. But there was nothing he could do. It flipped. "The time of impact goes down to zero," he said, "and nothing happens. I thought, 'Oh shit, did I screw it up?' One or two seconds later you see this massive blimp go through the front door. I mean, it's a massive blimp . . . a smoke puff comes out, and it's like, 'Hey, shit-hot!' It went all the way through the door, and then this stuff starts spewing."

Several seconds after that first hit, Dog and Wog's penetrator slammed into the mountain about midway up the hardened tunnel. It bore in so quickly that Wog didn't think that it had worked. "The skipper's [bomb] went into the door and just blew it to pieces; lifted up the steel plate that's in the side of the mountain that they'd covered with dirt. . . . As I see that happening, I'm going, 'Okay, ours should be hitting about' . . . and then this little puff underneath my crosshairs is my GBU-24 going in. . . . It didn't look like it penetrated. It just looked like it blew up. So we're going, Oh, I hope our bomb went in.' "

Once both crews saw the hits, they ripped back south and lit burners, climbing and distancing as fast as they could. Alvin and Loose were trying to put their penetrator into a protruding shaft at the far end of the tunnel. The shaft was hard to find. Loose was guiding the bomb, trying to find the shaft at the same time. When he finally did, it was too late. He moved the cursor to the shaft, but apparently it was too big a shift. The bomb couldn't hack the change in direction. It plowed into the mountain without penetrating and exploded on top.

Beaker and Toad too were trying to find a shaft. "I thought I had it," said Toad, "and at the last minute I realized it was the wrong [target]. . . . Actually, the only reason I missed is I was so involved in the planning, I [did] very little target study" — not words Beaker wanted to hear. It was the second miss with the penetrator for both of them. Beaker would take it so hard that he'd later question whether he had what it takes. Toad would call the mission his Kosovo low point.

Wrex and Squab missed the tower after a cloud broke their lock. But by the time the division was clear of the target and streaking home, the underground tunnel was a flaming inferno "hurling chunks of concrete in the air the size of my desk," said Dog. They didn't know it then, but twenty-six Serb jets, including Galebs and MiG-21s, were being destroyed in the holocaust. Billowing clouds with fire shooting out, characteristic of ammunition detonating, rose from the destruction. From seventy miles away, said Bru, it looked like "a nuclear explosion." The smoke and fire were so thick that when Slapshot and his strikers came out of the east to attack the tunnel's rear entrance, their FLIRs couldn't see through the erupting carnage to guide their bombs.

They dropped them anyway.

The third and fourth waves came in and destroyed the hangars and aircraft on the field. A Hornet driver later wrote in the *Hook*, the magazine of carrier aviation (summer 1999):

```
We had the greatest [Alpha] strike of all time . . .
crushed an airfield. I was the last aircraft over the tar-
get, so I got to see the whole thing. . . . It is awesome
what we can do if we're given the right targets and op-
portunity. . . . The only thing I need to make my career
in the Navy complete is to bag a MiG.
```

The Prowlers and Hornets ended up shooting seventeen HARMs and destroying numerous SAM launchers, both mechanical and human. Aviators praised them as the main reason they made it through that and many of the other actions of the war alive. In the span of some eight hours, the air wing had planned, organized, and executed a successful strike that the *Hook* would say in its summer 2000 issue "resulted in the greatest loss by the Serbs during the entire conflict"— and without a single casualty to the strikers.

"It could have gone the way of Lebanon," reflected Admiral Copeland, referring to the ill-fated 1983 carrier strike on Arab targets in retaliation for the terrorist attack on marines at the Beirut airport. Two strike aircraft in that raid had been shot down by SAMs, and crewmen were killed and injured. He had been a young fleet pilot himself when that had happened. He always worried about his men.

But Podgorica was a huge success. The admiral was thankful. The battle group had proven its worth in a single afternoon. No other U.S. force could have mounted a successful raid so fast. And Joey and the Black Aces had led the charge. The next day, April 16, U.S. Defense Department spokesman Kenneth Bacon told members of the press at a Pentagon briefing, "We hit the airfield in Podgorica last night with naval air and did a great job. I'll have some video of that tomorrow."

Twelve

The Podgorica success garnered little rest for the squadron and Joey, its skipper, in particular, although there was much high-fiving and backslapping celebration when the strikers returned. The admiral said personnel in the CAOC, listening to the raid live, broke out in cheers when the success became evident. But the war continued. The air wing had a no-fly day on April 16, a time to catch up on backlogged work. Its airplanes probably couldn't have flown anyway. The weather was too bad. On the 17th, weather again hampered flight operations. But Bru and Joey, with Wrex and Toad on their wing, flew a late-afternoon, early-evening, four-hour SCAR, which—frustratingly—again yielded zero results.

They were still using the old intelligence—photos from days or weeks past, coordinates from filed reports, and the rare, chance sightings by UAVs, satellites, or other airborne hunters. They needed fresher cueing. CAG and the admiral, who himself had helped pioneer TARPS, had forwarded a request to use the TARPs missions for SCAR but had heard nothing. Yet the SCAR mission, in the face of declining fixed targets and increasing pressure to find the Serbs' killing squads, was moving to center stage. One new result was that tempers began flaring.

Wog: "I can remember going down to CVIC and getting very upset with the guys . . . not being able to provide us with [pictures] because they were working on a brief for the admiral. . . . I went in and really roughed some feathers . . . goin', 'Hey, why don't I have this? Stop what you're doin' and get this!' . . . Bru knew I was doin' this. . . . He tried the indirect approach, kinda . . . talkin' to them. . . . That didn't work either, and [so] he went absolutely nuts, standing there with his flight gear on, sweatin' like a pig, just yelling at the CVIC commander, this O5 [numerical designation for rank of commander] in charge, tellin' him he doesn't know what the hell he's doin'. . . . 'Get us pictures.' 'Well, I can't.' 'Well, let me fly TARPS.' 'Well, we can't.' "

Bru, now beginning a schedule of grueling back-to-back SCAR missions with Joey, could get quite colorful in such tirades—his "Oklahoma-isms," often involving earthy images of cow manure and barnyard antics.

CAG: Bru "managed to get spooled up a couple of times against my guys and Intel for not getting the support he needed. . . . They took the tongue-lashing with great grace because they probably knew they deserved it. . . . They weren't giving him what he needed. They couldn't. They didn't have it. I always think everybody wanted to succeed when he was there. Everybody wanted to be on his team. Nobody wanted to fail because they knew *he* wasn't going to."

Some of Bru's loudest arguments would be with the Aces' intelligence officer, Lt. (jg) Kyle "Topper" Leese, who, because TARPS was an intelligence function and only VF-41 had the capacity, was also the battle group's TARPS officer, answerable to the CAOC directly.

As IOs frequently are, Topper was a scholar; a well-educated former high school soccer player from Haddonfield, New Jersey, with a master's degree in archaeology. He spoke Greek and at least one other foreign language. He'd wanted to be a pilot but had bad knees. As a consolation, he went into "air" intelligence. Twenty-seven years old and a lieutenant junior grade, he was one of the younger and lowest-ranking officers in the squadron. But he looked older. He was also conscientious and self-assured, and led a small and dedicated team of intelligence specialists. His job as head intelligence gatherer and disseminator for the squadron, and the fact that he was in charge of TARPS, put him in a pivotal position to help with the growing FAC-A and SCAR needs.

The problem was, said Bru, that Topper's immediate air-wing

bosses, administrative officers on various staffs, were telling him to do something else: "They were high-paid secretaries for the admiral's morning brief—you know, 'Put this on power-point. . . . And, oh by the way, for your TARPS report card . . . did you hit this image that the CAOC up in Aviano was wanting?' . . . That basic report card gave us no return on [the targets we were hunting]."

But when Bru pointed that out and suggested to Topper that he forget what the bosses wanted and start planning routes that would give the FAC-As fresh targets, the young intelligence officer understandably balked. "He said that would be insubordination," said Bru. "I'm not proud of it, but I had a meltdown. . . . We were yelling. . . . I'm going, 'What's our objective! BDA [bomb damage assessment] never killed a damn thing! . . . You need to find what we're supposed to kill.' . . . He [yelled back], 'But I can't. It's not on the order!' I said, 'I don't give a damn how you do it . . . just do it!' "

The blowups would become big gossip on the carrier. Joey was in the middle. The CAOC dictated to everybody. He wanted SCAR to work, but he wasn't skilled enough at FAC-A to lead the charge. He continued to support Bru, but following the April 17 failure, and mindful of the start-up friction in the cockpit, he wondered if he might be part of the problem. "It got very tense from time to time," said Bru. "[Joey] came up and said, 'Hey, this is tough. . . . If I'm making it more difficult by me flying with you to do this rather than you taking a FAC-A along, just do whatever you want to.' I said, 'No skipper, if you can tolerate it, this is how it's done. It's not easy. It's hard and we'd be going through the same stuff regardless of who I had in the backseat. . . . There's two heads in there and it's real easy to have independent thoughts, plus you being a skipper buys us a lot when it goes to getting the support we need to make this happen. Because if it's some O4s and some JOs doing this thing initially, I don't think it's going to get sold.' "

Wog: "Joey was, 'God, I can't take that five hours of listening to the KY58 radio cracklin' in my ear, trying to talk to guys. They don't know what the hell's going on, and it drove me absolutely bananas.' " Wog proposed that Joey take a day off from SCAR and fly a strike, diminished as they were becoming. He, Wog, a partially trained FAC-A, would fly the next SCAR with Bru. Joey liked the idea. "He goes,

'Yeah, you guys go try to see if you can sort this out . . . make some headway with it and give me a day off, and I'll jump back in.' "

It was a fateful decision.

Beaker and Joey were angling for a night trap, and the snakes were in the cockpit.

It was April 18, late in the evening. The weather was bad. The horizon was nonexistent. It was like they were powering through space made of piercing, driving rain.

Was the deck pitching?

Prestrike tanking had gone badly. Engine compression stalls, combined with the weather, had caused Beaker to miss numerous attempts to get gas. He'd finally plugged in — but not until he'd gotten irritated at Joey's comments from the back. "It's difficult enough," he said. "I just don't like flying with skippers." Joey remembers: "He's pretty capable. . . . I think he was just having a bad night." Then the strike had been called off because solid clouds over the target had rendered their lasers useless.

Now they were seconds from the carrier's deck. Their only aids, beyond Beaker's skills, were the red-orange lineup "ball" piercing the murky night like a serpent's eye, the line of tiny green lights pointing toward the invisible sea, and the now-silent, but hidden, LSOs watching on the stern. Trapping was the ultimate carrier pilot skill, and Beaker, as prideful as any, considered himself good, if not expert, at it.

Forget the string of bad luck he'd had bombing. He was a professional fighter pilot. He could handle the situation.

Any second now the deck would come smashing up, flattening their tires, jarring their innards — an unseen uppercut from a storm-tossed superweight.

Watching the ball, scanning his instruments, Beaker suddenly realized he was too high, had too much power. Instinctively, he jerked back the throttles, cutting gas flow. But then he waited too long to restore it. Only seconds. But that was enough.

"I have no idea why," he said. "But it just goes to show, in carrier aviation you can kill yourselves so quickly."

By the time he shoved the throttles forward again, it was too late.

The F-14As have the oldest, weakest engines of the Tomcats. It takes them two or three seconds to "spool up" again. The jet had already hit the deck, missed the wires with its tail hook, but the power had not kicked back in yet.

You always land at full throttle in case you have to take off again — as he chillingly realized he did.

The LSOs screamed, " 'Power! Power! Power!' . . . I made a critical mistake," he said. "It only takes a few seconds. . . . I screwed up."

They "boltered," the naval term for being waved off, or aborting the landing.

They were on one of the angled decks, heavy from the load of undropped bombs they were still carrying. Unable to lift instantaneously because of the time lag in the older engines, they "dribbled" off the side, heading for the water.

It was an emergency situation.

"I was pretty scared," said Beaker. From the backseat, Joey screamed, " 'You got it!? You got it!?' I slammed in the blower, and all I could say is, 'I got it! I got it!' even though I had no clue where I was or what attitude I was in. I'm like, 'Just please don't eject me [from the backseat] because it's so embarrassing. I'd rather die first.' "

Dog and Wog happened to be watching below deck on television monitors. "I see the airplane kinda fall out of the sky . . . go off the end, and disappear," said Wog. "I went, 'Oh, my God.' " Dog said, "Everybody's screaming, 'Power! Power! Get your nose up!' My heart fell out and hit the floor."

A Tomcat weighs upward of fifty thousand pounds loaded as they were. If they hit the water, some thirty-five-to-forty feet below, they were dead. "It's the force of the impact," said Joey. It would be like hitting a wall. "You're doing like 110, 120 miles per hour. . . . You stop pretty quickly. . . . Some parts keep going. . . . You may not die, but you'll be banged up. You may be unconscious. And the plane will sink within the next fifteen seconds. I've seen three or four F-14s hit the water. . . . Nobody got out. . . . You'd think they would stay afloat for awhile, but they don't."

Everyone watching knew this.

"Eject! Eject!" screamed an anonymous voice over the radio, probably one of the LSOs.

Joey: "We sink, and you feel it. . . . It's the dead of night. . . . Oh, my God. . . . There's no horizon . . . no references . . . a scary feel-ing. . . . It's a gut-wrenching feeling whether we stay or get out."

Because they were falling upright, ejection gave them a chance. Had they been turned toward the boat, it would have launched them into its side. Certain death. As it was, they both would probably land in the water very close to the ship.

Joey: "It's doing on the order of twenty-to-thirty miles an hour, which means it has tremendous pull. . . . By the time you land in the water, you've already gone probably one-hundred-to-two-hundred feet back, and you're getting close to the props. . . . It would have gotten pretty hairy."

The "saving grace," he said, was that in the few seconds it took them to drop, "Beaker was all the way up on the power, and he held the nose up more than what was optimum."

It kept them momentarily off the freezing waves, perhaps ten feet above.

There's a mysterious phenomenon in aviation called "ground ef-fect." Somehow, sometimes, when a plane is merely a few feet off the water, a "cushion" of compacted air can hold it up. Usually not for long. But in this case, enough to give the faltering jet, its engines churning the sea, a fighting chance to lift.

They were still flying. But barely.

Beaker: "I engaged the blowers and had some energy under it." He wasn't so much scared, he said, as realizing, " 'It's gonna hurt! It's gonna hurt!' " But they started climbing out.

Joey took his hand off the ejection strap.

Now they had to make another pass.

Both were badly shaken.

Beaker: "You don't let things affect you. You compartmentalize . . . because there's a task at hand that is much more pressing than what-ever happened thirty seconds ago. I said, 'Okay, I screwed that one up really bad, but I got to get this on deck.' And I got Joey in the backseat going, 'Hey, are you all right? Are you all right?' I said, 'Shut up! I got things to do. I got to land this frigging airplane. . . . I know I screwed up. I screwed up bad. . . . All I have to do is fly the needles and get on the deck. I don't need anything from you right now.' "

It wasn't pretty, but they landed on the next pass.

Once out and somewhat recovered, the two Aces met in the ready room. Beaker: "The skipper read me the riot act." The pilot said he was "so frustrated to hear ball-flying techniques from a RIO," but "bit my tongue." Joey recalls: "I got frustrated . . . but I didn't take it out on anybody. . . . The biggest thing was getting his confidence up. . . . I said, 'Beaker . . . everybody has their moments where they have a hard time.' . . . I told him, 'Just forget about this. . . . I have the greatest confidence in you. . . .' "

But he was still shaken. He talked with Bru and Dog and decided to fly exclusively with Bru. "Being the skipper and having all the pressures and then to have a guy have a hard time landing and nearly kill you. . . . That's like, man, a lot of pressure. So I said, 'Bru's safe. Bru is not going to be in the top ten tailhookers [pilots with the best landing grades], but he gets on board safely.' "

Beaker didn't know of the decision and said if he had, it wouldn't have mattered to him. "I screwed up. I was scared shitless." The tall redhead went back to his room. "I had a bottle of vodka that was completely illegal, but I got myself pretty stinking drunk that night because I was just scared shitless. That's the closest I really came to killing myself around the boat."

On the same night Beaker and Joey were fighting demons, April 18, Bru and Wog had a modicum of SCAR success. They found a Serbian Army communication tower and actually dropped on it—a first in the SCAR quest. But their bombs didn't explode. New procedures for fusing had been put into effect, and they weren't aware of them yet.

But the drop was an advance.

From there it was all downhill.

The weather that night was the biggest obstacle. Taking a midmission break from their hunting, Bru had trouble tanking. The tanker was in storm clouds at thirty thousand feet. It was hard to see in the rain and darkness. Wind jostled the jet. When they finally found it, others around them needed gas, too. They had to wait their turn. At that altitude, the Tomcat's vintage engines had to work harder to maintain flight. The air was thinner. There was less oxygen. Since the engines burned a mixture of oxygen with gas, it took more gas to maintain speed and maneuverability. They lost lots of gas as they maneuvered in and out of the clouds, ducking lightning, waiting their turn. When they finally got their chance, Bru had to go into burner to have enough gas to maneuver the Tomcat's probe, arcing up from the jet's nose, into the tanker's trailing basket. But he couldn't mate. For whatever reason—the storm's disruptive winds and vision obstacles, tenseness from the conditions, just plain bad luck—the probe kept coming out of the basket. Eventually they were so low on gas they realized that if they kept having trouble, they would quickly come to a point where they wouldn't have enough gas to break off and make it back to the ship.

They finally decided they would stop trying to tank and would divert instead to Brindisi, a land base on Italy, which was closer than the carrier. They calculated that they had just enough fuel left, about three thousand pounds, to make a slow descent without deviation right on down from the thirty thousand feet into the Italian base. There would be no room for maneuver or diversion. Then, as they began their descent, they ran into a forty-five-thousand-feet-high tower of thunderstorms blocking their way.

Wog: "Bru and I are just goin', 'Oh my God. What are we gonna do? How are we gonna.' . . . If we [went back to the tanker] and tried to fence with [the basket] and we run out of gas, we're gonna fall out of the sky."

It was a major storm front. They encountered it at about twenty-five thousand feet in their descent, up high where the turbulent air and thunderheads were. Lightning and hail threatened them. But they couldn't go back.

Luckily, nothing bad happened to them. While descending through it, they contacted the controlling E-2 plane in the area to tell the Roosevelt they dropped a bomb on the earlier target but were having to divert. They'd get gas at Brindisi and be back by the next recovery. Somehow the message got changed. By the time it reached the ship, they had gone too low, done something stupid, gotten battle damage, and almost lost their airplane—a report that not only scared the admiral, CAG, and Joey, but made the ship hierarchy wonder if there was more bad news. Everyone was worried about collateral damage and hitting civilians.

How could those guys be so stupid?

Bru and Wog arrived at Brindisi almost on fumes, but couldn't find anyone to help them with gas or even a phone call back to the ship.

They finally got fuel with the help of an air force C-130 cargo plane crew, and when they landed back on the carrier, they were told to report immediately to CAG's office, where they were called on the carpet.

Wog: "In the back of Joey's mind must have been, 'Oh God, these two guys are out there tryin' to make this [SCAR] work. And they're hotdoggin' and, you know, flyin' down real low and got in trouble.' And one of the things CAG said to me—we were explaining what happened—and he said, 'I thought you guys jettisoned your drop tanks.' " Wog said he looked at CAG incredulously a moment and then joked, " 'Well, actually, CAG, we did. Then we flew down below 'em, flipped inverted, and put 'em back on the airplane. Then we flew to Brindisi.' He just looked at me and then goes, 'Oh, Wog,' shaking his head. 'Get out of my office.' "

Wrex and Thing, flying their first SCAR, had their own comedy that night, although with different circumstances. A UAV put them onto an armored vehicle traveling a road. Undetected, they followed it to a large T-shaped building where the occupants of the vehicle parked and went into a nearby house. The FAC-As got cleared to drop and lased a five-hundred pounder into the building. But they too had missed the latest fusing information, and the bomb didn't explode. It just smashed into the building, came out the other side, and halted by hitting a car.

Now the comedy began.

Thing: "All of sudden we see these guys, it looks like ten guys, come running out of the building the bomb's gone through and head for the car. Then they realized there's a bomb sitting in it. You can see them gawk, spin around, and take off the other way."

Keystone Serbs.

But actually it was only funny in hindsight.

It's not clear what the outcome of the mission was. The two Aces have different recollections, one saying they left, and the other saying they vectored in some other bombers. But both recall that a SAM was quickly shot at them, which was scary, and that seeing the possible victims of their bombs—something aviators don't usually get to do— made them think of the personal toll inherent in their job.

Wrex: "This is when it hit me that there are people down there. . . . It's a tough job to do. . . . You want to know you are doing right. . . .

and I believe this conflict, our involvement in it, was definitely the right thing. . . . These guys . . . they're trying to kill me . . . if we don't stop them, they're going to take over another village and probably kill some more people. . . . That's your defense mechanism. . . ."

The next day, April 19, would be a breakthrough of sorts. Recovered from the frightening bolter, Commander Aucoin was back flying with his maintenance officer, Bru. The two of them resolved anew to make SCAR work—this despite continued resistance from those in the battle group who either still believed it was impossible under current conditions, or resented the departure it represented from established navy ways of doing business. Many of those tasked with the new mission still believed it was a waste of resources.

The continued resistance did not hamper Joey or Bru, or Dog or Wog, or most of the Aces either, for the squadron took its cues from its leadership and everybody knew where the leadership stood. The problem, at this particular point, was that little in the way of SCAR-FAC-A procedures or tactics had been standardized or even worked out. This was forging on the fly, trial by error, test and discard. They had bad intelligence. Their equipment, like the LANTIRN, while good, was not what was specifically needed for the hunting. The normal picture in the FLIR didn't have enough magnification to see troops and distinguish vehicles at the heights they were restricted to. And the narrow, magnified setting was like looking through a straw. If you lost the target, it was terribly hard to find again.

They only had two pairs of gyrostabilized binoculars, which meant that only one or two aircraft (if they wanted to split the pairs) could hunt with them at one time. The air threat had still not been neutralized. They weren't so much worried about MiGs or other enemy aircraft, which had all but disappeared after the first few days of the war and especially now after Podgorica. But SAMs were a very real danger, and inherent in SCAR was the loiter. You had to circle, stay in the area, check things out. Speed and maneuverability, the basis of SAM avoidance, were not an option when looking for targets. You had to get slow, dip down, hang around.

"My biggest concern was that we were going to get bagged out there as FAC-A and FAC-A escorts," said Dog, who, not being a FAC-A, would do a lot of the escorting. "It was a very risky thing. . . . This wasn't swooping in, dropping bombs, and getting out. . . . We're in the same piece of sky, very predictable. . . . The FACs and FAC escorts hung it out . . . no ifs, ands, or buts about it."

Meat, also not a FAC-A, wrote home:

```
Going after the troops and the tanks . . . is a totally
different ball game. Those things move around a lot and
it is hard to know where they are so we have to do what
is called Close Air Support with Forward Air Control-
lers. Basically now we have to send someone in to look
for the tanks and APCs and then they call in the strikers
to take them out. Very difficult to do from high altitude.
Initially they thought the Tomcats could do it with our
LANTIRN pods. But we found it to be harder than we
thought. So what we have to do now [is] go lower into the
SAM envelopes. Sound like fun. . . .
```

And finding and targeting weren't the only problems. They had to make sure the target wasn't civilian. They had to get clearance to fire from multiple headquarters, and then they had to coordinate the strike, which meant getting others to see it, and then maybe directing others with their laser, all the while hanging around, being a prime target themselves. And during the entire time they had to "deconflict" the airspace; in effect act as air-traffic controllers in the immediate area so the strikers they were using didn't have midairs.

There had been some progress in using TARPS to get more timely pictures—but not enough. On April 17, after authorization from the CAOC, which was beginning to understand the potential of TARPS for finding the Serbs' fielded forces, the battle group had organized its first photographic mission into Kosovo specifically to get leads for SCAR missions. It was to be led by Beaker. But bad weather had forced cancellation.

Such was the situation when Bru and Joey prepared to launch around noon on April 19. Bru said Joey had already gone up on deck when "Stalk" Thompson, one of the Hornet skippers, "called up right before I walked . . . and goes, 'Get down here. We've got a picture that just came in of a frog.'" "Frog" was the NATO code name for a Scud-like, truck-borne, surface-to-surface missile the Serbs were using to decimate and rout enemy villages. The pictures Thompson had, wherever they came from, were fresh and in the general vicinity that Bru and Joey were planning to reconnoiter. Bru gave them to Joey as he got in the Tomcat. Joey already had amassed some twenty-to-thirty pictures on his own, mostly from satellites. They were in the cockpit with him. But none were as fresh as Thompson's. They decided to go look for the frog first.

They launched into an anomaly—reasonably good weather. It appears they had some trouble finding the frog site, possibly because of problems with the GPS coordinates. But they kept hunting, using both the gyrostabilized binoculars and the FLIR's wide view. "We were just flying around the countryside," said Joey, "I happened to just, 'Hey Bru, that area looks real similar to the photo.' " The pictures had some farmlike buildings in it and an adjacent field. The area below them had similar features in roughly the same pattern. They were at fifteen thousand feet, too high to see details like the frog. They decided to take a risk and go lower.

They had already been dipping and popping back up as a cautious means of entering and exiting SAM envelopes. Now they swooped down lower than ever before. It paid off. "The buildings matched up," said Joey. It was a barnlike structure with other dwellings nearby. Near the barn was a "parking lot" with vehicles. And in the field was—the missile launcher! "It was on a truck," said Joey. "We suspected they stayed within this barn-type building and just came out to fire. Then they would run back in the barn."

They zoomed back up to safety.

Excited with what they'd found, they got confirmation to drop. It's not clear whether they hit the frog themselves or brought in Hornets to do it. Joey's recollection is that they used their own GBU-12 on the launcher and then brought in the Hornets for the other targets. Bru says they decided to wait for Hornets to do all the bombing because of the impact it would have on the SCAR debate.

"Anybody probably could have gone out with what we had and found the target and bombed it," he said. "The difficult part comes in when you've got different areas or targets and an allocation of airplanes with, say, a twenty-minute window. . . . I've got twenty minutes to go up there, circle around, confirm the target here, confirm the target there . . . get authorization . . . prioritize, deconflict . . . and start directing the bombing."

Regardless of whether they hit the frog themselves or not, they did have plenty of other targets to parcel out on the site. Bru wanted to make an example. Joey agreed. They had Hornets standing by. The Hornets were probably about eight-to-ten miles away. One of the advantages of using the Tomcats was that their LANTIRN system was stronger than the F/A-18s' Nite Hawk targeting system. The LANTIRN could see farther and provided a larger scope picture to its crew than the Nite Hawk did. With the Tomcat's sighting of the targets, the Hornets didn't have to get as close to it as they otherwise would.

The Hornets were carrying laser-guided Maverick air-to-ground missiles. These honed in on laser reflection and were unique in that they could be dropped and then the Hornet could fly away. Nothing else was required of the pilot. As long as the target was illuminated, the Maverick, which had wings, fins, and a motor, would fly to the laser spot on its own. It was an easy-to-use bomb for what would come to be termed "buddy lasing" — using the laser of one aircraft (in this case, the Tomcat) for the bomb of another (the Hornet). The Maverick was also specially made to destroy hardened targets like tanks and armored vehicles. It could easily penetrate farm buildings.

One by one, Bru and Joey called in the Hornets, which stayed out of visual range. They gave the Hornet pilots the target coordinates to aim the Maverick and the LANTIRN laser code so the missile could recognize and be guided by it. Once Joey had the laser aimed at a spot, the Hornet would make its run, still staying a safe distance away. When the Maverick located the laser, probably about five miles from the target, the Hornet would release the missile. It would then fly to whatever Joey was illuminating.

They decimated the area.

Joey likened the multiplicity of bombs being guided to playing a video game. "Did you ever play Missile Command?" he said. "I played it a lot as a young lieutenant . . . moving the cursor around . . . [the game was] a lot of fun."

The exercise provided a definite sense of power seldom experienced in normal bomb runs. It was almost point and shoot. The laser operator wielded a beam of concentrated energy that doomed everything it touched, with the rain of devastation relentless and seemingly unending depending on the number of bomb-carrying strikers being directed.

The concentration of one of the Hornet pilots sticks in Joey's memory. "A young lieutenant," he said, "I can't remember his name. . . . He couldn't pickle on his first run so he really bore down on the second." He didn't realize it, but he was pointed almost straight down, scorching the air at about eighteen thousand feet, approaching six hundred miles per hour. "All that is out of his scan. He just wants to get the thing off. . . . When he launches, he's almost Mach 1. . . . It comes off and blows up the support vehicle . . . just blew it to bits. . . ."

Not until the lieutenant got back and viewed his video did they all see the numbers recorded by his sensors showing such a thrill ride. He'd been oblivious. He had just not wanted to screw up.

Joey thinks the April 19 SCAR mission was the first time a Maverick was ever buddy-lazed in combat. But he could be wrong. Regardless, the mission was their first bonafide SCAR success—roughly two weeks after they'd started trying to perfect it. And although it by no means ended their SCAR-FAC-A problems, the mission had an immediate impact. "Once they do it," said Bru, referring to the Hornet pilots who were among the most skeptical of the mission in the air wing, "they suddenly come aboard."

Not every Hornet pilot was out there. Far from it. Nor were the skeptical F-14 crews or their doubting higher-ups. And they were still badly in need of fresh intelligence. But the seed had been planted. More important, CAG got a needed demonstration. Joey: "Once he saw the videos—and if we hadn't had the videos he wouldn't have believed it because we needed [them] for conformation and all that— he felt really good about it. . . . Hey, we can actually do this."

Thirteen

Through the rest of April, as predicted, the number of fixed targets the air wing was assigned to strike diminished greatly, while SCAR and TARPS missions increased. The killing of Albanians by the Serbs was mounting; pressure to stop it was heightening. Bridges, communications towers, and an occasional small ammunition or fuel dump would be assigned for elimination to a medium or smaller strike force, often including Aces Tomcats. But the big targets in Kosovo, the carrier's purview, were already decimated or only revisited for mop-up.

In the absence of ground troops in the Kosovo War, finding and eliminating the Serbs' fielded forces were now clearly becoming the battle group's main tasks.

Aware of the situation and inspired by their success of April 19, Bru and Joey increased their SCAR efforts even more. They began an almost round-the-clock schedule of SCAR activity usually involving two missions a day, which was about the limit they could fly. They'd jump into a jet in the early morning for two-to-three hours of hunting and return near noon. Still in their sweaty flight gear, they'd get a brief while munching a candy bar for lunch, pick up the best intelligence-supplied pictures or coordinates available, and launch back out for an afternoon-through-night hunt. And always there was unfinished squadron business, often a mound of paperwork and duties to attend to, when they returned late at night before they got some sleep.

Little by little they began to refine and create their SCAR techniques. For instance, where before they were dipping and quickly returning to safe altitude in order to check on possible targets, they began relying more on their wingman, Prowlers, and the E-2 plane in the area to signal danger and fight it. The wingmen would be their defensive eyes, checking the ground and the immediate airspace for threats. The Prowlers would jam or missile nearby enemy batteries that activated. The E-2 would alert them to distant hostile threats. All this meant that they could stay lower longer, concentrate on the search. The rules about *how* low they could go were not yet defined. Strikers were restricted to a twenty-thousand-foot floor, but the SCAR floor hadn't yet been posted. "It was one of those deals where we're not exactly sure we want to ask the question," said Bru. "So the strikers kept up there. But as FACs—I know I did [went lower]. It was more just doing it than asking about it."

Eventually they would be flying into the heart of the enemy's defensive envelopes—ten thousand feet and lower. They'd do so with wingmen who usually guarded higher and were FAC-As. These included pilots Dewar, Wrex, and Gooch, and RIOs Squab, Thing, and Toadboy. The idea was to always have a trained FAC-A crew in the area in case they went down. In the meantime, the wingmen, usually JOs, hopefully would learn from Bru and their skipper, Joey.

Dog, who, as XO, was saddled with a lot of the mundane squadron duties that Joey, because he was flying so much, couldn't do, was also used as a wingman crewed with Wog, who had FAC-A training. In fact, because of the danger inherent in the FAC-A loiter, Bru and Joey preferred to have either Dog and Wog, because of their experience, or Dewar and Squab, who were JO leaders rising to the top, on their wing.

Dog: "While they [Bru and Joey] are totally in the cockpit looking at sensors, looking at the ground, our job was to do top cover on them, call out SAMs, defeat the SAMs [that might elude the Prowlers], protect them. . . . I guarantee you, if they are heads down looking for things and there was a junior aircrew in the other airplane, they wouldn't feel so good."

The fact that Bru and Joey were taking the lion's share of FAC-A missions understandably caused consternation among the JOs, who, with the threats seemingly diminishing, felt they should now be getting their turns at combat. And they did. Only when Bru and Joey began kicking JOs out of good-to-go jets when their own jet went down, did the JOs start grumbling about the hinges hogging missions and seeking career-building glory.

The jet-taking was the leadership's prerogative, especially the skipper's. It happened maybe three times, the first time to Pappy and Money, who were not FAC-As, but the spare on the mission, and who therefore probably understood why they were being ousted. But when it happened to Gooch and Squab, the two senior JO FAC-As who felt themselves highly qualified decided they'd had enough.

They confronted Bru.

The situation was complex: Gooch had not redeemed himself from his earlier clashes with Joey and other squadron leaders. That may have been part of the problem. It was a night mission. The date is in question. Bru and Joey's jet had gone down on deck, leaving Gooch and Squab to take their place. The two JOs were in their jet preparing to move toward launch. A cockpit light wasn't working correctly. It wouldn't dim to the nighttime setting, meaning their Tomcat would be easier to spot from the ground. Gooch wanted it fixed. He was talking to the plane captain about the problem. Joey and Bru, according to Bru, were in maintenance discussing their downed plane and overheard some of the radio conversation between Gooch and maintenance.

"It was the same kind of deal like with the weapons thing [when Gooch had refused to man a CAP without missiles]," said Bru. Bru's solution was to put tape over the light and launch. But he was not hearing *any* solution from Gooch. Time for launch was winding down, and very soon the air boss, who controlled the deck, would take the Black Ace Tomcat out of the sequence—something that, for a variety of reasons, neither Joey or Bru wanted to happen. The squadron was measured by, among other things, how many sorties it flew.

Bru: "We go, 'Good God.' " They rushed up on deck. "We walked up to their airplane and said, 'Get out of the jet.' . . . It wasn't nice. . . . We didn't say please. It was, 'Get out of the jet. We're taking it.' . . . He [Gooch] goes, 'Well we just wanted to know. . . .' And we go, 'Too late. We're taking it.' . . . So they got out. . . ."

Gooch: "We're qualified FACs, and there was a misunderstanding there. I guess he thought that we weren't going to take that jet when, in fact, we were just trying to get the problem solved. . . . I think that was the climax of a long-growing . . . feeling among the JOs . . . of, 'Hey, we're just as capable. . . . [We felt like we] were just a turning spare for them. . . . I was upset. . . . I know Squab was very mad that night."

Later they confronted Bru. (Joey wasn't there but said he heard about it.)

Bru: "It was, 'What are you doing coming up there and taking our jet?' And then Gooch explained his part of it, and I said, 'Listen, pal. You either make a decision. . . . If the jet's down, then down it. . . . Make it unquestionable.' " He said he had no problem with Gooch's not flying with the broken light. By the letter of the law—just as in the missile situation—Gooch was right. "But what you're doing is sitting there dillydallying around and having a second-class petty officer tell *you* it's okay. What's with that? . . . That's why you're wearing wings. . . . Put some tape over it! Adapt. Overcome. Improvise. . . . Have a solution but don't just sit there and say weak voiced, 'Gee. I don't know.' I mean, jiminy Christmas. . . .

"And then Squab said, 'Well, by God, I'm not going to let that happen again.' And I said, 'Well, fine. Now you're growing up. That's exactly what you're supposed to do.' I said, 'The next time I walk over to your airplane, I hope you *don't* open the canopy. I hope you shoot off the front." He laughed at the recollection. "Jesus Christ . . ."

Joey agreed: "Initially I wanted to be [on all the FAC-A missions] because I was kind of concerned with collateral damage and hurting refugees. . . . That was my biggest concern, to make sure we didn't do something wrong. You know, our FAC-As are good, but I felt with my experience in the airplane, I'd rather err on the safe side. . . . I wanted assurance that we weren't going to start gunning down the refugees and blowing up Albanians. CAG wanted me there, too."

So they continued running roughshod, fighting the weather and lack of fresh leads, inventing and shaping by trial and error, and gigging those they felt were obstructing. Wog remembers Bru going to the carrier's intelligence office and demanding, " 'Get me a Yugoslavian field manual on how these guys operate!' " They wanted to know how the Serbs hid their tanks, on what types of terrain the tanks and other military vehicles could operate and where they couldn't. But nobody on the ship had the information. "We were navy. We didn't know army," said Wog. They asked the battle group's headquarters, Sixth Fleet in Italy, to send them an expert on the Serbian "order of battle." But despite the fact that there was a knowledgeable major at the headquarters, "they sent a lance corporal. All he could do was plot points on a map for us," said Wog disgustedly.

Meanwhile, Dog was having his own problems.

Right after Podgorica, he found out, quite by accident, that his wife back home was being threatened by a stalker at work. Charlotte Bauser worked for a civilian company doing secret communication setups for the navy. She looked like singer-actress Ann-Margret. She was very attractive. They had a five-year-old daughter Dog doted on. Prior to his leaving, Charlotte had fended off some unwelcome advances from a client representative whom she was forced, by virtue of a company contract, to do business with. Not wanting to worry Dog, who was leaving shortly, she had downplayed the advances, and Dog hadn't thought much about it.

Then, right after the raid on Podgorica, he had called her at work from the *Roosevelt*—a privilege the officers had for short periods when time and operations permitted. The client rep was there and became jealous and violent. His wife had tried to excuse herself from the man and take the call in private, but he had thrown a fit and had been physically removed by coworkers. "She was very upset," said Dog, and he suddenly realized he had a major problem. His wife was in danger, maybe his daughter too, and he was six thousand miles away fighting his country's war while "my own home was in jeopardy. . . . There was something wrong with that."

He had two choices. Fix the situation from the *Roosevelt*, or go home and do it in person. He wasn't going to waste much time. "If I didn't get the answers I wanted, I would have been on the next plane out of there." But he didn't tell Joey—not until he had to. "Joey had enough on his mind. I'll handle it myself." Losing the XO would have been a crippling blow to the skipper, who depended heavily on him. And to the air wing, too. Dog was one of its critical strike leaders who could plan and execute anything the CAG was tasked with.

He was a vital cog at several levels.

Calling his wife's boss, he detected hesitancy to act. He decided he didn't have time to argue. He went over the man's head. He called the head of the navy command for which the client rep worked. He told both her boss and the navy prexy that if something wasn't done quickly to insure his wife's safety, not only would he be there fast to take whatever action was necessary, but they, working for the navy, would have to explain to some of its highest-ranking admirals, currently fighting the same war he was, why "one of their seven prime strike-warfare leaders" in the battle had to remove himself to take care of a situation at home.

Dog: "I knew playing that card was the political thing to do. . . . I'm not an evil political person, but you start to screw with me, and I'm going to get downright ugly. Here's the thing. I'm flying two, sometimes three combat missions a day. And all night long I'm doing XO shit"—mounds of paperwork, personnel evaluations, write-ups for awards, manning disciplinary and administrative boards, making sure the toilets are unclogged—from 7 A.M. to 9 P.M.—all the "stuff that doesn't stop because we happen to be dropping bombs. . . . I'm tired. I'm pissed off. I'm angry. I don't need a bunch of people deciding whether they are going to go to Bennigan's or Olive Garden for lunch taking this situation lightly."

The hesitancy dissolved. He was deluged with e-mails pledging that a solution was imminent. An investigation determined that this wasn't the first time the client rep had harassed women. His bosses sent the rep away—in effect, a paid vacation. It wasn't the solution Dog wanted because he felt the man should have been prosecuted. But his wife didn't want to go forward with sexual-harassment charges because of what she felt would be a stigma on her ability to work in her field. Her boss assigned protectors for her at the office, and to and from it, and the actions did relieve Dog's fears for his family's safety.

And Dog wasn't the only Ace aviator with problems at home.

Lt. Ron "Mo" Vaught, a RIO and "Super" JO, meaning he was on his second tour and therefore was one of the JO leaders, learned while fighting the war that his wife was leaving him.

Such news is not uncommon on cruises.

Thin and soft-spoken, the thirty-two-year-old Redondo Beach, California, native was one of the squadron's Topgun graduates—the new, lengthier Topgun school that now incorporates strike warfare. He had no warning of his wife's intentions. "It was a shock to me. I didn't expect anything."

He had sensed the problem as the war heightened. "I knew something was not quite right because I was always sending e-mails and I wasn't getting e-mails back for a week." He finally called her from the ship, and she gave him the bad news. They'd been married three years. "No children, thank God."

At first he couldn't believe it and thought, "With time, she might change her mind." But that hope quickly dissipated, and he began a waking nightmare. "It was tough. Damn tough." Like Dog, he was six thousand miles away, and like a prisoner in a cell, he was incapable of taking action. Without telling others, he informed Joey and Dog. "I felt like I owed it to the skipper to let him know I had some issues. . . . I said, 'I'll understand if you want to take me off the flight schedule. I need a couple of days to figure things out.' "

Joey: "He said his wife didn't love him anymore and she wants a divorce. It was weighing heavily on his mind." The skipper gave him the days off and then asked how he was doing. "I said I was still shocked." He'd considered going home — a request he knew would be hard to get approved with the war on. He said Joey asked, " 'Do you think that will save anything?' I said, 'No. She's already made up her mind. I think she'd already made up her mind a long time ago. . . .' "

He decided to try and table the problem until after the cruise. "I told [Joey], 'I think I'm compartmentalized enough that I can still fly an airplane and go hit a target and do what you need me to do.' He looked at me and said, 'Okay. That's all I need to hear. If anything changes, if anything's different, you let me know.' And it was tough. I'm not going to say I was able to just forget about it. . . ."

But he endured, keeping it largely to himself. Some Aces didn't learn about his problem until the war was nearly over. "I wasn't going to sit out there on the boat the whole time moping," he said. "It's eating you . . . definitely a hurtful time." The hurt was least when he was flying. "You go out there. You do your missions." Those in the squadron who knew tried to help. "We're not a social-services organization," said Dog. "We're family." But they didn't need somebody breaking down at a crucial moment. "We watched him closely."

He wasn't put in demanding situations. His roommate, Razor, was asked by Wog to take over Mo's squadron job, strike-warfare trainer. It doubled Razor's work, but he didn't complain.

Mo: "I told him [Razor], 'Hey, you're gonna see me in a bad mood every now and then . . . a little depressed or whatever.' . . . He'd see when I came back, he'd look at me, and he'd know, 'Okay, he needs something to divert his attention. . . . Hey, let's play a little of this game,' or whatever. . . . You don't realize it at the time, but you look back and say, 'You know, this guy's pretty perceptive.'"

The hurt continued the entire cruise.

Not as devastating, but also tough both personally and professionally, was the professional problem experienced by Lt. James "Tab" Corlett. The call sign probably referred to 1950s Hollywood heartthrob Tab Hunter, a strapping blond actor often seen shirtless in beach scenes. Corlett was fairly tall and good-looking in a preppy, clean-cut way, but he wasn't blond like Hunter although he had been a surfer. A pilot, he was also call-signed "Jack," which he preferred. And as one of the few bachelors in the squadron, he had a reputation in port as a ladies' man.

The basic problem for Jack was that he was a nugget, a brand-new pilot right out of the training command. He had come to the Aces barely three months before it had left for war. He was inexperienced and hadn't had the work-up that the others, with one exception, had. That one exception was Lupe Lopez, the squadron's other nugget pilot, who had joined the Aces a little after Jack and so was less experienced but was adapting better.

Most nugget pilots have flying problems. The fact that the squadron had not had a new pilot in a year and a half meant that tolerance for nugget mistakes by pilots was low. They hadn't seen them in awhile. As Jack's mistakes mounted, some Aces began calling him "Gue," for "go ugly early." It was a derisive call sign that meant he was going to screw up, and after awhile it seemed fitting—to most but Jack, who hated the call sign and refused to discuss it.

Jack's problems had started even before cruise. In the last work-up exercise—the only one he'd been able to participate in—he'd had a bad landing. It was actually a bolter. But instead of being able to lift off and return for another try, he'd been too low. His tail hook had snagged one of the arresting wires as he was powering to go back out— a very dangerous situation.

Normally, the wing-rooted wheels are supposed to hit the deck first, cushioning impact. The nose wheel then tips down with minimum shock. But in Jack's situation, the three wheels hit almost at once, damaging the nose strut. The Tomcat would be out of service for an indeterminable amount of time. Even though he was a new pilot and therefore the mistake was "understandable," said Wrex, "we were going to war, and now you've got an airplane down, and people were pissed off."

Night landings became his nemesis. "I was moving the throttle too much, my scan [of instruments and ship-landing aids] wasn't correct. I wasn't looking in the right places at the right time. I was getting waved off a lot, boltering a lot, being real behind the boat." Making matters worse was the fact that he was being compared to Lupe, who was favored for his performance and attitude.

Lupe wasn't that much more advanced. But he wasn't having problems landing—a big flag for any pilot. And Jack, who, as a high schooler in Cleveland said he had been "a little rebellious" and embraced "the alternative side," was seen as a bit of a loner by some and not receptive to professional instruction, which was often curt and critical, especially from the LSOs. (Actually, his loner status may have stemmed from him wanting to stay away from criticism.) "Overall, the attitude [toward me] was, 'You know, Jack sucks, and he doesn't care that he sucks, and he's not fixing [his flying problems].'"

He began to feel that the squadron LSOs—Dewar, Brain, and Razor, whose job it was to correct his errors—were at least partly responsible for his problems. "Yeah, they were pretty hard on me. . . . Being the first new guy . . . is a lot of pressure . . . maybe it's personality. . . . I'm my own worst critic, so maybe people see that as I don't want to listen. . . . But you know when I suck, I know I suck. . . . They seemed to want to increase that. . . . I didn't feel they were there to help me," especially, he said, Brain and Razor. "I never really felt they were on my side."

LSOs have significant power. Not only are they the last word on actually trapping or not, and, in effect, preventing crashes and holocaust, but they are the landing graders, the "gods" (if they, in turn, are respected) in making a pilot's carrier reputation. After a recovery, they go one-on-one with the pilot, telling him what he did wrong—very little about what he did right—and assigning a grade. "Okay" is the highest grade, showing the emphasis on negatives. Negatives kill. There is no "excellent" or "good." Safety is what is important.

If you can't land, you can't fight.

It's that simple.

Pilots live or die on the grades posted on the squadron "greenie boards" (so called because an "OK" is always written in green). The boards are in the ready rooms for all to see. (RIOs have no such grading and thus are spared the personal humiliation of a bad effort.) The Ace's greenie board was a replica of a blackjack table hung on the wall near the walk-in door. Everybody saw it. Jack didn't get many greens. His reputation was going down, not up. He likened some LSO criticisms to being "punched in the throat kinda. . . . I was kind of down on myself, real critical of myself."

His loss of confidence caused more problems.

CAG, concerned with the big picture, worried that he would damage another plane. Joey was supportive, believing he'd mature as most nuggets do and come out of it, but said, "He was my weakest pilot." Jack began finding mechanical problems with his jets, especially at night. A joke started among the RIOs that if you didn't want to fly, get scheduled with Jack. He'd find a reason not to launch. He was scared, said more than one Ace. That made RIOs in his backseat and the LSOs landing him edgy.

It was a downward spiral, publicly viewed.

They gave him an occasional CAP to see how he'd do. Wog flew with him on August 14. He wanted to see if he could help. Jack had trouble tanking. Then he boltered on the return. "You kinda had to treat him with kid gloves," said Wog. "If you rattled him, things went right out the window. . . . He lacked confidence in himself to make him be better."

But everyone agreed he had skill. And he also had persistence. And despite the fears and setbacks, even the convening of a "Human Factors Board" to see if there were any hidden problems like a pregnant girlfriend or dying parent to explain his behavior, he didn't give up. "I knew what I needed to do to be a good pilot," he said, "and basically, I would strive to do that." He avoided the critics and found refuge in "Eight-Ball," the crowded little stateroom he and seven other nuggets and junior JOs shared.

No one on the carrier had luxurious accommodations. The ship was built for war, not comfort. The admiral, understandably, had about the best, an expansive set of rooms that included a spacious, multiroom office, dining room, and bedroom and probably his own bathroom. Joey's stateroom, as a comparative example, was like a Motel-6 single —

but smaller, without the bathroom, and including the deafening thunder of a catapult shot periodically shaking the room. But at least Joey's room was private, as was the XO's, the only other Ace who had private accommodations.

By contrast, Eight-Ball—so designated by a black-and-white JO-affixed cue ball sticker on its metal door—was a far cry from even the Motel 6 unit. It was small and cavernous and cramped eight aviators into its confines. Multiple bunking filled one wall (bulkhead). The bunking was claustrophobic, like small stacked coffins except for a foot-or-so-high opening separating each, which allowed an occupant to crawl in—carefully. The other wall had a desk or two and closets for all eight to share. But at times it was special for the newest and youngest Aces because when they needed it, it was their sanctuary.

Jack's roommates were Mental, Rhino, Lupe, Topper, Moto, Lt. J. Eric "T-bone" Tidwell, a new RIO who was doing well, and Lt. (jg). Christian "Mookie" Stover, a nonaviator maintenance officer with a penchant for comedy and partying. Rhino, missing his new bride, was having trouble, too. Because he was a naval academy graduate and had done well in training, the squadron had expected him to excel fast. But he'd had trouble working the LANTIRN and not studied it like Wog and Dog thought he should.

He, too, was literally behind the eight ball.

"The guys in Eight-Ball kept me sane," said Jack. "We were all in the same situation, all first-cruise guys, all making mistakes. When I got into my room, I was in my little—you know—world there. I had the support of my buds."

He could get away.

The next tier of JOs, senior to the Eight-Ballers, lived in "Six-Pack," a stateroom a little bigger and less cramped. It was home to Pappy, Meat, Money, Dewar, Brain, and Squab. They'd cleared out some lockers to make room for a sheet on the wall onto which they projected Nintendo, VCR movies, and TV, which was run by the carrier and included CNN. The projector was an old one from the ready room that had been replaced. "That was our entertainment on the boat," said Meat. "It was kind of nice."

Hinges like Bru and Wog, Alvin and Loose, and senior JOs like Gooch and Thing and Razor and Mo rated double staterooms, which usually had bunk beds, a table for each, and maybe a sink for toothbrushing and shaving. The most notorious double was that shared by Wrex and Lt. Frank "Salami" Silebi, a wiry, skeptical former A-6 pilot who'd transitioned to Tomcats. The reason it was notorious was because Wrex had surreptitiously "hot-wired" an Internet connection into it from the CAG's computers.

The squadron had about six personal computers in the ready room, which were used by the pilots and RIOs to e-mail home. Each aviator had a password and thus could use the connection whenever he had the time. The computers were connected to CAG's LAN-hub (Local Area Network or main computer terminal), which, in turn, was connected to the ship's.

Wrex was the squadron's computer officer. He'd been responsible for hooking up the ready room and knew how to do it. The stateroom he and Salami shared was right next to the CAG's LAN, and they decided they'd get their own private connection that they could use in their room.

One night, when things were quiet and the carrier's tunnel-like corridors were lit only with dim red lights, they dismantled the lights near their room so that it was dark and went over to the LAN, which was attended by only a night clerk. They said they were just checking out the wiring because they had some problems in their ready room, and the clerk bought it. When she resumed her work, they pulled wire from their flight suits and began attaching it to the LAN in a mass of other connections and then fed the wire into a vent that went out into the hall.

The clerk never caught on.

Done, they thanked her and went out into the hall, where the wire was spooled out all over the corridor. They quickly set about taping it over the corridor along grooves in the ceiling and wall. Several times they were watched by curious passersby but each time were able to talk the gawkers into believing they were fixing a legitimate problem. When they got to their own room's vent, they were done. The tape job was almost invisible. They had their own Internet connection and could send e-mail from their beds.

They used it for a good while, even shared it with some neighbors, and no one would have found out, said Wrex, if some inspectors "who hadn't done their jobs since leaving the U.S." finally did. Checking the CAG's connections, they found the unexplained wire and followed it out into the corridor and the stateroom, where they promptly ripped it out. Wrex shrugged. He was in the ready room later with Dog and some others when they called to have him disciplined, and what happened is still laughed about at every retelling.

Dog, incredulous, said they must be mistaken. He looked at Wrex and asked, "You gotta computer wire from the CAG in your room?" Wrex said, "No, sir." Technically, he didn't. They'd just taken it out. Dog told them they had the wrong man, but his facial expression betrayed him so the accusers persisted. He finally went back to Wrex. "You know anything about this?"

"No, sir. I mean. . . . Maybe, sir."

"Maybe sir?"

Dog lowered the phone. "Outside!" he said.

Wrex followed. "Actually, we just kind of had a little laugh amongst ourselves," said Wrex, "and then he [Dog] said, 'Did you really do it?' I said, 'Yeah, I did it.' Actually, I said, 'Yes sir, I did it.' And he said, 'All right. You don't need to BS me. I'll work with you. . . . You just need to come clean.' . . . He saved my butt."

But Wrex's caper would come later in the cruise.

An earlier one, even more infamous, served to rally the squadron, particularly the younger JOs, who could always be counted on to uphold, if nothing else, the squadron's honor. This caper involved a certain award so hallowed and yet secret in the intramural competition of navy fighter squadrons serving in the Mediterranean that to name it publicly would break a decades-old tradition — not to mention blow the cover of many a salty or daring aviator who would prefer to remain anonymous regarding his particular distinction, awe-inspiring as it might be.

Phrases like "colorful" and "sustained performance on the beach" are used in describing the criteria for winning.

"Let your imagination run," said one Ace, reluctant to give details.

The award, both an infamous honor and an inscribed figure with plaque, is kept on the carrier currently in the Mediterranean and transferred to the relieving ship when it enters the territory. The squadron holding it — meaning the squadron with the current winner — then transfers it to the arriving squadron of their choice. Does that mean that a new winner has been crowned? The answer was never revealed. But 41 was indeed contacted surreptitiously and told the bulky award would be arriving on the *Roosevelt* in a crate labeled "F-14 TARPS," which, of course, was the Aces' sole domain.

But a spy somehow found out about the transfer and told sister squadron VF-14, which, because of the competition between the two Tomcat units, saw an opportunity to best its rivals. The crate was delivered to the *Roosevelt's* hangar bay. Unaware of the security breach, the Aces sent a lone officer to retrieve it, which he did. Making his way back, he was jumped by a gang of Tophatter JOs, who held him, injuring one of his ribs, while they made off with the award. When Joey heard, he was incensed. Regardless of the winner, the award—like the grail, or ark, or other hallowed but missing artifacts of other traditions—was not with its rightful and righteous owners.

It had to be returned!

Making matters worse, at dinner that night in the ship's officers' mess, the Tophatters were laughing at the Aces.

"I'm pissed," said Dog. "Joey's beside himself. But we've both got bigger fish to fry." They had to fly. "I grab the JOs and go, 'You better fuckin' do something.' "

It was not as if the JOs had to be bribed or prodded. They knew they'd screwed up in letting the Tophatter JOs get it in the first place. It was an unwritten law that such matters were the purview of the younger guys, who were more trained in pranks and bloody noses. A group from Eight-Ball, possibly with Six-Pack participation, sprung into action, Rhino leading them—and not a moment too soon. The Tophatter ready room was only a bulkhead away from the Aces' ready room. The Aces could hear the hammering as their rivals worked feverishly to prepare a place on their own wall for the award.

They had to act fast.

Wrex was the duty officer that night so they had a crafty enabler. They bribed the Tophatters' stateroom cleaners to find the award, which was hidden, the Tophatters teased, until they were ready to mount it. Not long after the bribe, the "coop cleaners," as they are called on the carrier, discovered the award in the Tophatter XO's room, hidden behind a desk. The Aces who stole it back were actually confronted on their way to the XO's room by Tophatters, who teased them again. They acted shamed but continued on. By the time they got back to their ready room with the prize, Wrex had ship's solderers making a weld for the award on the ready room wall that would assure that no one could steal it again.

Joey: "I come back from our flight, and I'm surprised like all hell. Like what happened? And I see our JOs, a half dozen of them sitting in the back like they just ate the canary. You know, there are feathers in their mouth."

Such fraternity pranksterism was diversionary fun, even though it heightened intrasquadron squabbling. In fact, Joey and Slapshot, the two squadron skippers, ended the evening in a shouting match over what had happened. But as the Aces moved into the last days of April, they faced more-serious problems. One of their primary concerns—besides the main one of keeping their airplanes flying—remained getting up-to-date cueing. Without it, the FAC-As were still hunting basically with rolls of the dice, arriving at long-abandoned enemy strongholds, guessing more than knowing.

They were still groping.

Bru had talked Topper into putting suspected targets onto the CAOC-ordered TARPS runs, but then the young intelligence officer had dismissed the early results—a move that produced another tirade from Bru that he wasn't proud of. "He [Topper] said, 'There's nothing there.' I go, 'Bullshit! How can there be nothing there when we fly up there and I look out the window and I'm seeing it every day! . . . You're just not looking hard enough. . . . Either that or you don't know what it is you're supposed to be looking at!'"

Part of the problem was that Topper and his personnel weren't trained at finding moving soldiers or their vehicles, or clues, like tracks, to their whereabouts. Their training had been in bomb damage assessment and other static recognition. The analysis Bru wanted was like that done by police at a crime scene—clues, indications, leads that could be followed up. Finding in the film a tank or artillery piece ready for targeting would be the exception. More likely, the intelligence specialists would only find *signs* of the Serbs—abandoned campfires, places where they supplied themselves and hid out, trees or dwellings with pieces of camouflaged weapons protruding. "It was like finding ants at a picnic," said Bru. "At first you don't notice them. Then you see one. Then another and another. . . . Pretty soon you're seeing what they're doing and where they live. . . . It's a little *Hunt for*

Red October-ish. Somebody had to start asking the right questions."

Topper wanted to help, but it wasn't easy. "Just because you've got someone looking at film," he said, "doesn't mean he can catch every detail." He said it was a Catch-22 situation. Yes, he and his shop were derelict. They didn't have the training; they weren't doing what Bru wanted. But they also lacked necessary information from the FAC-As. "How do you grab a guy [for a brief] who just gets off a six-hour hop, has two hours to get some food and get up on another six-hour hop before he goes to bed to get up for another one? . . . And if, in fact, we found tank tracks [or other clues] but could not [pinpoint them to] within five or six miles because the FAC's gone back out on another hop—well, those are not necessarily excuses, but those are causes behind our problem."

Like the rest, Topper and his specialists were learning on the job. Such training involved months in the designated schools. He might have been headstrong in coping, but he said he actually welcomed the screaming matches with Bru because they "made me so miserable that I *had* to work it out."

Still, the solutions came slowly, piecemeal.

On April 20th, spurred by Bru, Joey, and Topper, the air wing decided to make another try at sending a TARPS mission over Kosovo expressly routed to aid SCAR. "We were going to map the main lines of communications," said Wog, who was the mission commander, "the main roads, the places where we'd see stuff like tanks and things." Wog's pilot on the mission was Brain, who had volunteered to work on TARPS after hearing Bru ranting one day in the ready room about SCAR problems. Two other Tomcats, crewed by Beaker and Mentul and Gooch and Money, were also on the mission.

The two RIOs were already helping as aviator liaisons with Topper.

The three Tomcats streaked over the early-morning route and brought back pictures. But whatever their cameras found was quickly overshadowed by the fact that when Sixth Fleet learned about the mission, it banned any more. The reasons are not clear. Those at the squadron level weren't privy. Some suspect it might have been politics—part of the ongoing squabble between Sixth Fleet, which owned the battle group, and the CAOC, which ran the war for NATO and thus, ultimately, told the battle group what to do. Or it might have been shock that such valuable fleet assets as Tomcats were being used in a dangerous extra mission the importance of which, for equally unclear reasons, had not yet been sufficiently conveyed to fleet head-quarters.

Whatever the reason, Sixth Fleet halted any non-CAOC-ordered TARPS runs over Kosovo proper, in effect thwarting its own battle group's mission. The coast was as close as they'd let the Aces take their Tomcats on non-BDA TARPS missions. As it so happened, however, a situation soon arose that would ultimately show what TARPS could do in the way of unearthing Serb fielded forces, and that would pave the way for the airborne cameras to finally be approved to help with SCAR.

Thing had taken his early failures on the LANTIRN to heart. When he wasn't reading writings from his wife about the progress of their nine-month-old second son, whose crawling and walking milestones he was regrettably missing due to the cruise, the RIO was likely prac-ticing on the LANTIRN simulator. On the 20th, he flew a SCAR mission with Dewar and got a measure of redemption.

Even though Wog was in the backseat of the other plane, Dewar, increasingly being relied upon, was the lead in the section. Dewar and Thing were the FAC-As. Wog was there mainly to see what Thing was doing wrong. But the SCAR was a bust. Bad weather and no targets forced the two Tomcats to a "dump" target, so called because bombs dropped were a measure of a squadron's success and because pressure was increasing to drop if one could.

This dump was an SA-6 refueling facility on the outskirts of Pristina. "It was really easy to find," said Thing, "—easy because of the land-marks. It was right next to a ridge and a river. You could see it twenty miles away. . . . I remember looking at the LANTIRN picture and say-ing, 'Wow, that studying really helped,' because that's [the picture in his screen] exactly what I'm looking for."

One of their two laser-guided bombs took the roof off the building he targeted—a perfect hit. The other one, however, missed by three hundred meters. He'd forgotten to finger a switch to the attack mode.

Bittersweet.

But the hit, he said, "made me feel I could do it."

•   •   •

On April 22, during a morning Aces' TARPS mission, a small Serbian submarine, called a "Sava," approximately 180 feet long and capable of launching ten torpedoes, was photographed moving in the Bay of Kotor off the Macedonian port of Tivat. Surrounded by a towering fjord — the southernmost fjord in the world — Tivat was the Serbs' main naval base (one of two on the Adriatic) and as such had worried Allied leaders since the *Roosevelt*'s arrival. While the battle group purposely kept its distance from the enemies' shores (in order to stay out of range of its missiles) and had a network of protectors, including its own submarines, the Sava, although technically a coastal submarine, was capable of sneaking out of the bay and attacking the American carrier.

Details are lacking (some being withheld for what were stated to be security reasons), but it appears NATO had been looking for the sub since the air wing had earlier bombed its pen (or pens) in the fjord. "We destroyed the tunnel that had been storing it," said Admiral Copeland. That was why the submarine was in the bay, which was some ten-to-fifteen miles southwesterly of Podgorica. "The Serbs knew we could penetrate their [sub] pens." For political reasons, however, the battle group was forbidden to strike the submarine unless it ventured out.

That latter possibility worried the Allies.

As a result of the sighting, TARPS missions increased. Aces began flying them along the Macedonian coast every day, presumably to keep tabs on the Sava. Early on in these missions, the evidence indicates, the sub disappeared again. NATO put out an order to find it. Not only did the Aces' daily TARPS missions become a priority, but other Allied searchers, like the air force and member countries with their own reconnaissance abilities, began hunting.

Meanwhile, as a result of Joey and Bru's interest in TARPS as a SCAR aid, as well as normal detailing, several Aces' aviators had been sent to Topper to help liaison between the Tomcats and the intell shop, which prepared the TARPS missions. RIOs Money and Mentul began helping with mission planning. Brain helped from the pilot's perspective.

Brain, who said Bru was the pilot "I would most like to emulate," had won praise from the MO for voluntarily jumping into the breech. "I was kind of venting in the back of the ready room one day," said Bru, "going, 'Goddamit, we need somebody to fucking stand up to the plate and micromanage this problem [the use of TARPS for SCAR]. I'd do it, but I'm not here enough.' He [Brain] hears me and just walks up, 'Well shit, I'll do it. What do I have to do?' No questions asked, just, 'I'll make it happen.' "

Others helped out, too.

TARPS is a "nonsexy area," said CAG. "They tend to put younger guys in it. . . . It's a temperamental system that requires a lot of care and feeding. . . . Pods can collect moisture. . . . It eats into [the squadron's striking ability]. A TARPS-configured airplane can't be a bomber. . . . [But] it's vitally important to me. . . . [Those detailed to it] never gave up the ghost. I mean, they never lost enthusiasm when we had missions canceled."

When the call went out to find the sub, the TARPS section jumped at the opportunity. Tivat was heavily defended. Its missiles could range fifty miles out. NATO wondered if the sub's absence meant something was imminent. An impending Serb attack? The Serbs were believed to have other subs. Were Allied higher-ups preparing to order the *Roosevelt* to strike the base?

The squadron didn't know. But there was a sense of urgency about the task. Topper, Money, and Mentul readied and briefed the missions and gave them to the scheduled aircrews, which often included Money and Mentul.

Alvin was one of the pilots. "I was with Mentul, I think. . . . There was a thought that we were going to sink all their ships, which never happened because of political reasons. . . . We get out there . . . and the weather's shitty." Their floor was fifteen thousand feet. "I'm not gonna get slammed for it now, but we said, 'F this. We're gonna get it.' "

They were over water. He took his Tomcat down to six thousand feet.

"We're just balls to the wall trying to go supersonic — if we can get it. Pretty much can't with the TARPS pods on. But we're fast as we can. . . . There was an SA-6. We blew over it . . . cranked up the [cameras] so we're taking pictures every nanosecond. We go over this thing — we're so low — I'm thinking if I'm on the ground looking up, I would be pretty damn scared. I would be calling my president and saying, 'They're coming lower and lower. They're looking like they want to do this.' "

And Alvin wasn't the only pilot to take it lower than authorized.

Brain did, too. And probably others. In order to make it appear that they'd stayed above the mandated floor, they coerced the squadron intell processors to change the computer-generated altitude printed on the film.

They changed it to an acceptable number.

Several days later, on April 27—if not before—they found the sub—still in the bay. The excitement and rush to print the film meant that they'd be unable to change the altitude.

Joey came up to him, said Alvin, who had piloted the lead plane. " 'What happened?' 'We got the pictures.' 'Good. Good.' 'No, you don't understand. We got the pictures, but we had to go a bit lower.' He's like, 'Okay, we'll see what happens.' "

Actually, they probably weren't pulling the wool over the admiral's eyes, or the CAG's either. The admiral had commanded one of the first TARPS squadrons in the navy and did, at some point, realize TARPS flights were going lower than allowed. CAG said, "He took me to the woodshed" when he found out. "He said, 'You got to keep me informed.' "

But both men wanted success, and pinpointing the sub was cause for celebration.

Topper: "It was huge. We released its location—latitude and longitude. There was confirmation through a thousand different systems that we may have in the intelligence world . . . NATO can't find it. Nobody can. But one VF-41 jet launched off the carrier does. . . . It was a big deal. . . . I remember if we had had champagne, we would have been drinking it. So instead, I think I actually went and bought all my ISs [intelligence specialists] candy out of the ship's store . . . twenty dollars' worth . . . Pretty incredible."

Finding the sub proved TARPS's worth as a valuable hunting tool and alerted the CAOC and Sixth Fleet to its varied possibilities. It didn't immediately cause TARPS to be used for SCAR. But now Bru, Joey, CAG, and the admiral had ammunition for their arguments that it should.

Fourteen

As TARPS was evolving, the FAC-As kept searching.

"It was a good thing I was in decent shape," said Joey. Otherwise, he said, he couldn't have kept pace. The constant missions, "the concentration. . . . If you're not talking [on the radios], you're listening to all these different voices, and having to divvy up your time between looking out the cockpit, working with Bru, staring at the damn LANTIRN scope. . . . You're constantly moving around [in the cockpit]. . . . It was really, you know, a lot of squirming. You hear people screaming on the radio, and your heart rate goes up. 'SAMs in the air! SAMs in the air!' It was really a drain."

He'd brought a treadmill from home and installed it in his room. He'd return from missions "frazzled. . . . You don't have a lot of time." Even so, "I would try to do something every day, even if I was dog tired. If I couldn't run, I'd at least sit on the floor with my little mat and do a couple hundred sit-ups and push-ups." The constant pressure meant they were all on edge. "It doesn't take a lot to get you going."

Wog remembers a fight he and Alvin got into over a stupid thing like coffee. His wife had sent him Starbuck's coffee beans, which he'd fresh-grind every morning and brew in the ready room. He didn't like others "screwing with it until it was properly done." Alvin did, and "I just spooled up through the roof." Alvin took offense, and the two almost squared off. "I was wrong," said Wog. "I said it too gruffly, thinkin', 'What the hell are you doin'?' . . . We talked about it later and got it all worked out. But, you know, I overstepped my bounds. . . . It was that kinda time."

More pertinent were the frustrations of Dewar and Squab, FAC-As who flew a lot together and had developed an almost unspoken synergism. "I knew what he was going to say, and he knew what I was gonna say," said Squab, whose journal entries for late April are peppered with phrases like "no photos yet" and "unable to find any target." Weather was a recurring problem, causing cancellation of several missions or generating so much cloud interference that they could not have lased even if they had found the Serbs.

Squab was still without a successful employment of bombs, and Dewar did have one hit on April 20 (coupled with a three-hundred-yard miss). But he was "driven," said Squab, "and part of the frustration of not succeeding [with SCAR] was that it was hitting him hard too. . . . We couldn't drop our bombs. We had problems with the jets. We would try to pickle, and nothing would come off." He remembered one night when "we couldn't find a thing and Dewar was actually yelling on the [radio] and beating on the cockpit going, 'What the fuck are we doing out here!' " But they didn't give up. "What we did for the next time was try and get a more organized game plan"—more prospective targets, pictures, coordinates—"just stepped up the effort to try and crack it."

A bright spot was that Topper, spurred by his confrontations with Bru, had begun plotting enemy sightings and squadron bombings, and any other pertinent intelligence he could acquire, on a big map he called the "TARPS Grid System." NATO had divided Kosovo into two areas, east and west. He did the same. Using existing intelligence data, especially CAOC-ordered TARPS runs, and the daily debriefing information he could get from strikers, "we devised a system where we essentially did search patterns on a grid." If there was a potential target, they'd mark it on the map and try to route a CAOC-ordered TARPS mission to cover it. If there was no evidence of any kind of enemy activity in an area, they'd give it a different mark, one that would tell the FAC-As they probably wouldn't find anything there.

In addition, he started a database that enabled him to catalogue all existing intelligence information about the area from all sources available, including photos. Thus a FAC-A going out on a mission could retrieve an up-to-the-minute folder and briefing on areas he might want to search.

"We were putting some method into our madness," said the young intelligence officer.

It was the type of action Bru had been begging for.

Meanwhile, on April 22, Bru and Joey had hit the jackpot.

It was late in the afternoon, and they'd been scouring the countryside. Their assigned strikers had already gone on to secondary targets. They were going to have to go back soon themselves. Joey was using the LANTIRN from fifteen thousand feet and saw what looked like a convoy. It was in a little town south of Pristina.

They circled.

Some of the larger vehicles looked like tanks. But could they be tractor trailers driven by fleeing refugees? He couldn't tell. "At that altitude, tractor trailers and tanks, those kinds of things, all look the same."

They dove to eight thousand feet but still couldn't make a positive identification, even with the binoculars. "There were shadows." They couldn't be sure.

They'd heard an air force A-10 Warthog in the area, hunting like they were. They called it over and asked the pilot's opinion. The A-10 jets, formidable gun-and-missile platforms, were the big hunter-killers in Desert Storm. Spotting tanks from the air was one of their fortes, although they didn't have the pinpoint laser that the Tomcat did.

The Warthog pilot was glad to oblige. He swooped down. Soon, said Joey, they heard, " 'Yup. You guys are right.' " There were three tanks, "eight or nine" jeeps, APCs (armored personnel carriers), "that kind of thing," and "more targets off to the side," said Joey. "They were all clustered up."

Apparently, they'd finally found a sizable Serbian fielded force — and it was out for all to see.

"The big thing was to make sure they were hostile," said Joey. With the A-10's confirmation, they were now free to attack. Alvin and Slugz were their wingmen. The A-10 wanted some of the action. He had Mavericks. Joey said fine. Two other A-10s in the area heard the talk over the radio and wanted in, too.

Joey said fine again.

"It was like a turkey shoot," he said. "We circled like vultures." Joey

put a GBU-12 in the center of five vehicles, destroying them all.—
"They were close together." He was lasing a tank when a bomb being
guided by Slugz hit it first. "I yell over the radio, 'Hey, that's mine!'
We were playing around. It was something else."

At some point, the occupants of the tanks and vehicles jumped out
and started running away. The "vultures" blasted trucks in the air,
raised giant fireballs, and decimated the convoy.

"It was pretty spectacular," said Joey, "like an action movie."

It was around this time that Joey broadcast a kind of demonic cackle
over the radio that still brings smiles to those who remember it. "Yeah,"
said Bru, "there were a couple of instances where that happened. I
think it was more a nervous reflex. He'd been a twenty-year fighter guy
only exposed to bombing in the last couple of years. All of a sudden
he's got this wizard machine in front of him, and he can put a bomb
in a trash can from twenty thousand feet. Of course, you play it back
[on the cockpit video], and it sounds like he's having anything from a
Silence of the Lambs moment to an orgasm. But that was early on.
After that, it became kind of sterile and absolute. Because the few
conversations we had transiting back and forth, I'm going, 'Do you
believe what we're doing to this country. We don't even know these
people.' And he goes, 'Oh, God, Bru, I can't even begin to fathom
what we're really doing.' And I think that was when he looked at the
human element of it."

April 25 was Joey's birthday. The squadron decided to throw him a
little surprise party in the ready room. Word came down that they
could wear their special black flight suits—the ones Joey had said *not*
to wear during the war because he thought them ostentatious and
inappropriate for a combat cruise, even though he'd helped pay the
expensive tab for them so "Black" Aces who wanted could wear something distinguishing at the officers' club or other places at home. They
had a cake baked for him, and everybody was preparing for a good
time.

Razor remembers being on the way to the ready room in the snazzy
suit made of fire-retardant "Nomex" (which was why it was so expensive), carrying a camera for party pictures, and unexpectedly running
into Joey. "What's going on?" said the unaware CO. (He'd told everybody that he didn't want a party, that they should concentrate on the
war.) "Oh, I don't know, Skipper," said Razor coyly. "Why don't you

come on down to the ready room and find out?" They had a good relationship, based on kidding, especially about others trying to "kiss the skipper's ass," said Razor, who prided himself on not doing so.

Joey, he said, smiled and followed him.

But when they entered the ready room, the smile disappeared. There were already a number of Aces there wearing their black flight suits. Joey suddenly was mad. He ordered them out, engaged in a pointed exchange with Razor, and said no one would be readmitted unless he was wearing khaki.

"I couldn't believe it," said Razor. He went back to his room and changed. "I'm pissed. Why would he do that?" When they all reappeared sans the fancy suits, Joey gave them a speech. "He says, 'You guys are all probably pissed at me. I don't care. I want you to set the tone around here.'" The flight suits were for later, not war. "'We got guys that are sweating their asses off downstairs in the hangar trying to put jets together, and we're up here having a party looking like dandies. I don't want that. . . . Until this is over, I want everyone in here with the mindset that we're in a war. We are not the cushy officer types, and I don't want to see that.'"

Razor said he continued to be mad "until I was like, 'You know what? He's right.'" Some of the JOs stayed mad. "But to me, it was like, 'Wait a minute. . . . If he cares about those guys sweating their asses off, he's going to care about me. . . .' He told us, 'It's nothing personal, but that's the tone I want to set.' . . . As good a relationship as I felt that I had with the skipper, he was willing to get pissed at me or anyone . . . just put on the skipper's pants and make a lot of people mad for something that was important."

Joey: "It turned out they were having a surprise party for me, so it made me feel like a tremendous heel. I apologized . . . but I still wasn't going to take it back. I don't care if it *was* my birthday . . . It wasn't like we were on the French Riviera. We were going out to kill people that day, and we had guys working their butts off, and we were prancing around like peacocks. . . . I'm sorry. . . . We're in combat. Let's act the part of warriors and put those things away for another time."

Another confrontation was more controversial.

One of the things you didn't want to do as a squadron member on a carrier or see happen as a squadron CO was a failure to launch. Missions were very tightly scheduled to fit into the carrier's launching cycle. You can't launch when planes are being recovered, and vice versa. If you are launching a jet that has just returned, it must be serviced, and any problems it has have to be fixed. It has to be fueled and rearmed, and different missions require different armaments and fuel loadings.

All of this took time. Generally, two hours was a minimum to work on a just-recovered plane before it was ready to launch again, although faster turnarounds were effected in the demanding war situation. Joey was strong in his directives that all crews make scheduled launches. The war effort demanded it. His own performance rating depended on it.

One day, Bru and Joey, with possibly Dog and Wog on their wing, after long hours on a SCAR mission, were late. They'd probably stayed out a little too long searching, and then, racing back, knowing the squadron needed to launch the jets they were in, they had been ordered by a theater commander to check out an unidentified aircraft that could be threatening the battle group. They had to obey the order. By then the sun had gone down, said Bru, and "it took us fifteen minutes to consummate the intercept."

So they were that much later.

The aircraft turned out to be a stray B-52 from England. No sweat. But by the time they got back to the carrier, there was little time to effect the turnaround. The squadron tried but missed. Joey got mad. He called an AOM and blasted the JO crews who missed the launch and the squadron in general for the failure. There was considerable grumbling among the JOs afterward. Why were *they* being blamed when *he* was late? Was the skipper losing it? Was he mad because not launching looked bad for him? Even the squadron's high-ranking hinges thought he was wrong, although they kept it to themselves.

"His response was pretty callous," said Bru. "His words were to the effect of, 'While the rest of the air wing is out there engaging Kosovo, we're sitting here because we didn't take the steps necessary to get our airplanes in the fight. And I want you all to think about that and, you know, evaluate it.' . . . I'm just paraphrasing, but I wasn't very happy. I was kind of, 'Why not share the blame?'. . . . and go, 'Hey guys, there were areas we could have improved.' . . . But none of us said anything. We just sat there kind of pissed off."

Joey remembers the incident somewhat differently. "I'm not completely guiltless on this . . . but I'm a reasonable man . . . I'm pretty sure I didn't just stand up there and say, 'Hey, I'm blaming you guys' " —a contention that still puts him at odds with the others. What was really concerning him, he said, was the fact that the waiting crews themselves had not been ready to launch even if he and Bru had brought the plane back in time. They (the JO crews) had not, in the admittedly shortened period they had to get the jets turned around, done the things they could have to increase the chances of the launch no matter how small those chances were. This had happened a number of times, he said, and "I wanted to get it through everybody's head that we have really got to be ready to go."

Apparently, said Bru, the crew or crews that were scheduled to launch were "a bit passive at that particular time with communicating the status of their airplane," especially the fact that they hadn't even commandeered a "huffer," a device on deck that blows air into the Tomcat's engines to turn the turbines and help get the motor started. There weren't a lot of huffers, and the flight-deck crews move them from plane to plane. A crew had to be assertive in getting one, or another crew would take it. "Apparently the requests by the guys flying weren't made with a sense of urgency," said Bru.

"You've got to go out there and do whatever it takes," said Joey. "We need to be ready to go, in all our gear and all that, and do whatever maintenance needs from us. . . . I felt like we weren't giving 100 percent. We weren't doing everything we could. . . . Sure, we brought it back late because we had to go do something [identify the B-52]. But don't just sit around. . . . We can launch late. . . . We did it a number of times. . . . You've got to lie, cheat, and steal . . . bribe those yellow shirts because we're held hostage to huffers. . . . The sooner you get your plane started, the sooner you're ready to go flying. . . . That was a big thing. I was very vocal on this."

Bru said: "The burdens of command can be extreme, and I don't have any perspective on that . . . [but] there was a point [in the war] . . . where tensions [for all commanding officers] got kind of high. I can imagine that, as the CO [Joey] probably wasn't sleeping more than about three hours a night. He was flying anywhere from five-to-eight hours a day dealing with the resource limitations we had to overcome. You know we had girls getting pregnant having to leave the ship. We had one guy come out and say he was homosexual just to get off the ship, and then later [he] came back when he realized he wasn't going to get off and say, 'Well, okay, I'm really not.' . . . I'm kind of speculating . . . but the mission at hand was production, production, production, and by that I mean, figure out how to get our airplanes fixed, maximize the assets we've got. . . ."

Later, said Bru, after he'd had time to contemplate the AOM, he reevaluated. "I saw it as a human-interaction hurdle. Was it pleasant? No . . . but so what? We've got a bigger issue at hand. So let's deal with that." When several JOs approached him to complain about what had happened, he said he told them, "Sure, we were late, and that was part of the problem. But that being said, what else could *you* have done to do better?" He said they had to become "more aggressive" and "maintain situational awareness . . . not only while flying, but on the flight deck. . . . And they [the JOs] go, 'We'll, you're right, but we don't think the skipper was right in how he addressed it.' I said, 'Well, that's fine, but he's the old man. That's his, you know, job.' "

The issue of whether Joey was momentarily bending under strain, acting to further his career, or only trying to better the squadron's performance went unresolved. There was a war to be fought, and Joey anyway tended not to worry about those under him disagreeing once he'd made his decision. It doesn't appear he even knew they were questioning him. "But one thing I can tell you," said Bru, "the effect was an elevated sense of urgency when it came to getting our airplanes off the deck. . . . We turned into—I don't think the ship liked us at all—because we were the most, I mean we turned into the squeaky wheel that said over and over, 'Okay, why is somebody else getting the huffer before us? We need it. Give us this. Give us that. We need to be accommodated because we need to get off the ship. If nobody else makes it, fine. But we need to launch.' "

Whatever the internal politics, Joey's squadron became that much better.

Topper's grid map was twenty feet by fifteen feet. He hung it on the wall in seamed sections. "If you picture an Indiana Jones movie with Germans in the war room with pointers and little flags, that's what I did." Shortly after the map was up, at the very end of April, probably on the 28th, he said, CAG and Joey came into his office and told him, " 'Topper, go to town.' "

It was what they all had been waiting for.

NATO and Sixth Fleet had finally authorized TARPS to be used as a SCAR hunting tool over Kosovo proper. Now the squadron could begin planning daily missions to check suspected sites, or at least put their own targets on CAOC-ordered TARPS missions without worrying that they'd be flagged for doing so. It was the beginning of a rare integration of intelligence and operations. "Historically," said Dog, "intell and ops don't get along. The intell guy doesn't know what the operations [pilot] guy needs, and he's close to the vest with what he's got. The operations guy really doesn't know what to ask the intell guy because he knows there are so many security issues. So they just stare at each other. They don't mesh."

Now, because of necessity, those barriers had been broken. "We would have a way to control our intelligence, focus our reconnaissance," said Bru. "It was the biggest key." They could begin to look forward to SCAR operations with up-to-date, systematized information.

It would make a difference.

At least that's the way they all felt when the welcome news came down.

The first such TARPS mission since April 20 launched on April 29 around noon. Beaker, with Moto in his backseat, was the commander. He had been delegated to become sort of the unofficial hinge of the TARPS-SCAR effort, which was not something he relished because it took away from time that could have been spent bombing. But he dutifully accepted—just as he accepted teaching and thus flying with nuggets like Moto, who was doing well. (The lowest-ranking hinges, including Alvin and Loose, were each having to tutor the inexperienced.) Razor and Money, Meat and Mentul, were in the other two Tomcats.

CAG said they could go to ten thousand feet. They probably went much lower.

Like Indian scouts galloping through an unsuspecting enemy village, the three jets—one in the lead, another about a mile in trail, and the third guarding from above—barreled into Kosovo airspace low and fast. "We blew out all their windows," joked Beaker. Each Tomcat was in full blower, eating gas at a rate in excess of a thousand pounds per minute. Their six- or-seven-minute run at six-hundred-plus miles per hour had to be perfectly timed so that Prowlers, or air force F-16s, which also shot HARM, would be at a station on the periphery ready to jam or missile any Serbian air defenses that tried to fire. But the run was too fast. They brought the first sanctioned SCAR film back without the Serbs being able to effectively react.

On the same day, April 29, Dewar and Squab, and Wrex and Thing, went out on a SCAR mission. As frustrated as they were, the four were learning more each day and earning reputations as who among the JOs could most be counted on to produce results. Wrex and Thing were the leaders of the section; Dewar and Squab, the escort. Once they were airborne, Squab's LANTIRN scope stopped working. He had no picture with which to pick out a target and designate it, or on which to hold the cursor. Basically, he was going to be blind when performing his job. When the four found a bridge to drop on, they innovated. Dewar did a lot of the visual-acquisition work on his smaller scope while also piloting and verbally fed Squab information he needed in order to do what Dewar couldn't. "Dewar got the pod on the target very nicely, and we dropped one bomb," wrote Squab in his diary. Then Dewar did "an awesome job of verbally talking me on to the target and telling me all the necessary slue inputs to keep the laser spot on the bridge."

They blew a span out of the bridge.

Who or what might have been on the bridge is not written. But in one video from the squadron's hits on bridges, several vehicles, which look like ordinary cars, can be seen driving right through the cursor's cross as the RIO holding it urges anguishingly on the radio that the driver hurry up. Moving the cursor, of course, would have alleviated the worry by making the anticipated bomb miss. But the aircrew had worked hard to get it there and wasn't going to do that. The bridge was a hard-to-acquire objective, so he just hoped, it appeared, that the driver would make it far enough away in time that the blast, expected any second, wouldn't hurt him.

Squab said that with the pressure to find the Serbs and drop bombs, and the problems inherent in high-altitude identification, the squadron's crews were constantly mindful of making mistakes. He remembered seeing a bunch of what looked like tanks in a field and then deciding that they were bales of hay. But when he got back and played the video—"you can play it on fast-forward"—the bales were moving. "They were too small to be armor because, you know, you can stop the tape and use things to estimate what size they are. They were either cows or horses," which he said sometimes were bombed.

One pilot in another squadron, he said, made the mistake of targeting what was later determined to be a cow. "They were gonna get T-shirts made up for him: 'Cow killer.' They gave him a lot of shit." Although others said they were not aware of it, Squab said the laser they used could explode eyeballs if it hit the face of something living, like a cow or horse. "It's similar to a microwave oven," he said. "It heats. The eyeball has a very high water content. There's nowhere for the heat to go so it explodes. It's not pretty."

The next day, April 30, Squab flew escort with Brain for Dewar and Toad. They'd learned enough to follow clues. "We found some tracks in some fields that led to a tree line" and located a "hot contact" inside. One bomb guided and presumably hit what Squab doesn't describe. But the other bomb didn't work. "It failed to guide or had a fin failure," he wrote.

Frustration again.

And the scariest FAC-A mission—one that would almost get the FAC-As killed—was to come the next day.

Book 3
TIP OF THE SPEAR

Fifteen

The Aces' "Air-to-Ground Delivery Tracker," a tabulated accounting
of all the bombs dropped by the squadron's various aircrews on daily
missions, shows mounting bombing success as April drew to a close.
The missions counted included SCAR, also, by this time, called "KEZ
Ops" for Kosovo Engagement Zone Operations, and K9 missions,
which were strikes on the smaller fixed targets in Kosovo, such as radar
installations, radio antenna towers, bridges, and what was left of the
larger fuel-and-supply depots.

On April 25, Bru and Joey, cued by coordinates they were given,
found tracks that led them to a heavily wooded area where "four or
five" Serb war "vehicles" were hiding in the tree line. After lasing their
own bombs to the targets, they called in some Hornets, whose pilots
finished off the rest. Later, they found a tank in a parking lot "next to
a store on a road that had traffic." But Joey had no problem lasing a
wingman's bomb onto the tank and destroying it without hitting anything nearby. (A note by the entry for Brain and Thing, who were also
out hunting that day, indicates they were talked on to a "cow" as a
target by an apparently fooled air force FAC. According to the sheet,
they didn't lase.)

On the 29th and 30th, Bru and Joey also found targets, because,
according to the delivery tracker, they buddy-lased for several different
Hornets. So the two were most probably in good moods as they woke

Saturday morning, May 1, for a daylight SCAR. Bru recounts that he was up by 10 A.M. He then presumably went and had something to eat, probably with his roommate, Wog, since Wog was going to be flying wing for Bru and Joey. He next went to CVIC to check the latest weather and ship's war intelligence, and then to see Topper to discuss what TARPS was doing. It so happened that the day's TARPS mission, which had left hours before, was going to be photographing the same area he and Joey would be working—a valley area in the eastern part of Kosovo. If the Tomcat cameras found anything, he and Joey would be close enough to strike almost immediately.

Around 11:30 A.M., Bru briefed forty-five aircrew from various squadrons. The weather was surprisingly good on May 1, and a lot of missions were planned. Beaker and Alvin were leading separate K9s. Dog and Toad in two other Tomcats were going to be flying close air support in addition to some other missions. Despite his domestic situation, Mo Vaught was in charge of a CAP, with nugget Jack Corlett as his pilot, and Gooch and Mentul on their wing. As the most knowledgeable FAC-A doing the carrier's priority mission (SCAR), Bru had the job of informing the aircrews about the previous day's engagements and what else was new. This included the enemy's latest strengths and weaknesses and changes in the navy's tactics, codes, radio communications, and refueling, and other matters pertaining to their operations over Kosovo.

During the brief, the TARPS mission returned. When Joey and Bru went by Topper's office to see what they'd found, the two were shown what appeared to be pictures of an SA-6 battery near some artillery and tanks. The photos were of a rural area approximately four miles south of Pristina. The suspected targets were near some dwellings. It was just the kind of hot intelligence they'd been hoping for. They grabbed the pictures, along with the coordinates, and ran up on deck.

Piloting Wog's Tomcat was Lt. Frank "Salami" Silebi, Wrex's roommate and a slightly older JO than most. Married and with three daughters, a Colombian-born, naturalized citizen, Salami was thirty-one years old. He'd flown A-6 Intruder attack jets before transitioning to Tomcats and thought himself a bit more skilled at bombing than the average. Thin and wiry, with a frequent wily grin, the dark-haired pilot, who some joked was a "lounge lizard" in port, fancied himself a comedian. But squadron mates usually groaned more than laughed at his punch lines. Salami didn't seem to care. He was a tireless worker, the squadron's main scheduler, and had the reputation of being able to function with the least amount of sleep. More than once, he'd taken over unfinished paperwork, and thus helped another Ace who was too tired, confused, or multitasked to continue.

But he was also under somewhat of a cloud. During work-ups, with T-bone in his backseat, he'd busted one of the Tomcat's main wheels while landing. It had been a stormy day, and the deck had been pitching. He'd come in off center and was waved for another pass—but too late. He couldn't lift. The jet hit hard. It had careened a little, and firemen sprayed foam as the broken strut spewed sparks. No one was hurt, but the Tomcat was out of service, and Salami was put on probation. Some thought it was the LSO's fault, but Salami was still accountable. It could ruin his career. He'd been cleared to continue flying, but he was still waiting for the final disposition, and most of the Aces, including Joey, who had gone to bat for him, thought he was handling the pressure of possible flight-status change well.

He didn't seem too worried on May 1. Having flown mostly CAPs and HVAAPs and a few noneventful SCARs, he said, "I hate to say it, but I really wasn't nervous. It was just a job." He didn't feel he'd been challenged yet. At the altitudes he'd been flying, he said, "you see Triple-A every now and then, but it's not getting anywhere near me." He actually wished it would get closer so he'd have a more exciting time.

He was soon to get his wish.

They launched shortly after noon. The sky was deceptively beautiful—clear, blue, sun-swept. They hadn't seen it like this in weeks. The Tomcats gleamed. It was a good day to be flying.

They had little trouble tanking. When their Prowlers were in position, they started working "the box," which was what they had begun calling an area that was ready for search, meaning it was guarded. They were south of Pristina. Both the E-2, controlling the area, and their own cockpit RHAW gear (Radar Homing and Warning Receiver), which signals if they are being targeted, indicated that ground-missile batteries in the valley below were being turned on and off.

It didn't concern them as long as they weren't being tracked.

After about fifteen minutes, they found what looked like a group of surface-to-air missile launchers. The potential targets weren't exactly where they'd been photographed by the TARPS mission. They were in a field. But they were in the same proximity. The two Tomcats started circling, Salami and Wog staying high, Bru and Joey, beneath them, going lower, trying to get a positive identification. The two jets were at approximately twenty thousand feet, which was too high to get a good look with the LANTIRN.

Bru decided to go down, "staying above ten thousand feet, as CAG had ordered. But not much." They were going into the heart of any SA-6's envelope. If what they had were indeed launchers, they were like the mongoose challenging the cobra. "That thing can tap you," said Bru. "It's a perfect shot for them, but we had to make an ID."

They didn't want to hit civilians.

They went down several times, each time getting a little lower. "I'm looking out with the binoculars, and I can't quite correlate what I'm seeing on the FLIR with what I'm looking at out the window. But I think I'm getting close."

Joey was having the same problem.

They decided they needed one more descent.

Above them, still at around twenty thousand feet, Salami and Wog circled. They were watching their RHAW gear because it had been giving fleeting indications of their jet being "spiked," meaning they were being hit by a beam of radar. The type of indication had Salami at first thinking it was just another plane trying to identify them. Wog thought the intermittent hits more sinister, "like they were about to lock us up and shoot us."

But they weren't going to overreact. (One of the jokes around the ready room was about a young pilot, not a Black Ace, screaming over the radio about a SAM shot at him, only to realize he was reacting to a HARM shot by a friendly aircraft nearby.)

Suddenly, they heard the high-pitched *deedle, deedle, deedle* that the RHAW gave off when a surface-to-air missile locked on. The gear's visual display showed "6," for an SA-6, and indicated the spike was coming from their five o'clock position, which was aft, or toward their tail. "I looked down, and there's a missile airborne at us," said Wog. This was no phantom. He jumped on the radio. " 'Sam launch coming. Six o'clock! SAM launch!' " Simultaneously, Salami, the squadron's SAM expert, amazed by the sight, instinctively slammed the

Tomcat into afterburner, called for the release of decoy chaff, and began defensive maneuvers.

The cobra had struck.

Bru and Joey were just coming out of their latest descent and were in a hard right turn when they heard Wog's excited warning over the radio. The intensity of his voice, almost more than what he said, scared them both. "We plug in afterburner and start climbing up," said Bru. "I'm looking outside, and I don't see it. He [Wog] calls another one [a second SAM launch]. I said, 'Say bearing.' He goes, 'West.' I was headed east, so I kicked it around, and right there at our five o'clock are two surface-to-air missiles looking like Saturn rockets coming up."

He estimated that they were about five miles away—which was not so far, given the missiles' supersonic speeds. As he looked, a third SAM rose. Then a fourth! "I've been shot at before," said Joey, "but not that many right at us. . . . At first it was like, 'Oh, God!'" Adrenaline shot into their veins.

They were climbing and spewing chaff when the first three missiles rocketed past their stern, continuing on a straight-up course. The missiles were ballistic, like bullets shot from a gun. They weren't guiding. Whoever fired them had probably turned off the guiding mechanism so that the Prowlers couldn't home in. The two Aces calmed somewhat. But then the fourth missile abruptly turned, a very hard maneuver for the speed it was traveling—unless it was guiding. It pointed its evil head right at them, narrowing its tubular profile. Spearing forward, an orange plume propelling it like a tiny hidden sun, the SAM, Bru remembered, suddenly resembled an "eclipse."

But it was no benign crescent. It was a conscienceless, relentless persuer, hell-bent on catching and killing.

More adrenaline.

"We go up, and the missile goes up. We go down, and the missile goes down."

In a move to outsmart it, Bru decided to stay down. The missile continued up. His RHAW stopped warning. "I'm like, 'Yes!'" he said, indicating a fist-in-the-air-type reaction. He'd defeated it—or so he thought. "I come up [on the radio] and go, 'Hey, One's naked,' meaning I don't have this thing on me anymore [their section code was 'Dash One'], and Wog goes, 'Not us. It's still guiding!'"

Apparently it wasn't stalking the lower Tomcat after all.

Since calling the SAMs only seconds before, Salami and Wog, still above but now closer to Bru and Joey, had been desperately trying to defeat the missiles, which they saw as shot solely at them — not at Bru and Joey. (The two Tomcats were now almost stacked one on top of the other, although separated by thousands of feet, and the perspectives looking down at the missiles could have made each think they were the sole targets.) In addition to sending out decoy chaff, they'd roared up and then abruptly down, just like Bru and Joey. The maneuvers were an attempt to get the missiles to expend energy by following an erratic path.

Although separated by a chunk of sky, the two jets, from the ground perspective anyway, probably had seemed to perform a synchronized dance, so alike were their defensive reactions. But the maneuvers were no ballet. They caused about as rough a ride as a Tomcat can give. Going up, said Wog, the pilot suddenly reverses the jet, doing a hard "G" turn, and then comes back down on a dime, so to speak. Such a quick-change reversal is analogous to the moonshiner flipping his car in midchase and roaring back past his pursuers. As he did this, said Salami, he also tried to keep himself "abeam" of the radar source, which, in this case, was the ground launcher.

"Abeam" meant at a ninety-degree angle to the projected Serbian radar beam, or, in aviator terms, keeping the radar beam at their three or nine o'clock (ahead and behind being twelve o'clock and six o'clock, respectively). The missiles, they believed, were tracking with "pulse Doppler"–type radar. "In pulse Doppler," said Salami, "all they are working on is the difference in speed between you and it. If you are moving towards it [or away], it can see you. But if you are moving abeam to it, or parallel to it, it can't see you. But you have to be very precise. No kidding, no motion toward it [the launcher], which is really hard to do."

In effect, he'd had to hold the ninety-degree angle off while executing the violent reversals.

Then they'd noticed that the first three missiles were ballistic.

They'd relaxed too.

Then the fourth missile had launched — the one that *was* guiding.

"Now I've maneuvered for the first three missiles so our plane doesn't have the energy I'd like," said Salami. "We're down to about three hundred knots and closer [in altitude] to the missile's operating envelope. I'm thinking it's about four miles away. . . . I can't go up any more cause I'm running out of airspeed." The jet didn't have the energy. He'd have to go down to regain it. "But I don't want to because that will really put me in the heart of the [missile's] envelope."

They were in trouble.

" 'Fuck, they got us,' " Wog said he told Salami. "The pucker factor was intense."

They tried two more maneuvers, but neither worked. "At this point," said Wog, "it's getting really close — less than a mile."

They were losing more airspeed, becoming, in effect, sitting ducks.

It was time for the last-ditch maneuver.

The missile's tracking mechanism was able to calculate where they were going. Its reaction to their moves was somewhat delayed, but it always turned. Salami decided to take the missile head-on — like two cars in a game of chicken. He'd barrel-roll it at the last second, which would take him swiftly up and past the missile. Hopefully it wouldn't be able to hack the turn, or at least wouldn't be able to turn quickly enough to follow them and would overshoot. There was a chance it might explode just because of the close proximity. But with any luck, they'd be out of its explosion radius. The radius was about three hundred feet. They also had other measures, which are classified.

They'd employ them, too.

It was their only chance.

According to Wog, Salami said, " 'Okay, we're going in.' I said, 'Roger that.' " He knew what Salami had in mind. "As we pull into the missile, I drop the last bit of Bol chaff [decoy strips]."

The streaking killer was aiming for a point in front of them. Salami pulled a hard 90-degree turn. It was a fast, wrenching change of direction, leaving them pointed toward the missile and the missile, they hoped, still heading for their old course. But to their dismay, as they came out of the turn, moving to the barrel-roll — their cockpit glass the only thing between them and the missile below — they saw it had done an unbelievable "270-degree" about-face, and was "pointing right at us."

It was only seconds away, standing on its tail beneath them, orienting to the kill — a vision of death neither wanted to see.

But they couldn't take their eyes off it.

It was speeding toward them.

Time suddenly slowed. "I can see the missile clearly," said Wog. "It's about ten to twelve feet long . . . the rocket motor burning in the back. I can see the fins. . . . I'm going, 'Oh, I just hope it hits back aft, not up front at the cockpit.' But it's coming right at us. Right at the cockpit."

A surreal calm flooded him. "It was like someone else got in the cockpit with us. I kinda. . . . It was . . . okay . . . my grandfather, and Donna's grandfather, who just died. They're both in the cockpit. . . . It was like we had all the time in the world." They were telling him "it was okay. . . . If I die, I die. It's my time. God has called me." At least his good-bye letter was still in the stateroom drawer. On the other hand, he said, if they survived the hit, "I don't want to land on the ground here. We've pissed these guys off enough."

Salami roared into the barrel-roll. They were going over the top of the enlarging missile when it "just blew up." It was probably eight hundred feet away, said Wog. "Not yards. Feet. Very close. . . . It looked like a firework going off. Flash. Then a big puff of smoke. I remember it very vividly. . . . My first thought was, 'Okay, that's how it detonates. Now when does the shrapnel hit us?' "

But they didn't feel a hit.

They finished the barrel-roll, astonished that they weren't dead. "I couldn't believe it," said Wog. "Yeah, there but by the grace of God go I," said Salami later.

It's not certain what caused the missile to explode prematurely. Almost simultaneously with its detonation, a HARM from one of the Prowlers hit the launcher. "They'd finally decided we've had enough," said Bru, who saw the HARM hit. But Salami says destroying the launcher won't necessarily cause the missile to explode. Bru thinks it might have detonated on one of the expendables. Wog guesses it was the HARM. The missiles sometimes are programmed to explode when they've missed their target but are still close. It could have been a malfunction, or an operator could have detonated it.

Whatever the case, a *fifth* missile was launched, and Bru and Joey thought it was tracking them until the HARM hit. Then it went stupid. Salami and Wog never saw either. They had been too busy with the fourth missile and were now thanking God, wobble kneed and thinking they were done. But Bru and Joey had other ideas. Up and out of the SA-6 danger envelope by then, they were readying to turn on their attackers. The smoke trails (some say "vapor trails") from the missiles, quite thick and visible, all led to a clear point of origin. Joey designated it on his LANTIRN and told Bru to get ready to drop. Realizing what was happening, Salami, in turn, told a surprised Wog to do the same, and turned their Tomcat back toward the missiles. "It was like, 'Okay, motherfuckers,' " said Wog, reluctantly steeling himself again, " 'you shoot at us, we're going to kick your ass.' "

Barely a minute had passed since the first SAM had been shot. Both Tomcats had five-hundred-pound GBU-12s. They lased what they had left. It's not clear what went wrong. Bru says he pickled late. Joey says they "landed wrong." But none of the bombs hit the mark. "We were a little excited there," said Bru. Now they were out of ordnance. He got on the radio, asking for help. " 'Anybody have any bombs out there?' " Tophatter hinges C. J. Deni, a FAC-A, and Slammer Richardson, the sister squadron's XO, responded. They were tanking for another mission. Deni radioed, " 'How many do you want us to drop?' " Bru said whatever they had. It didn't take the Tophatters long to get there, and together with the Prowlers, who shot some more HARMS, and Joey doing some buddy-lasing, the navy jets decimated the site.

It was a defining moment in the FAC-A adventures.

Instead of frustration, both crews had a sense of payback. They'd done their job under extreme circumstances.

When it was over, the two Tomcats had expended most of their fuel, and it was time to tank. On the way to the tanker, Salami asked Bru and Joey to check them for damage. Bru later said he felt "silly" for not thinking of it sooner. They were still coming down from what they'd just gone through.

Their wingman's jet was untouched.

"Divine intervention," said Wog.

They'd had a lot of excitement, not to mention their brush with death. Bru, Salami, and Wog thought they'd just go home after tanking. It was getting late, and they'd just been through the first big counterattack FAC-As had experienced. There would be a lot to discuss in the debriefs; a lot of hand-flying stories to tell in the ready room. But Joey, mindful that strikers might be holding in designated areas, waiting to be called in by FAC-As—or, who knows, maybe just wanting more action—had other ideas. "All of a sudden," said Wog, "the skipper pipes up, 'Okay, boys, we're going back.'"

Roger that.

Since the earlier site was now just embers and ashes, they went to another on their list. It was on the west side of Pristina near an ammunition facility that had been hit before (once by Wog) but still offered some targets. Sure enough, two Hornets were racetracking in a designated nearby area, waiting to be directed or lased by FAC-As. Four other Hornets, including one being piloted by CAG, were arriving over the ammunition dump. They too needed FAC-As.

The two Tomcats began buddy-lasing for the Hornets, which were armed with the self-propelling Mavericks. The targets they picked out were in the ammunition facility. But before they'd done much, two SA-6s were launched from a nearby area. Wog saw them first. "I'm looking outside, and all of a sudden I say, 'Hey, I've seen this before.' There's a missile in the air. I'm looking at it and going, 'Those stupid fucking idiots. We killed 'em [at the other site], and they're doing it again! Okay, 'SAM launch! SAM launch!'"

He had no RHAW gear indications, so he didn't think they were guiding. "They come up at us," said Joey, "but they don't make a midcourse adjustment. They go straight up by us and explode overhead." CAG, who tried to fly as much as he could, had a policy that strikers were not to engage SAM sites that were firing. They were to exit the area and let HARM-shooters (Prowlers, air force F-16s, or HARM-equipped Hornets), whose weapon was specifically made to destroy such sites, duel the shooters. CAG didn't yet know that the Aces directing him had engaged the earlier missiles that had launched at them, and they were a little apprehensive about him finding out.

But they needn't have worried. When CAG saw the missiles go up, his ire too was tweaked. Close to them, he could see the smoke trail to their origin. He wasn't aware they weren't guiding. "All I could think about was, 'I know where it is,'" he said. He started radioing his GBU laser code—what the FAC-As needed in order to buddy-lase his bomb into the pinpointed launcher. CAG was going to violate his own "don't attack" policy.

At the same time he was "screaming" his code, he said, "the E-2 [controlling the area] is screaming for me to get out of the area because [the Prowlers] are out of HARM and gas and need to leave station." No other HARM shooters were available. "We finally just said, 'Stand by, we're busy.' . . . Basically, I told him to shut up . . . I wasn't thinking that I was violating any policy. . . . It was just one of those reactionary things. We had tally on it. We'd survived the initial volley. It was probably going to shoot again, and if I could get a sensor on the area, my bomb would be there in about twenty-five seconds."

Joey already had his cursor on the target. With CAG's four-digit code, he could guide the Maverick. He lased the target, giving the self-propelled bomb a beam to look for. CAG came around and dropped. Joey guided it to a direct hit on the launcher's control van, the vehicle that hauled the missile launcher. There were more launchers at the site. The other Hornets lined up and dropped as well, lased by either Joey or Wog.

They decimated their second site of the day.

CAG: "It was kind of morbid LANTIRN video. We actually can see the guys getting out of the vans, bailing out of them [before the bombs hit], because I think they saw immediately that we weren't exiting the area, and that the Tomcats were still there and other airplanes were rolling in on them. . . . They start running, and I mean the bombs hit. It just knocks them down. We thought, 'Oh man, he's dead.' And then Joey says, 'Nope, watch this.' Boom. He stands up and starts running again."

How did he feel being faced with so vivid a picture of human terror?

"We don't live in a sterile world," said CAG. "There's no doubt that we can kill, did kill probably. Nobody knows for sure. We have pretty good evidence on some cases where we know people were there. But that's the job. If you haven't figured that out ahead of time, if that's not already resolved in your mind, then, well, I mean, no one hates war more than the people who have to fight it. So it's just part of the job. I don't know how else you can deal with it."

When they got back to the carrier, hands and stories were flying. It was probably here that they figured out the Serbs' SAM tactic of firing a few missiles ballistic, hoping they'd get the navy jets defensive and vulnerable, and then guiding some. But it hadn't worked. "It was a thrilling, thrilling hop," said Joey. They'd been out for five hours. "CAG called it a red-banner day for the air wing." He'd seen FAC-A working as it should, and he'd been impressed.

As Slapshot wrote after the war in *Wings of Gold* (winter 1999), "Before, when encountering a SAM under such circumstances, we would have gotten out of there and come back to fight another day. That didn't happen this time. . . . The FAC-As took control and, working in concert with available strike aircraft, employed laser-guided weapons to take out the SAM sites."

The Serbs had been impressed, too.

As Bru put it, "They learned that pushing that launch button could have lethal repercussions."

The bombing near Pristina wasn't the only FAC-A mission on May 1. That night, a second SCAR took off, with Wrex and Squab leading it. It wasn't as important as the "Sambush," as the May 1 missile attack became known to the Aces, but it made a little military technology history.

By this time, Wrex was being recognized as one of the warrior JOs. As CAG remembers, "I didn't know him well and thought he had a tendency to be what we call a little 'Sierra Hotel.'" The term, because of the first letters of the two words — "S" and "H" — is another way aviators have of saying "shit-hot," sometimes uttered to mark a great experience but also applied to flashy pilots in the "Maverick" mold who might do something rash in the air. But that impression changed when CAG saw Wrex as a FAC-A on the "Keystone Serb" mission, April 18.

"That was when they [the FAC-As] still had to work through the system in order to get clearance," said CAG. "I was in a section of F-18s. . . . It was hilarious. . . . He [and Thing] found the target. . . . He's trying to get authority to hit them. At the same time, he's busy trying to get our eyes on target and keep the whole thing going." When the Serbs had dashed out of the building hit by the dud, Wrex had given a running commentary. "And then the SA-6s came up, and I mean all hell broke loose."

Wrex had impressed him with his ability to function in such a pressured situation.

Wog added, where Gooch would stay high, "not breaking altitude restrictions . . . not loitering like you need to do to find a target," Wrex, on the same hop, would be down at "five thousand feet . . . going, 'I got this. I got that. . . . Give me more bombs.' . . . He's out there, you know, with the club, calling for more people."

Squab, too, by this time, was gaining a reputation. His was for competence and persistence—and lately, a newfound can-do attitude. "I really got on board when we got photos," he said. "Things on the LANTIRN aren't very big. They are hard to pick out. But with pictures they're annotated. . . . This is a bunker. This is an artillery piece. So I saw how we could do it."

Following the frustrating night of April 25, Dewar and Squab had acquired some pictures of a suspected Serb command post. It had revetments surrounding it, and although intelligence said it might be abandoned, they were happy to have a "no-kidding confirmed target." They planned to investigate it as soon as possible. But bad weather and other missions kept them from doing so. When the weather cleared on May 1, Dewar wasn't on the flight schedule. (He probably had other duty.) So Squab was going with Wrex to check it out.

The command post was near Prizren, a city in the extreme south of Kosovo. A lot of the killing was concentrated there. They were going to match the photos with the picture their FLIR would make. But the FLIR broke. Even swooping close wouldn't help in that case. It was too dark. Other FAC-As might have turned around and gone home. Not Wrex and Squab. They had a new searching device, brought out to the carrier just a few days prior by navy strike-warfare officers aware that the FAC-As needed help. It was called an "IZLID II." IZLID stood for "Infrared Zoom Laser Illuminator Designator." It had never been used in combat before. The device resembled a large flashlight. It operated like one too—as long as those looking for the laser beam it projected were wearing night-vision goggles.

They decided to try it.

The IZLID posed some danger to its user. The operator had to keep the beam away from his eyes, even with his goggles on. But the lighted circle it threw on the distant ground wasn't a problem. Anyone with goggles could look at it freely, which is what they told the strikers to do when they called them in. With the photos and the IZLID, Squab found the revetments. Inside them was the command post—an antiquated but functional building. It was a valid target.

Their first strikers to arrive were Dog and Slugz. The XO had taken a personal interest in helping some of the nuggets. But IZLID was even new to him. "I'm pointing things out to them," said Squab. " 'See this road intersection? See this little grungy smudge here? That's actually a revetment.' " From the XO and Slugz's perspective, they were following a spot of light similar to what police helicopters use on fleeing criminals but without the originating beam back to the cockpit. Defenders on the ground couldn't see any of it. They destroyed the command post then left to attack a radio relay antenna elsewhere.

Next came Alvin and Moto, another teacher-student crew. They put two GBU-12s into some of the revetments as Hornets arrived. Wrex and Squab guided a few of the Hornet's laser Mavericks, then switched to the IZLID to show the Hornet pilots the new gadget they had. It was a hit. With their FLIRs, the Hornet pilots could easily pick up the IZLID-illuminated targets. It wasn't the kind of complicated situation of relayed coordinates and descriptions that so many of them didn't like. "We'd just hold the spot, and he'd make his delivery," said Squab. The Hornets blasted the remaining revetments.

When Wrex and Squab got back to the carrier, they were surprised at the reception they got from the normally FAC-A-skeptical Hornet drivers. "With the pressure to get the bombs off the jets," said Squab, "the Hornet guys are all stoked. They got to drop all their ordnance so there's a no-kidding carnival atmosphere. . . . It's one o'clock in the morning, and they're all high-fiving me, saying, 'That was awesome!' They loved the IZLID."

It had been such a hit, he said, that another Hornet section told him they had seen the spot from far away and had tried to raise them on the radio in order to get in on the action. But they hadn't been able to find the frequency.

"To me," said Squab, "that was the start of the upswing."

Sixteen

Lt. Comdr. Eric "Double" Pfister, the Aces' administrative officer and
a seasoned RIO, had attended too many funerals. It's one thing to lose
parents and grandparents. As hard as that is, burying elders is the natural order of things. But like most Aces, Double had seen several young
friends killed in their prime.

In 1994, as a JO in the VF-74 Bedevilers, one of Dog's old squadrons, he'd scheduled a pilot he'd usually crewed with on a flight from
which that pilot had never returned. "I was devastated," he said. The
pilot was a good friend. The Bedevilers had been involved in a round-
the-clock offshore exercise during the Haitian Crisis, and the pressure
was on. He and his pilot had returned from their night mission, but
Double still had the next flight schedule to write. An extra plane was
added unexpectedly, and he didn't have a crew. His buddy, about to
get some rest, volunteered. "I can still hear him saying, 'Yeah, I'd hate
to turn that down.' "

Double hadn't gone with him because he'd still had to finish the
schedule. "I felt a lot of guilt," said the RIO, a married 1989 Virginia
Tech graduate with a young son. "It was crushing. We had come over
together [to the Bedevilers] from a previous squadron. My wife knew
his fiancée very well. We'd socialized for a long time." The pilot had
died in a midair crash. They suspected that he'd become disoriented
while following another Tomcat close behind and that thus the two

had collided. But the exact cause had never been determined.

"They searched all night but couldn't find him. When they called off the search, I had to go. . . . Actually I volunteered to go with the CO to [the pilot's] fiancée's house. That was devastating, too." Double had to remove himself from the flight schedule for two weeks before he resumed flying. At his next squadron, VF-101, the Tomcat training RAG where he'd been an instructor before joining the Aces, he'd seen two more deaths. "In one," he said, "the airplane had a flight-control failure." The pilot couldn't do anything but ride into the ground and was killed. "I wasn't real close to that one, but it hit me hard because I had seen him two hours before the accident."

Because the RIO in a Tomcat doesn't have any flight controls, instructing student pilots was always scary, said Double. "The only thing you can do is talk to them and hope they respond and not second-guess you because there's usually not much time for a lot of discussion." Because Double had joined the Aces just before cruise and wasn't familiar with the LANTIRN, he was sent, in the beginning of the war, to the CAOC to be a carrier liaison. When he returned, one of his assignments was to help Jack Corlett as much as he could (an ironic assignment, given his aversion to novices, but one that he liked because he and Jack would become good friends).

Before coming to the Aces, Gooch had been in the squadron that had the navy's first woman combat-pilot fatality. Lt. Kara S. Hultgreen had boltered in October 1994 during routine carrier qualifications and had lost an engine. Her plane had stalled coming around and fallen like a rock into the sea. The RIO had gotten out, but Hultgreen, call-signed "Revlon," was never found. Gooch, who joined her squadron shortly after the accident, said she was well regarded, and the death, one of several the squadron suffered and controversial because the navy was accused of trying to cover up mistakes she allegedly had made, slowed the squadron for a considerable time.

Joey and Dog, by virtue of their time in service, probably were the Aces who had seen the most death. Dog said that over a period of two cruises plus work-ups, seven men died — and not just aircrew. "I've seen some horrible things. . . . A pipe breaks in the shower, and a kid gets scalded to death. A kid is walking next to an E2 and the next thing you know all this red stuff comes up, and parts of this guy's body are splattered against the side of the airplane. . . . Sometimes the men don't understand why we get angry, but if we see something about to happen, we go off the deep end."

Joey: "You go on a cruise like this, and you do a lot of combat, and every once in a while you think, 'Shoot, we're invulnerable. We're not gonna get into any harm.' But I remember the one Dog was talking about, the kid who walked into a prop. Yeah, the guy just went away, and body parts were all over the tower. . . . I've seen guys sucked down the intakes. I've seen that in an A-7, A-6, and F-14. . . . There are so many dangers out there."

Now Pappy and Money, eager JOs, were going to have their brush with death.

Pappy Anduze was the squadron's sole Hispanic aircrew member. He looked the part. The twenty-nine-year-old Puerto Rican–born pilot was tall, dark, and handsome and had a mild Spanish accent when he spoke English. But that's where the stereotype ended. He was a devoted family man, loved racing, and had been educated in private schools. He'd graduated from the Naval Academy in 1993 and liked the military. "I'm a pretty laid-back guy," he said. "In Puerto Rico, things move a pace slower. You hang out by the beach . . . go to lunch . . . go back to the beach. . . . So I don't mind following orders. It gets me in a routine, and I need to follow routines."

Squadron members kidded him about getting animated on the phone when he talks to his wife and children in Spanish. They didn't know what he was saying but knew he was passionate about it. That's how he got his call sign. "Pappy" is "daddy" in Spanish. His own father was from Venezuela. His parents divorced when he was ten, and his father then moved back to South America. They didn't see each other much after that. But the elder, an auto mechanic, left his mark. He'd loved racing, and Pappy grew up in garages, attending races on the weekends. They always had motorcycles and a need for speed, which is what ultimately got him in Tomcats. "The surface navy moves at six knots. I like moving at six hundred knots."

Pappy and Money were good friends. In port, they'd hang out together, sometimes looking for CDs they could buy and bring back for the ready room. On the night before "no-fly days," held weekly on the carrier as a periodic break, the two of them plus Dewar, Squab, and others, mostly from Six-Pack, would stay up to 4 or 5 A.M. playing poker. To Money, the all-night sessions were the good times that he said he'd remember most from the cruise. But neither aviator was on the FAC-A or on the A-Team, so on May 3, they were flying wing for Bru and Joey, holding in a racetrack at about two thousand feet above them, when they had an engine stall.

The stall wasn't a big deal. There were routine procedures for re-lighting. But it was that just-after-dark time when night had fallen but they were high enough to have remaining sunlight interfere with their night-goggled vision. Dealing with the stall, they'd lost sight of Bru and Joey and were low on gas. Pappy's repeated attempts to relight didn't work. Because they were on one engine and the solution involved descending to make air turn the turbine, they were losing altitude, falling closer to the heart of SAM envelopes. Lighting the burner on his good engine would have lifted them, but Pappy was afraid of putting "a big torch in the sky for anybody to take aim at."

He finally decided he had to take the chance. He lit burner and radioed Bru, and they decided they'd meet right outside Kosovo, thus lessening the danger, and then go for gas.

"So I'm in afterburner, climbing," he said. "We're getting our airspeed back, and I'm just looking around going, 'You know, what's gonna come up at me now that I have this big old candle lit and everybody can see me?" Suddenly, they heard a warning from "Magic," the air force AWACS plane. It said there was a "bogey" in "Derringer," the code name for the airspace they were in.

A bogey meant an unidentified aircraft, possibly hostile.

Money: "Pappy and I are like, 'Wow, how about that. There's a no-kidding bad guy somewhere out here.' We didn't think they were flying."

Magic had given some coordinates. "I'm like, 'Money, where's that?'" said Pappy. "He starts looking through the system, trying to figure out exactly where it is. . . . I'm going, 'Man, it's really close to where we are.'"

Throughout the war, the navy and air force manned CAPs around Kosovo to shoot enemy planes. Magic directed an air force section from the nearest CAP to intercept the bogey, all of which Pappy and Money heard. Pappy remembers it was an F-15 Eagle section. Money remembers it as two F-16 Vipers. Whichever it was, both remember the two fighters were coming with "hate and discontent," ready to kill.

Then the two of them realized that *they* were the bogey. The stall they'd experienced had involved some electrical wiring, they later found out, and might have short-circuited their Mode 4 identification box. As they'd entered Derringer, they'd not been broadcasting the proper code.

They were in real danger of being shot.

Money: "Pappy comes up, 'Tell 'em we're friendly! Tell 'em we're friendly!' I go on the radio and say, 'Hey, Derringer, so and so. Friendly F-14.' Then you hear [from the interceptors], 'Knock it off. Knock it off.' You know, disengage. I can't remember specifically what they said. But about twenty seconds later, two F-16s came screaming by us supersonic."

Pappy: "We hear the AWAC go, 'Friendly. Friendly.' And at that point I'm like, 'We almost got shot.' . . . About fifteen seconds later, we merged with the F-15s. . . . I don't know if the loss of the motor spiked the system . . . and just took our codes out. But as soon as we get our motor relit . . . they have no problem figuring who we are."

The two Aces were pretty shaken. Nobody wants "blue on blue," the mistaken shooting down of friendly aircraft. But it had come close to happening. Luckily, a bogey meant the interceptors had to make a visual identification before firing. Had they been declared "hostile," the two Aces most certainly would have taken an air-to-air missile.

The air force interceptors turned a quick circle around the Tomcat and sped back to their station. Nobody exchanged words. But they were probably as shaken as Pappy and Money.

"It was pretty eye-opening," said Money.

"That was the time I saw myself closest to dying," said Pappy.

Early in the war, Admiral Copeland had secretly worked out a schedule with Sixth Fleet's Admiral Murphy that would give all serving on the carrier a week's break from combat after about thirty days "on line." That break, unannounced until just before it occurred, came on May 6. There were a lot of attractive ports in the Mediterranean for the "sabbatical," as the admiral called it. But the farther away the port was, the more transit time to it would eat into the short respite. Greece was close but represented a political problem because of the country's proximity and ties to the Serbs. Antalya, Turkey, an ancient coastal city on the "Turkish Riviera," then became the most desirable spot. It was out-

of-the-way and steeped in historical sites for touring, and was also relatively cheap for the sailors and quicker to get to than Tel Aviv, Israel,
the next closest port.

The carrier steamed out of the Ionian at thirty knots.

Most of the Aces were thankful for the break. "We were tired," said
Beaker. "The guys had been flying almost nonstop and really needed
to get away." Standard squadron procedure in any port was to rent the
suite of hotel rooms called an "admin," where any of them could
"crash," hang around, or just have a base from which to do whatever
they wished. The admin was stocked with beer and liquor. Everything
was supposed to be paid for from the squadron social fund. But there
wasn't enough. Razor said Joey called him aside, gave him money from
his own pocket, and said he wanted to take care of the JOs. "They
don't need to know," Razor said Joey told him. "And he never really
said anything. . . . Some of them didn't like him. He didn't care. He
wanted them to be happy."

The port call was a time to unwind, have fun, and be with squadron
buddies. Joey believed it built closeness. A bar was picked out and
designated the squadron waterhole. Usually it was a place someone
knew about from a previous port call. If you were looking for an Ace,
you'd go to the bar or the admin. It was in Antalya that the wrestling
matches started. "There were like ten or twelve of us," said Razor, "and
the skipper's ordering food, and we just had a ball. I wrestled the XO,
and a couple of other guys wrestled the XO. And then we started
wrestling each other."

Antalya had a crescent-shaped beach, but it wasn't Honolulu or Las
Vegas East. Its main attraction was its ancient history, which included
early Roman, Christian, and Turkish sites. There was also the exotic
Islamic culture, most exemplified by the periodic calls-to-prayer by
Moslem imams from the tall, spindly minarets that dotted the city.
There were breezy sidewalk cafes with tasty Middle Eastern food. And
shopping. "Merchants from hell," one Ace termed the tugging vendors
on the city's ancient streets. But the prices could always be negotiated,
and a beautiful piece of jewelry or an oriental rug could be had for a
fraction of what they would cost in the United States.

"They were really scared about terrorists," said Thing regarding
warnings from security. "We couldn't wear America logos, flags, that

kind of thing. Yet we stood out like sore thumbs. Everybody said, 'There are the Americans.' So we didn't fool anybody." Thing went to a place that St. Paul visited in his missionary journeys. Jack, smarting from his flying troubles, avoided the admin and stayed largely to himself. Other Aces ate roast lamb, a succulent Antalya specialty, and undoubtedly went seeking what night pleasures they could find. And at least one Ace had a heartfelt experience.

While Topper Leese was having arguments with Bru about what TARPS could and couldn't do, he was also going through a situation that would end in divorce and had met a girl he wanted to wed. When he learned about the port call before the official announcement, he said all he could think about was calling the girl and getting her to Antalya. It was going to be quite a feat. They hadn't planned the trip. She was eight thousand miles away in Canada, and the carrier would be arriving off Turkey within forty-eight hours. "But once I knew, it was the only thing on my mind."

Her name was Joanne. They'd met months before on St. Maarten Island in the Caribbean. He'd been on a liberty during a training exercise off Vieques Island near Puerto Rico. She was on a vacation from her job at a Toronto-area museum. They'd both gone with friends to eat at the same restaurant. The attraction from across the room had been instant. "Something happened," he said. "Within a millisecond I knew I was going to marry her. . . . I can't explain it." Joanne, blond, soft-spoken, said the same thing. "It was just one of those moments you read about or see in the movies where time stands still and you're in this kind of tunnel-vision state. It was phenomenal, like I had blinders on."

But neither of them knew what the other was thinking. He was nearing a divorce. She was shy and turned away. He walked over and said, "Hi." They began talking, soon finding they had much in common. An assistant curator, she had a degree in classical history. He had a master's in nautical archeology. "It wasn't, 'Hey, have you been to Spain?,' " he said. "It was, 'Do you remember that park in Spanish history? And did you see those tapestries?' "

They talked so long that they were booted from the bar at closing time. He walked her back to her hotel, and they ended up talking outside almost until dawn. "We didn't profess anything," said Joanne.

"I grew up very proper. Even though I was feeling what I was feeling, I certainly wasn't about to tell Kyle." He too wasn't sure where he stood. He just knew he had to see Joanne again.

They had chaperoned dinner the next night—Pappy, Meat, and Dewar in tow—and he'd taken her and a friend on a VIP tour of the carrier. "We felt like royalty," she said. But then an onboard emergency as she was leaving had caused him to break away without proper good-byes. They still had not even voiced their feelings and she was leaving later that day. It had all been platonic. Not until she was gone and he was back in Eight-Ball undressing did he realize he didn't even have her address.

He spent "four or five days calling every museum in and around Toronto" in his spare time, but he had no luck. She had gone back feeling, "I had met someone very special who I had connected with. But I lived far away, and he was in the navy." But she couldn't get him out of her mind. "It was a really tough decision for me," she said, "because it went against everything I'd been taught—that women do not chase men." But on the advice of a friend, she sent him a cautious telegram: "For further conversations on Greek history and nautical archeology, please e-mail me at . . ."

It was the "best telegram I ever got," he said (despite the fact that telegrams were rare on the ship, and by the time it was handed to him, a crowd of Aces was preparing to have to comfort him over news of a family death). They began "a period of getting to know one another," said Joanne. " 'What movies do you like? Do you know this poem?' " They discussed their jobs, their pasts, what they were looking for in the future.

As the e-mails mounted, the talk got more intimate, said Topper. "Not in a sexual way, but personal way. It went from, 'These are my favorite movies and food,' to *why* these are my favorites." She told him about a painful four-year relationship that had ended just before she met him. He explained his own personal situation (which he didn't want discussed here). Joanne said, "We were educating ourselves about each other . . . sharing what really struck a chord in our own heart . . . I just never felt so connected."

Once he'd arrived back at Virginia Beach, they started planning to see each other again. They each got some time off. They made plans to meet in Washington, D.C. She came by train. "It was fantastic and wonderful," he said. "That same feeling was there as soon as I saw her again." They spent four days going to museums and art galleries. She'd never had sushi or eaten lox and cream cheese on a bagel. "And it was there," he said, "that we realized how much we meant to each other and what it had become to us at that point in time."

His divorce proceeded. A month before the *Roosevelt* left for Kosovo, he got some time off and went to Toronto. He met her family and friends. "I knew I was in love with her, and I could feel the cruise looming," he said. He asked her to come back to Virginia Beach with him for a few days. At first she couldn't because of her work. But then she got the time off.

"A couple of days before we pulled out, we were on the beach, and I told her I loved her. . . . I didn't propose, just let all my feelings out. I didn't want the same thing to happen that happened in St. Maarten. I was leaving, and who knew what would happen? If she had said no, oh well, I'd get on the boat, and nobody would see me cry."

But Joanne "was feeling the same things, hoping the same things." They didn't get into specifics, but a promise had been made. When he learned about the midwar port call, he e-mailed her to meet him in Antalya. She e-mailed back, excited and scared. "I mean, I'd only been as far as St. Maarten in my lifetime. This was a predominantly Muslim country halfway around the world." Because of secrecy, he didn't even know the exact dates. And how would she pay for it?

He had a credit card that he kept for emergencies. He told her to get the ticket, and he'd reimburse her with that. It was almost one thousand dollars, very expensive. She withdrew the money from her savings. He couldn't wait to see her. She phoned with the arrival time. He was at the airport two hours before she arrived. He sat at the bar talking with a German businessman and having a beer to calm his excitement.

She flew to Frankfurt and then Istanbul before landing at Antalya. "I was a stranger in a strange land. It was surreal. Phenomenal. Finally getting into Antalya was a huge relief. I had so much excitement to see Kyle and hear how he was doing. I didn't think about the war. I had no knowledge about the navy and the military. I didn't even know what questions to ask."

She wasn't expecting him at the airport. They'd left it that they'd meet at the hotel. But as she was walking along the exit area, "I just got this feeling in my stomach. It was like, 'I'll bet he's here.' I remember thinking that to myself and looking into the glass on the wall and kind of fixing my hair. And then there he was, standing there." They ran to each other, oblivious to the stares.

They'd made reservations in an eighteenth-century Ottoman merchant's mansion turned into a hotel. It was in the city's Old Town section, its historic, ancient core. The furniture, paintings, courtyard, and fountains were all from that era. It was dusk. Their room had eight-foot-tall hardwood framed windows with shutters opening to the city. Outside, a call for prayer was just beginning. They could see the minaret. "We threw down the bags and were in each other's arms," he said. "It was magical, exotic." Just "the euphoria of seeing each other," she said.

Later, when she'd had time to take stock, she said he looked "very thin . . . seemed tired but still very sure of what he was doing and why." The war was frightening to her, and he didn't talk about it. "My understanding was that a lot of it was classified, and anyway this was supposed to be a break from that." They went to dinner atop an old castle wall overlooking the harbor. For dessert he ordered chocolate soufflé. "That's what she loves." The next day, they rented a car and toured Greek and Roman ruins, famous sites that they'd read about but never seen.

At the end of the second day, he took her to a jewelry store in the Old City. "The prices were cheap," she said. "I thought, great. What woman doesn't love jewelry? Sales over there are not like here. It's a sit-down affair. They bring you coffee, tea. Whatever you buy, they are showing good business and faith by spending time with you." When the merchant brought out a deep blue sapphire ring with diamonds, he said it was "exactly what I wanted for her . . . classic. . . . Just made me think of who she is and all the things we shared and experienced. . . . She began to realize I was in the process of buying it for her, and we ended up having a wonderful time during the purchasing process."

She shrank from the price, but he said in America it would be five times as much. "I was almost in tears," she said. "He was making me feel like a princess." He bought her a bracelet and suede jacket too. They went back to the hotel and up to their room. He sat her on the bed and pulled out the ring. "This is for you," he said. All she could say was, " 'Oh, my God. Oh, my God.' "

Seventeen

There was a new atmosphere in the VF-41 ready room when the *Roosevelt* returned to daily combat operations on May 13. It wasn't something the Aces necessarily talked or even thought about. The war was still there and each one had to resume fighting it. But, as was hoped, the time off had a rejuvenating effect. For many, it had bred a new resolve, one that was less clouded with questions about combat and each aviator's ability to deal with it. The warfighters and those not so inclined or proficient had been identified. The squadron had made its adjustments and was a functioning combat unit. Joey knew who he could count on and who needed work. And the task at hand was more clearly defined. They were returning, it appeared, to what basically was going to be a FAC-A war. There still would be periodic strikes on stationary targets, CAPs to man, training flights that had slowed but continued during the war. But the Ace's main job was going to be continuing to find and destroy the elusive Serb army, and they now, despite the dangers, had a good handle on how to do that.

A personal example of the rejuvenation was Topper. During his "oasis in the midst of a great adventure," as he called his Turkey respite, he hadn't consciously thought of the war or his problems with finding up-to-date intelligence. He'd concentrated on Joanne. But the problem, he said, was always lurking. "In lulls in the conversation. In the back of my mind. As I'd look out at the horizon." When he'd returned, he said he had a new attitude. "I can't say I'd had any rev-elation, you know, 'Eureka! I've found it!' But the break had taken me out." It had been his island in the storm, a time of subconscious per-colation. "And when I got back, things just started clicking. Hey, I need to look at this from a different angle. What we're doing isn't providing solutions. There's got to be a better way."

The new attitude bore fruit, he said, on the first day back when, alerted by his analyzers, he noticed heavy vehicle tracks in photos of the ground taken during the morning TARPS run. It was the first time he and his intell specialists had actually spotted such clues, which were very subtle in the celluloid. The tracks, feint and crisscrossing, were in an open space, a field of some sorts, and seemed to lead to the edge of a heavily forested area, a "tree line" as it was called. The Serbs, aware by now that the Tomcats and others were after them, were being more deceptive, hiding more. The forest was a perfect hiding place.

Topper had some non-TARPS intelligence that indicated the enemy was believed to have a concentration of tanks in the area, perhaps a mechanized battalion. But the TARPS pod, on the blink that day, hadn't stamped the latitude and longitude on the film. They couldn't verify the coordinates. "Wouldn't you know," he remarked about the breakdown. They were having to calculate the exact location of the area from aerial navigation charts. When they finally determined the coordinates, they were identical to the intelligence pinpoints he already had. "It was literally, you know, what's that called, serendipity? You could hear the harps playing in the distance as we, pardon my French, said, 'Holy shit. That's exactly where it's supposed to be. Right fucking there!' "

They had concrete evidence of what another source had given them. And it was fresh! Bru and Joey were there when they'd made the cal-culations. They grabbed the pictures and walked.

"We got it," Topper remembers Bru saying.

In little more than an hour Bru and Joey, with Brain and Loose on their wing, were over the target, which turned out to be an approximate ten-acre clearing bordered by a forest at one end and the intersection of several roads on the other. They quickly found "two tanks and a personnel carrier on the edge of the tree line," said Bru. They bombed those and saw tracks "going further into the trees." The more they looked, the more they found, "like ants at a picnic," he said. Secondary explosions indicated there was more there than they could see through the forest canopy.

Out of bombs, the section radioed the Hornets scheduled to be their strikers to bypass tanking and come quick. The Hornets did. "It looked like the Serbs had come down the roads and then turned off into the grassy area," said Bru, "then they'd gone up into the wooded area to hide." He estimated there might have been as many as "fifty-to-sixty vehicles and 250 people" there. When the Hornets arrived, they started raining death, "like rabid dogs chewing on a piece of meat . . . I remember looking down and just going, 'Man, this is carnal. . . . These guys [the Hornets] are assassins.'"

Among the Hornet bombs were "Rockeye," antipersonnel, antitank bombs that blast superheated bomblets in every direction just above the ground. Rockeye are dumb bombs, not guided. Three or four of them could spew enough of the nasty little balls to saturate most of the airspace hovering directly above a football field. Bru said his strikers probably dropped, in the short span of two-and-a-half minutes, "eight tons of ordnance" on the area. And when he and Joey left, succeeding FAC-As, aided by low-flying UAVs from the CAOC whose administrators wanted in on the frenzy, directed bombardment of the area for the rest of the day. Finding the staging area was a major coup for the Aces and there was hearty celebration when they returned to the carrier, especially in Topper's intelligence office.

It was a precursor to stepped-up Serb activities.

The Serbs, time would show, were on the move.

In the coming weeks, Topper's Bru-instigated system of big target map and comprehensive data base would see fruition. FAC-As could check the area they were going to for recent activity and leave with a folder full of the latest pictures and intelligence on the area's suspected and known targets. The system was updated and replenished by the airwing's ongoing cycle of missions. Morning TARPS runs ordered by the CAOC or the airwing would be plotted to include suspected FAC-A targets. What was found would be given to the first FAC-A missions that left the same day around noon. The returning FAC-As would then give new information and suspected sites to briefers who would use it to plan the next morning's TARPS run. Sometimes returning FAC-As, afraid the enemy might disperse, would simply radio a hot target to a fresh, inbound crew. Returning strikers, who often saw potential targets or had other valuable information, added more up-to-date information to the map and data base.

The day after Bru and Joey found the tank battalion, Dewar and Squab, with Dog and Wog on their wing, located an enemy concentration of revetments near Podujevo, a town northwest of Pristina. Podujevo had recently been the scene of Serb action against the town's Albanian population. The concentration was perhaps an enemy staging base. The FAC-As had been told about it by air force A-10 pilots who had been in the area previously. The area was similar to the one Bru and Joey had observed the day before: a large clearing bordering a forest. But this clearing had six or seven built-up revetments in it. In his diary, Squab called them "fighting trenches." They had camouflage over them—and perhaps supplies under the camouflage, speculated Wog.

It appears that his speculation was right. The two Tomcats bombed the stone-walled revetments with GBU-12s and then called in Hornets, for which they lased. "Some of the revetments really went off," said Wog about secondary explosions in the trenches. He guessed the camouflage covered boxes of munitions. "They [the revetments] probably had artillery in them at one time. Now it's just a staging area." The Hornets then dive-bombed the adjacent forest with Rockeye. "We didn't see any secondaries, but something burned," said Wog. On his FLIR, he could see the continuing heat.

Out of bombs and low on gas, the two Tomcats left the area, tanked, returned, and found another group of revetments six miles from the first. They called in a new group of Hornets. Even if the revetments were empty, the Aces would bomb them in order to make them less useful to the enemy should he return. In the later propaganda war, the Serbs would claim that NATO planes were being tricked into hitting useless decoys. Wog said their practice of bombing the empty sites might have helped the Serbs make that claim. But in this case, he said, there were enemy troops in the woods because they saw them scrambling from the bombing in their vehicles. "They got out and went on the highway," said Wog. "If you couldn't absolutely identify it [a vehicle] as military, you had to leave it alone." He said they didn't take the time to make the ID because they wanted to concentrate on the revetments. "But you could see the dust marks as they hightailed it away."

For the next week-and-a-half, with the system up and working, the Aces continued having SCAR success. "The weather started getting better," said Thing. "The intelligence was better. Guys were getting better at recognizing what they were lookin' for." Familiarity with the terrain made it easier to discern targets from higher altitude. "You stare at the ground long enough," said Wog, "and instead of targets blending in, you notice, 'Hey, that's not right. That's a sharp corner there. There shouldn't be anything like that in those trees.' And then looking at the FLIR. . . . 'Hey, there's a hot spot in the middle of that field. What is that? That shouldn't be there.' "

With the air threats lessening (but not gone), the FAC-As and their strikers ventured ever lower. Where they had started the war with a twenty-thousand-foot floor, which was nearly three and a half miles up, the FAC-As eventually would come down to five thousand feet, sometimes lower, to make identifications. (The official floor for the strikers eventually came down to eight thousand feet.)

They began deciphering Serb tricks. "They [the Serbs] would go right back into areas we'd bombed, thinking we wouldn't look there again," said Bru. "You got into the habit of looking out the window at everything you'd already hit." Updates on the map in intell would also alert them to any reoccupancy. The Serbs started using fire trucks as refueling vehicles, thinking the Allies wouldn't know. But the Aces caught them at it. "The trucks went up in flames," remembers Wog, who directed Rockeye on them. Following tracks and looking closely at tree lines became second nature, and finding a target in one area usually meant another was nearby.

The Aces were becoming experts.

And they were getting wily about what they were doing.

The Aces' hierarchy continued to believe spies in NATO were passing mission information to the enemy. "I wasn't comfortable with that," said Dog, "but we were good enough to where it just didn't matter." Much of the SCAR mission, anyway, was spur-of-the-moment opportunity that couldn't be forwarded in time to benefit the enemy. However, some Aces believed the Serbs could listen to their radio transmissions, probably by receiving the secret frequencies. Relatively cheap Radio Shack–level technology was all that was needed. Evidence for this, said Beaker, was that in at least one instance, a known enemy concentration disappeared just before strikers arrived. Consequently, countermeasures that slowed operations had to be instituted. Conversely, intelligence from Albanian fighters was reaching the air wing. "We would get word from them saying, 'Don't hit around these coordinates,' and we wouldn't," said Beaker.

The implication was that the Albanians, gathering for a counteroffensive, were operating in the area.

As a result of the Aces' success, squadron confidence grew. "It got to the point," said Wog, "where we'd take off with a full load of bombs, and unlike before where we might get just one off, I now know I'm going to slick off the airplane." Operations sometimes almost became routine. There was time to appreciate some of the perks on the carrier, like round-the-clock food availability, especially ice cream and desserts. And "the girl on Cat 2," a particularly curvaceous airplane handler on one of the catapults. Even in the bulky, unflattering deck gear, she was unmistakably female.

In early April, briefs had been thirty-minute, tension-packed affairs with multiple power points and minutiae on every aspect. By mid-May, they'd shrunk to casual five-minute check-off meetings. "Bru would just come in and put the overview on the board," said T-bone. "I was getting more sleep," said Bru. Because of the expanded TARPS coverage, photo study became the mainstay of FAC-A mission preparation. For the strikers, there was even less sweat. "It was like an office workday," said Alvin. "Go up, get our gas, check in with whoever are our FAC-As. 'Okay, we're here. We're holding. Whatcha got?' "

Aircrews got bolder. "After you've been in combat for awhile and nobody gets shot down," said Admiral Copeland, "you start becoming a little bit comfortable, then more comfortable. And then you can become complacent." All the commanders worried about it. Not only did the Aces go progressively lower, but they started loitering longer, holding over the target. "Basically we go out there with two Tomcats," wrote Meat to his wife, "and . . . fly circles over the Serbs . . . and wait for them to shoot AAA at us or a SAM, and then we drop bombs on them if we can see where they were fired from." Their "biggest goal," said Dewar about the FAC-As, was to get the enemy "to shoot at us, shoot at us so we can roll in and drop something." Near the end of the war, supersonic TARPS crews were going as low as three thousand feet to get their pictures. "There aren't many windows left unbroken in Kosovo," wrote Meat. "We wanted to show we were real tough guys," said Alvin. "We'd zip through the mountains . . . kinda kick ass, sayin', 'We're here. You can't touch me.'"

But the Serbs too were getting smarter. They'd stopped moving in the open and on highways. When they did move, they favored night and did so in smaller groups. Joey said that if they saw a target out in the open, they'd suspect decoy. Then NATO bombers (not navy) mistakenly hitting refugees and the Chinese embassy in Belgrade caused a renewed tightening of rules about when, where, and who to hit. While the Allies were now clearly in charge in the air, the Aces, as well as every NATO bomber, again had to be extra careful about dropping their bombs.

It was like taking a step backward.

One night Brain, who said he was frustrated because "I don't think we're hitting them as hard as we could," dove on a Serb artillery site that had impotently but aggressively shot at him. (He was too high to be hit.) He'd not had authorization to attack, and since he was out of bombs, he'd used his twenty-millimeter cannon from a height just a little below ten thousand feet, which was violating the official floor. He didn't know if he'd hit the battery, but he said the attack made him feel good. When he'd returned to the carrier, he'd decided he had little choice but to confess to Joey. "When you shoot the gun, there's a lot of oil and residue. It leaves a big mess. Plus, I was missing about two hundred rounds of ammunition." Joey warned him that if he did it again, he'd be grounded. "It's worthless to do something like that," said Joey. "You're risking your life, a $50 million airplane, and you can't do anything [with guns] at that altitude anyway."

But when the FAC-As found a validated target (and a lot of UAVs were shot down validating them), they had carte blanche.

Wrex: "It was quite a neat thing to [be] part of, to be in control of a battlefield as a lieutenant, just an A-3. I am driving what is going on in Kosovo right now. Whoever's in my backseat, the two of us together coordinate the whole battlefield management."

It was a power trip few aviators experience. The best FAC-As were dealers of death, executioners literally from on high.

Wrex: "We put the strikers on. Tell them what targets to hit. Coordinate the whole SEAD, the suppression of enemy air defense stuff that's going on in an area. To have all that power is just amazing."

Fear, however, was always near. Meat wrote his wife:

I had a mission . . . that really scared the piss out of
me. There were two of us, me and a nugget Tomcat guy from
VF-14. We were doing a night strike into Kosovo against a
fixed target. The weather was shitty and we weren't sure
we could see the target. We proceeded in country and
started getting SAM indications on our RAW [RHAW] gear
out in front of us but we couldn't see the ground because
of the cloud cover. We had no way of knowing if there had
been a real SAM launch. We started doing our defensive
moves and turned to get the hell out of there. . . . Then
after aborting the strike we go to the tanker and have 2
or 3 near misses with Hornets trying to get on the
tanker. This is probably the scariest thing out there,
trying to find the tanker at night with 5 to 10 of your
closest buddies all at the same altitude. . . .

Pressure mounted to drop bombs. "It was a no-no not to drop bombs," said Loose, who would end the war with the best bombing rating in the squadron. Aircrews pressed hard to find targets, not only to stop Serb killing, but to prove their own, the navy's, and the squadron's worth. "You didn't want to send a section back with ordnance on it," said Dewar. If you did, "you had to apologize in the debrief because you couldn't find a target for them. . . . When I took off, it wasn't the threats we talked about. It was, 'How are we going to get these guys' targets?' "

To their chagrin, the carrier started running out of laser-guided bombs. The reason was similar to why the Aces were flying old airplanes. "We don't have production lines that even make them anymore," said Bru in a slap at planning or priorities. (It wasn't clear who or what was at fault.) As a consequence, the air wing began partially loading dumb bombs on its aircraft along with laser-guided bombs in an effort to ration what guided bombs were left. "We'd send a laser-guided bomb in to pinpoint the target, and then [the strikers would] use the free-fall bombs to follow up," said Bru.

The shortage didn't hinder good FAC-As. "Dewar and Squab, Wrex and Thing—they were the air-wing favorites," said Bru, who, along with Joey, was setting the standard. "When [the strikers] heard their voices, they'd go, 'Oh, boy, we're going to get our weapons off tonight.' . . . Dewar and Squab in particular. . . . Those guys exercised more power and authority in a lethal engagement than practically anybody senior to them."

Through will and preparation, the three crews consistently went out and found the enemy. "It was absolutely amazing to me," said Bru, "especially after Joey and I would go out [in the daytime] and come back and I'd be sitting there worried about them, hoping that they were all right and that things were going good. And really those guys had the worst problem because they did it mostly at night. . . . And then you'd watch the recovery of the airplanes coming back, planes that had taken off just loaded with bombs. And they would be empty. And then you'd go, 'Oh, my God, the stories are going to be good tonight.'"

Dewar, after initial excitement in the first days, was actually disappointed in the war as it continued. "We aren't even close to what those guys saw in Vietnam," he said. He didn't like bombing. "There's not much to it. Steady up your headings. Push the buttons at the right time." Dogfighting was what he wanted. "You still want to beat somebody. Talk shit after you've gotten him. Get in close, call the Fox Two [code for 'a heat-seeking missile away']. That is something you are not going to forget."

But he enjoyed FAC-A. "I thought it was cool to be part of the full cycle. I'd go out and fly TARPS and then use the pictures I just took to hunt. No one else has that capability. And it's phenomenal since we've got this twenty-five-year-old airplane. What the hell is going on with the navy that this mission can only be accomplished by a twenty-five-year-old plane? They've got the Hornets. And the Super Hornets are coming. But guess what? Neither one of them could do what the Tomcat did. . . . Somebody fucked up."

The exact circumstances under which Gooch got back into Joey's good graces are not clear. He says he did so on the night of April 30 when he and Thing, sitting spare for Bru and Joey's afternoon SCAR mission, had to launch in place of the scheduled wingmen, Meat and Wog, whose jet suffered a mechanical problem.

"The turning point," said Gooch, "was, first of all, when we realized the threat was not this big gargantuan monster like we perceived in the first few days. Yes, there were some SAMs out there. We knew where they were. We [learned] how to avoid them. So we could come down to altitudes that were more workable for the LANTIRN pod. And also being able to utilize those other assets [like TARPS] to help us locate and identify the targets . . . I think you're talking about . . . shoot, I would say, maybe Skipper and Bru thought my skepticism changed . . . when I went on an escort with them, me and Thing . . . and we were able to perform FAC-A functions on their wing. I think that might have impressed the skipper a little bit."

Checking his logbook, he identified that date as April 30. "We were only there in an escort role initially, but since we're a FAC-A crew, they [Bru and Joey] were able to delegate some responsibility to us — stack management, providing air-to-air deconfliction, finding targets for them. . . . I remember they wanted us to take out a bridge that ran from Kosovo into Montenegro." The mission had air-wing Tomcats and Hornets arrive as strikers, and Gooch and Thing buddy-lased for them. The bridge, he said, eventually came down, and then they went up to the Dakovica region near the Albanian border and helped hit more targets. At some point, according to the squadron bombing tallies, Triple-A was shot at them.

Neither Bru nor Joey remember the turning point coming that soon. To them it was later — more like the latter part of May. "We were the primary FAC-A, and he was on our wing," said Joey. "A couple of times he pointed out targets that we needed to look at. I always knew Gooch was confident. He was extremely talented. It was just his aggressiveness and his willingness to be part of the team and work in a hostile environment [that I questioned]. Those hops showed me that he was getting into it and was a team player to the extent that he was able."

Bru: "I think what happened was, he became more comfortable in the environment we were operating in. The threats had minimized, and he found a level of . . . anxiety that he could manage and operate under, which is what happened to everybody. But his ability to do that came later. . . . Towards the end, he was as productive as anyone."

In fact, after the war, Gooch was as good at instructing FAC-A as any of the Aces. "A real FAC's role," he said, alluding to the fact that they didn't have ground controllers, "is close air support. Close air support is defined as coordinated arms on enemy units in close proximity to friendly forces. In Kosovo, instead of friendly forces, read neutrals or civilians. So we're trained to control weapons close to people you don't want to hit. . . . Lasing a weapon is the best control you can get. The other way you control is by talking a person's eyes on . . . As a FAC you make sure his eyes are on the correct target and that they have visual of all the friendly or civilian positions they are not supposed to hit."

Concerning deconfliction, he said: "I'll tell you, the air force FACs did not do a very good job of it. . . . I don't know if it's a training issue or the fact that their FACs are flying single-seat airplanes [A-10 and F-16] and they're not as aircrew-coordinated as we are in a dual-seat airplane, where we can divide tasks." He said there were "several close calls with aircraft in the same piece of sky" during the war, a near midair suffered by Brain among them. Brain said a jet that was supposed to be stacked several thousand feet above him "dipped" and came within "ten-to-fifteen feet" before pulling up sharply. It scared him badly. And when the air force was in control, continued Gooch, "they would routinely say, 'Okay, we've got targets here,' . . . and start bringing all these strikers in but provide no altitude deconfliction. . . . What's worse, they wouldn't tell you that there were other aircraft operating [in the vicinity]. . . . There were a couple of times when an airplane went by you and you went, 'Where did that guy come from?'

"The first thing a FAC-A should do is assign you an altitude and a place to hold. . . . The way it worked in my cockpit was, the RIO was in charge of airspace deconfliction. When a striker would check in with him from the E-2 and say, 'Hey, this is Snake One and Two checking in,' you say, 'Okay, Snake One and Two, hold at Beck's [a CAOC-designated point] at twenty-one k [twenty-one thousand feet]. You have Viper at twenty k and Muskrat at nineteen k.' Now they know who is in the area and what altitude they're supposed to be at. Then, when you find a target, you say, 'Okay, Snake. I got a target for you. Go ahead and proceed to this latitude and longitude and hold overhead at twenty k. You'll have twenty k and above. I'll be nineteen k and below' . . . And once he gets overhead and established, you say, 'Okay, now start your job,' and you talk him on. And if you're going to have more than one section come in, you start stacking them above. . . ."

Gooch took issue with his skipper and Bru: "They say that I was not a team player and not aggressive. I would say to them, yes, I had issues with some of the ideas put forth. I didn't think they were feasible. . . . My issue wasn't that I didn't want to go out and fly under a high-threat scenario. My issue was that I didn't think [Bru's] tactics would work under that scenario."

Gooch, when all was said and done, was a respected member of the Aces; opinionated, confrontational sometimes, and often at odds with others because of it. Most of his junior officer contemporaries regarded his early war estrangements from squadron management as mainly the result of his by-the-book, no deviation-from-the-rules attitude.

Thing said: "He was one of the most tactically knowledgeable guys, one of the guys who always forced me to hit the books harder to learn more. . . . I always respected him for that. He knew stuff. He was careful, by the book, not a haphazard guy. . . . He wasn't afraid to tell management, 'Hey, you're wrong, and this is why you're wrong.' . . . Every organization needs that even if they don't want to hear it. . . . I always felt very confident with him, loved flying with him. If I would have flown with him the whole time [during the war], that would have been fine with me."

Gooch said he believed he flew as much combat as any JO and that classified records, could they be examined, would bear him out on that.

Whatever the timetable and exact circumstances, Gooch, by the end of May, was a proficient and aggressive FAC-A.

The squadron was going to need him.

Eighteen

Toward the end of May the war on the ground took a crucial turn. Time was running out for the Serbs, who, although they were talking big, were steadily losing men and war matériel. More important, the Albanians began launching a counteroffensive of sorts. They didn't have a large army. But what they did have was concentrated in northern Albania along the border of southwest Kosovo. From there, the KLA, or Kosovo Liberation Army as the Kosovo Albanians called themselves, were infiltrating fighters in small groups. These groups began challenging the Serbs. Cognizant of the infiltration, their own deteriorating situation, and the fact that the area was a crossing point for fleeing refugees—the same they were trying to eliminate and who might come back and hurt them—the Serbs decided to move men and supplies down to southwest Kosovo in what can now be termed their final military thrust. It was this thrust that would provide NATO, and consequently the Aces, with their last test in Kosovo.

While intelligence from the war is still classified and hard to get, it doesn't appear that the Aces themselves were aware of the thrust as it began (although higher-ups in the chain of command dictating missions might have been). As May advanced, there were increased sightings of enemy encampments and movements, but these could be attributed to the improvement in the weather and thus in flying conditions as summer beckoned, and also to the fact that the aviators, especially the FAC-As, were improving at their jobs.

The Serb thrust was hidden and piecemeal.

One of the first times the Aces ran into the buildup appears to have been around May 26, according to Wog, when, he said, he and Dog led three other Tomcats, two from the Tophatters, on a mission to seal the main railroad tunnel going south out of Pristina. "They [the Serbs] were moving tanks," he said. "We wanted to stop them from bringing their stuff down." The weather was bad, and one section took the south side of the tunnel, and the other section took the north. He and Dog delivered a two-thousand-pounder, which he said went "right in the mouth" of the tunnel, spewing an enormous amount of dirt. The mission is on the squadron's cruise video. They flew away believing they had done their job but not cognizant that what they had stopped was part of a larger thrust south.

On May 27, Wrex and Squab, the night FAC-As, found a series of enemy positions that together appear to have made up a sizable staging area—probably one of those from which the Serbs were to launch their subsequent offensive. They too didn't realize the implications. Nevertheless, they prosecuted as hard as they could, and what subsequently transpired would have made the air wing's FAC-A highlight reel if there had been such a thing.

Actually, the mission started out badly. Their assigned wingmen (Pappy and Double Pfister) and the backup spare (Gooch and Thing) went down on deck. The two FAC-As had to launch into the darkness with a section of Hornets as their escorts. The Hornets were going to be their strikers. They had photos of a "battalion command post with a shit-load of revetments and mortar pits around it," according to Squab's diary. They found the place easily. Then their laser went down. They'd been through that before. The FLIR was still working so they could see the heat contrasts of the target in their scopes and use the handheld IZLID to throw a spot on it for the strikers. The Hornet pilots could see the spot because they had night-vision goggles.

After a few reconnoiter circles, Wrex and Squab had the command post visually located. They also saw in their scopes "three or four tracked vehicles" on the command post's south side. The building was two hundred feet long and about fifty feet high, with a long north-south axis—a juicy target. There were revetments around it. Squab trained the IZLID's beam on the part of the building where the vehicles were, and the Hornets, after being talked onto it, each dropped an MK-83 thousand-pound dumb bomb, scoring a hit with one and missing with the other.

Suddenly, the Tomcat's temperamental laser flicked back on. Now the FAC-As could guide the Hornets' Mavericks. "Things get a lot easier here as all we have to do is get the target under our crosshairs without the intermediate pain of getting their eyes on the target," wrote Squab. They guided the Mavericks onto another of the vehicles and "on one mortar pit that looked occupied." Then the Hornets were out of bombs. They left. Wrex and Squab finished by lasering two of their own GBU-12s and then left to tank.

So far, so good. But they still needed a wingman. Now they used their power as FAC-As. When they got to the tanker, Alvin and Loose, both ranking lieutenant commanders, were taking gas. Having finished a mission, they were on their way back to the carrier. Wrex and Squab had another idea. They requisitioned the two hinges. "Even though we're lieutenants, we're in charge," said Squab. "We can take strike assets. . . . We decided on our own that we are extending them for the double cycle. . . . It's kind of cool to have that ability."

Hinges in tow, gas tanks refilled, the two FAC-As left the tanker to hunt for more targets. They still had a lot of timely reconnaissance photos, most of them probably from TARPS. The photos led them to a field with eight revetments and a small airstrip. Five of the revetments were arranged in a pattern that, from the air, looked like the famous Olympic Rings—three on the top, two on the bottom, all interlocking. They were near the airstrip. Three other revetments were on the far side of the field.

A division of Hornets was inbound. Not wanting to waste any time, especially on a target that might be alerted, Wrex and Squab decided to lase their remaining two bombs. "As we drop one, we go to the next revetment," said Squab, "and as we're in our target run [for the second], our Hornets are checking in. I'm saying, 'You know, hold on a second, let me drop this bomb right quick.' We drop, and as we're guiding it, I'm giving them coordinates. 'Here's my laser code, come on in,' and so on. . . . Everything is going like clockwork."

Coming back around, they started the Hornets on their runs. Now Alvin and Loose had a part. Squab lased for the lead Hornet. Loose, increasingly becoming known as perhaps the most accurate RIO-bomber in the squadron, lased for the wingman. As the lead Hornet was about a mile from his release point, Squab's laser failed again. "Fortunately, I noticed it in time to tell them, 'Hey, abort our striker, but let the other guy drop his,' " said Squab.

Loose lased his bomb to a direct hit.

Returning for another pass, Squab gave all the Hornets Loose's laser code. "Now we are the FACs, with Loose as our external laser. So we talk with them on one radio to confirm DMPIs for the strikers, and we do the normal target com with the strikers on the other radio," Squab wrote. "The thing that was awesome was the coordination required and how flawlessly it went," he later said. "We'd come up like, 'Olympic Rings or group of three,' and we'd get, 'Roger that, we're gonna hit the targets with the Olympic Rings.' " Back on the carrier, Squab wrote: "The [five-hour] hop was a superb example of crew coordination between jets as well as within our jet for IZLID employment."

But he didn't mention the buildup.

Two days later, Serb intentions would became obvious.

On May 29, Wrex and Squab flew wing to Tophatters skipper Slapshot and Scooter Moyer on a morning mission to blow up a mountain tunnel in southwest Kosovo. The tunnel entrance was deep in a ravine and hard to get to. Weather further obscured the target. The Tomcats were only able to knock overhead dirt and rock into the tunnel's entrance. The debris could be cleared in a matter of hours. The urgency of the mission at that time, if there was any, was not alluded to in Squab's diary entry. But that afternoon, when Dog and Wog were given the assignment to go back and finish the job, blasting the tunnel had become a priority. Waiting to use it was a large Serbian force whose objective was to attack a nearby village. "They were trying to clear the tunnel out so bad guys could come through and wreak havoc on this little town," said Dog.

The tunnel, near Prizren, Kosovo's largest southern city, was surrounded by curling mountain ranges. The only way to get to it was to fly down a deep and steep ravine, a valley of sorts, and hope the laser beam could be held on the entrance long enough for the bomb to arrive before the pilot had to rise sharply and disappear over the mountains at the far end. Any deviation, including going up and over the mountains, would break the beam. "They were telling us, 'hey, they're trying to open it up again,'" said Dog, "'and we don't want that because there's a lot of fighting going on with the rebels and whatnot and we don't want them to get through. Go get it.'"

Obviously, the chain of command was now aware of the offensive.

So Dog and Wog launched. Details about the mission makeup are sketchy, but they carried a two-thousand-pound penetrator. When they got there, the weather again was bad. But they were determined. "We had to get this thing, or there's gonna be hell to pay for this village," said Dog.

They took a low track to delivery. "We kinda cheated a little bit on the [official] altitude [floor]," said Wog. There was no other way. On the run in, Wog was looking at the tunnel entrance in the FLIR and had his pipper on it. But the entrance seemed to be moving. "I'm wondering, 'What am I doing wrong? The tunnel's wobbling.'" As he got closer, they realized the movement was a bulldozer pushing debris.

They had to work fast. When the tunnel was opened, the waiting Serb army would rush through.

They made the bomb drop okay, but as they counted off the seconds until impact, the mountains at the far end of their route were coming up fast. Dog had to keep the jet from blocking the laser beam while also weaving through low-hung clouds. It was tough and precise flying. "We're going real slow, and I'm doin' a bunch of turns," said Dog. "The ridge is coming, and [the laser] can't see through the mountains."

He couldn't fly through them either.

At one point, trying to delay the inevitable, he got down to about two hundred knots—so slow that he thought he was going to stall the jet. "If a missile came up at us, we would have been dead," said Dog. "But we gotta make this thing, you know, because . . . this is our only shot."

The bulldozer, oblivious, continued to remove debris from the earlier raid.

On the video of the strike, Dog can be heard grunting to the bomb, "Come on, come on, come on." At the same time, he was vigorously working the Tomcat's controls, teetering the jet on the brink of falling out of the sky in front of the mountain in order to prolong the run.

Their dangerous efforts worked.

"The two-thousand-pounder misses the bulldozer by about three feet and hits right where we wanted it to," said Dog. "It caves in the whole tunnel."

Freed of the lasering, Dog gunned it, and they roared skyward.

But swinging back, they saw the mangled bulldozer on a ridge below the caved tunnel. It was still smoldering from a horrendous fall. The sight brought a sudden realization. "I said to Wog, 'We've killed a lot of people, but today we actually saw the guy.' . . . You think, 'Boy, he's part of the bad guys, and the bad guys are not doin' good work down there.' But, you know, maybe he has a family. Maybe he has no choice but to be there. . . . Milosevic, you know, is not an equal-opportunity employer. . . . This is my job, and we do not pick the war. . . . However, I'm an American who saw a terrible injustice going on and was in a position to stop it, and that certainly makes you feel better about what you do."

Wog said: "The bomb took the bulldozer and blew it off the side. . . . As I was flyin' home, I realized, 'I went, I killed someone.' . . . It wasn't just me droppin' a bomb in a hole somewhere or blowin' up a piece of dirt. There was somebody operating that piece of machinery, and he's not goin' home to his mom or dad, or wife or kids, tonight. And I kinda thought about that for a little bit. It didn't deter me from what I'm doin'. But I actually stopped and . . . said a little prayer for the guy and his family. . . . I saw that vehicle moving. I knew there was some-body drivin' that vehicle, and he wasn't drivin' it anymore. It was layin' on the floor of that cliff."

They'd helped save a village—anonymous people they'd never met, but whom they knew in a general sense from CNN and other news sources and for whom they had risked their lives.

It was more than political talk.

And that was just the beginning of the slaughter.

In the coming days, Dewar and Squab would find a line of tanks near the Albanian border. Being careful not to hit Albanians, whom they now knew were operating in the area, they guided Hornet hits on five of the eight tanks—not a terrific score, but one good enough for the normally skeptical Dewar (skeptical about what they actually hit) to call the hop his "Fun FAC mission." Bru and Joey would actually find a Serb tank hiding on a college campus, so desperate would the Serbs be to get to their objective. "Towards the end," said Beaker, "they finally came out, and it was like turning the lights on and seeing all the cockroaches at night. We were able to swoop down and whack them."

What was developing as the FAC-As found the Serbs in increasing numbers could be called the "Kosovo Turkey Shoot." The Serbs knew they were beaten. The air war was relentless, and they had limited war supplies. In their all-out push to inflict final damages on the Albanians before the inevitable end of hostilities, the Serbs were abandoning their cat-and-mouse tactics and coming out in the open to kill or be killed.

Mostly, it was the latter.

Bru's first awareness of the offensive, he guessed, was in early June, when he and Joey were called by air force A-10 pilots to an area south-west of Dakovica. It was late in the afternoon. A UAV had seen refugees streaming out of the city and being shelled on a main east-west artery leading into Albania. The A-10 pilots, who were FAC-As, had been sent down to stop the shelling. But the area was mountainous and had a lot of hills and valleys, and the late afternoon shadows were prohib-iting them from seeing their prey.

"They wanted us to use our FLIR," said Bru.

Almost as soon as he got the call, Bru said he knew exactly where he'd start looking. He and Joey had frequently passed the mountainous area going to other targets. It had a hill that overlooked the road. It reminded him of a mound on the west side of Bartlesville. "I always said, 'You know, if I was a military guy, I'd be up on that high ground shelling down into the valley.' "

When they arrived, Bru trained his binoculars on the hill. "I just go, 'Holy cow!' " What he saw was "three tanks, a couple of really big trucks, and a couple of armed personnel carriers." Eventually, after further reconnoitering, he guessed he and Joey identified twelve "pieces" on both sides of the hill. They were attended by a good num-ber of soldiers. All were taking part in the shelling. The FAC-As had received reports on ship of increased killing of fleeing civilians by Serbs, including one report that stuck in Bru's mind. It was about a "Serbian with a gun who had told his neighbors, who were ethnic Albanians, to leave and then burned their house."

He'd thought the action particularly treacherous.

"I'll tell you when it got personal to me," he said. "There was this time when I was watching CNN and they showed little kids being run out of their country. And there was this one little boy that was just, he was walking along and whether it was just the camera angle or what, you saw the refugees and this little four-year-old just crying his eyes out. He looked like the most lonely orphan you've ever imagined. And I thought, 'You know, somebody has got to make this stuff stop.' . . . And the other time was the first of May when that volley of SA-6s and stuff came up at us. That really, 'cause that's when I thought of my daughter Baily, my wife, and Mallory, and I thought, 'You guys, now you're pissing me off.' "

Now they were seeing proof of the reports with their own eyes.

Realizing the better detection capabilities of the LANTIRN, the A-10 pilots turned control of the area over to Bru and Joey, who started, with a vengeance, trying to stop the slaughter. The A-10s had Rockeye, which Bru termed "particularly nasty." The navy FAC-As had one of the Warthogs go after the Serbs on the western side of the hill and the other hit them on the eastern side. According to Bru, one of the air force pilots asked, " 'How many do you want me to drop?' I said, 'All of them, of course.' He goes, 'Roger that,' and rolls in. It was hell on earth down there. It's just like a bunch of popcorn going off. And then the fires started. I mean vehicles started bursting into flame. Second-aries were going off. . . . That Rockeye killed a bunch of guys. It was pretty sick. . . . Then me and my wingman, I think it was Dog and Wog, we went around and started circling the wagons, popping the lids off those tanks."

As they were directing the fire, other FAC-As in the area heard the carnage and were attracted. Comparisons could be made to sharks or vultures. But killing was their business, and their arrival would help stop the shelling of innocent civilians. Among the arrivals were C. J. Denny, with Slapshot in his backseat. There were still targets left. Bru and Joey wanted to reconnoiter nearby. They told Slapshot and the others to finish up. The targets were clearly marked by then. They went south with the two A-10s, each of which still had a Maverick left. They were betting that they could find other enemy concentrations.

They purposely went high so that the Serbs couldn't see them from the ground. They followed a side road from the hill. Joey worked the LANTIRN looking for heat signatures. About ten miles away, they found what they surmised to be an armored personnel carrier and a five-ton truck pulling an artillery piece. The targets were traveling down the road in a direction away from the hill. "At first we're going, 'Well, let's hit that,'" said Bru. "But then we got to thinking, 'Well, wait. Let's see where they're going.'"

They followed the vehicles.

"Sure enough, they go on down about five more miles and pull into what looks like a burned-out building," said Bru. "But it's really not. Just the top floor is burned out. They have a headquarters or something on the bottom floor. These two vehicles pull in, and there's about thirty other vehicles all staged in this area. Armored personnel carriers, artillery tubes. All sorts of stuff. The only weapons we've got are the Mavericks on the two A-10s."

They were low on gas, and some Hornets were due to arrive as strikers. They lased one of the A-10s' Mavericks into the lead vehicle that had just pulled up in front of the burned-out building. As the rocket-bomb sped to its DMPI, "we see [in the FLIR] the guy getting out of the vehicle that was pulling the artillery tube," said Bru. "He's sort of walking toward the building. He gets right to the door when the weapon hits the truck that he just exited."

The truck blew up, either killing the driver or emphasizing to him what a very close call he'd just had.

They do not know which.

As they continued, eight Hornets had shown up, including one piloted by CAG. They were carrying Rockeye and laser Mavericks. This new area was also mountainous. Twilight and bad weather were approaching. The combination of clouds and peaks made it hard for lasing. "We're trying to get where we can shoot a laser down to take out these other vehicles," said Bru. But the topography and increasing low clouds meant the Tomcat would have to go lower if they were going to get the job done—a dangerous situation.

"We sent out wingman to the tanker," said Bru, "and we've got these F-18s overhead covering us while we're down trying to get to where we've got laser line of sight so they can shoot their Mavericks." The mountains were about eight thousand feet high. Bru and Joey descended to about twelve thousand feet on their altimeter. Technically, they were above the ten thousand-foot minimum floor established to keep Allied planes safe from the enemy antiaircraft fire, whether Triple-A or SAMs. But in reality, they were only 4,000 feet from the mountain peaks—and from any enemy weapons on them. That meant they were actually in range. Suddenly, Triple-A started bursting all around them. "It's a screwup on my part," said Bru. "I've gotten low enough where they can shoot us."

Simultaneously, they hear C. J. and Slapshot, back at the site they left, calling a SAM shot. The missile appeared to be fired at the Tophatters, but the curvature of its route made it also appear as if it might be threatening Bru and Joey, who were only about ten miles away.

Suddenly, they had a very tense situation.

Bru: "I look down and see the muzzle flashes [of the Triple-A] as they are coming up. . . . So I plug in the afterburners and put the jet on its ass and go straight up. . . . I'm going, 'Dear God, let me get above this stuff before one of those lucky BBs ends up hitting us.' In the meantime, I'm kind of aiming towards Albania so that if we end up having to jump out we'll at least land over there and not in Kosovo."

As he climbed, he instinctively started directing fire.

"While we're climbing up, I'm explaining as best I can to the lower Hornets [one of which is piloted by CAG], 'You see the triangle lake? . . . Go just north of that to an east-west road. You see that?' He [the Hornet] says, 'Contact that.' I go, 'The road makes a zig and a zag and runs north. The zig to the west is where Number One [Hornet] needs to drop his Rockeye. And the zag to the east is where Number Two needs to drop.' "

As they powered up, the two F/A-18s roared closely by them going straight down and obliterated the SAM sites with Rockeye.

Nearby, C. J. and Slapshot had attacked the SAM launching sites and destroyed those.

Bru and Joey didn't stick around for the results. They were now in serious need of gas. Coming out of their climb at a safe altitude, they turned due south and sped for the tanker. They still had the additional obstacle of bad weather to go through before they could get the gas. As they streaked, they asked one of the Hornets whether either of the sites was still shooting."

The Hornet pilot responded, "Oh, no. You ought to see it down here."

It was another slaughter.

•   •   •

By June 3, Yugoslav officials had accepted in principle the NATO peace plan. But last-minute objections by Milosevic meant the fighting would continue. Both sides upped their military efforts. In the meantime, other Aces had their own encounters with the heightened Serb presence:

Thing remembers finding four targets on one hop. The first was a mobile Triple-A truck that had been disabled by an earlier bombing but still appeared capable of shooting. They had TARPs pictures of it sitting in the middle of a Dakovica intersection. When he arrived, they destroyed the truck with one of their own bombs, then found other enemy vehicles in nearby revetments. They called in Hornets and buddy-lased for them, blasting the revetments. After tanking, they got coordinates from an airborne radar, probably AWACs, which had spotted an artillery piece shelling a village. "That was amazing," said the RIO. "They got it to us real quick, right after the piece had started firing. We dropped a bomb on it. Blew chunks everywhere." Their last vector was to a field dotted with artillery. They lased their final bomb and then brought in a section of A-10s to finish the job.

Wrex and Squab won Joey's praise for their action on a night mission — but then found out that what they'd done had almost caused an international incident.

The mission had started out routinely. They were wingmen for Razor and Slugz; both sections working as strikers for the air force. They'd hit targets down south in the buildup when the A-10s controlling them ran out of gas and left. Instead of going home, as was their option, Wrex and Squab requested permission from Moonbeam, the air force AWACS, to do a little FAC-A. Permission was granted. Leaders now, they took Razor and Slugz back to an area along the Albanian border where Squab with Dewar had earlier hit a line of tanks. With the heightened Serb activity, they figured it would be a good place to recheck.

To their surprise, the armor was still there — or at least it looked that way in the night-penetrating FLIR. "I'm wondering why they hadn't run away," said Squab, cognizant of Serb tricks, "but I don't consider that for very long because, hey, we got targets." Because they hadn't been scheduled as FAC-As, they only had about ten-to-fifteen minutes left before they'd have to go "feet wet" (fly back to the ocean) in order to make their recovery time on the carrier. Antsy, but wanting to squeeze every productive moment out of the night they could, they radioed Moonbeam for quick permission to attack. While waiting, they circled, preparing for the strike. Permission came with only a few minutes left. Mindful of how close they were to the border, said Joey, who commented later, they queried the AWACS, " 'Are you sure you want us to take them out?' "

The answer was an emphatic yes.

It was all the Aces needed to hear. They were already set to drop. In a mere ninety seconds, they lased five bombs and destroyed every-thing they'd targeted. "It was a work of art," said Joey about the FAC-A job. "Really incredible how precise and timed out they had it." The skipper gave them an "attaboy" when they returned, wrote Squab, "for being proactive and driving the show." But what none of them knew until later that night was that the targets weren't Serbian; they were Albanian. The "tanks" were actually covered Albanian pillboxes that were part of an Albanian border station. "Furthermore," wrote Squab, "there happened to be a news crew on the road at the border station as our bombs begin blowing up a few hundred meters from them."

Luckily, the Albanians had exited the pillboxes prior to the bombs hitting. "CNN had footage that we saw in the ready room," said Bru. "There's this guy [a reporter] saying, 'As you can see behind us, there are NATO airplanes. . . .' All of a sudden the bombs start going off right behind him. . . . They [the news crew] are like, 'Shit!' They started running away. . . ."

Neither Wrex nor Squab got into trouble "because we had been so careful with release authority," wrote Squab. The mistake was the CAOC's, said Joey, who had to explain it to CAG.

Luckily, they had the tapes to prove it.

The ground fighting got so furious at the very end, said Joey, that he witnessed hand-to-hand combat. "You could see it escalating," he said, "tanks firing, men running. Vehicles fighting one another." He remem-bered a hill about twenty miles south of Dakovica on the Albanian bor-der, called Mount Pastrik by some Aces, as a scene of clashing armies. "It was vehicles and tanks going up the hill chasing small packs of guys run-ning back into Albania. It's hard to distinguish people in the LANTIRN, but you could see muzzle flashes and smoke from the tank barrels." Bin-oculars confirmed what the LANTIRN indicated. "The hills were 6,000 to 8,000 feet high," he said. "We would dip down to around 12,000, and then you'd only be 4,000 or 5,000 above it. You could see everything. . . . We went after the tanks. . . . Basically, the armored stuff was the Serbs, and the Kosovars were the packs of men."

Certain areas amid the clashes were off-limits. These were the areas where the KLA was operating. After dropping their own bombs, Joey and Bru began directing A-10 fire at the Mount Pastrik battle. "We specifically went after big targets, moving targets." The clashes got so big that a B-1 bomber was sent. "I think it was from England," said Joey. The big stealth jet's pilots wanted to make sure they had the right coordinates, and since Bru and Joey were the FAC-As in the area, they used their laser to update the bomber's drop information. It spread a line of some thirty Mark 82 free-fall bombs on the hill, blasting tanks and armored personnel carriers. The explosions progressed like machine-gun fire, said Joey. "Pretty impressive."

In another action, Bru and Joey deconflicted airspace for three B-52s from England that were preparing to carpet bomb from 45,000 feet up. The FAC-As declared a ten-mile-square chunk of sky off-limits so that no Allied aircraft would be hit by the falling bombs. Ironically, the leader of the flight was an old friend of Bru from the days when both had flown Hornets. Bru, unaware of it at the time, joked with Joey that he knew one of the B-52 pilots, and wouldn't it be funny if he was in the flight? After the war, Bru found out that the friend had been leading it. On another occasion, they chased Serb helicopters hoping for an air-to-air kill.

They never found them.

But the rout was clearly on.

With FAC-A established and the threat diminishing, more missions went to the second and third teams, including the nuggets. A kind of competition set in. "I think by the end, everyone wanted to drop the last bomb," said Thing. "You know, 'Hey, yea for me!' If someone else goes out [on a mission], then I need to go out. Everybody got comfortable. . . . Yeah, I'm over bad-guy land, but they're not going to touch me, or I can get away. . . . We started breaking every rule you could think about."

The younger Aces who hadn't performed started making their marks.

Lupe had already proven himself. For instance, flying wing to several senior aviators on a Pristina mini-strike, he and his backseater, Mo

Vaught, suddenly were thrust into the lead when mechanical failures in the other planes forced the scheduled leaders home. Lupe "did just an awesome job," recalled Mo, a senior RIO, about the mission. "I'm assholes and elbows because I'm not expecting to lead." The two found the target, led the others on their runs, and put a bomb "right through the front doors" of a Serb ammunition vault. Rhino eventually got his confidence up by finding a target on a mission with Dog. They didn't drop because weather kept breaking the lase. But on his next mission with Meat, he delivered a bomb that destroyed a radar tower.

He considered it an adequate deflowering.

Jack Corlett, however, had to wait until June 8 before he got some joy. The young pilot had dropped his first bomb in mid-May. But continued landing problems, plus a near tanking accident, had kept him in the doghouse. Then, sitting spare for a FAC-A striker mission during the Turkey Shoot, he was launched as Dewar and Squab's wing-man with Double in his backseat. As an LSO, Dewar was one of his constant critics, and he must have been uneasy. But he'd attended the briefs and felt "mission-capable." Because of Double's experience, he'd been detailed to help Jack, and the two had become friends. After tanking, they joined Dewar and Squab and headed to the border area south of Dakovica.

Their targets were some tanks firing into a village from a hillside above it. The weather was lousy, and Dewar and Squab were having trouble lasing their bombs. They had to go under the clouds. Being the spare, Jack and Double's Tomcat didn't have a LANTIRN. Although they had a two-thousand-pound bomb, they were staying above the clouds, acting as cover. Jack, trying to do the best he could, kept tabs on his leader with a cockpit monitor called a "fighter link." The device, resembling a video display, showed him where Dewar and Squab were relative to his own position. As a result, when Dewar and Squab popped back up through the clouds, having run out of their own bombs, he was able to quickly join them and return with them for another bomb run on which they would lase his two-thousand-pounder.

"We're going through the clouds," he remembers. "I'm not sure what our altitude is. It's a real varsity condition [i.e., demanding skillful flying]." They broke out from under the clouds, pointed down and rapidly gaining speed. "Squabie found a tank right next to a tree, and they say, 'Three . . . two . . . one . . . pitbull.' I drop my bomb and pull off high and left. They lased it all the way in and ended up getting a direct hit on the tank."

The buddy-lase had largely been possible because of Jack's awareness and flying ability. When they returned to the ship, Dewar congratulated him in front of everybody in the ready room. "He was actually singing my praises, saying I did a real good job. . . . Whenever you hit the target like that, I mean those tanks were dropping bombs into a village. And, you know, it's kind of lopsided. And when you can . . . make it a little more even, you feel pretty good. . . . I was always [Dewar's] problem child. But for him to see me do this really cool rendezvous, you know, in the clouds, he probably thought in the back of his mind that, you know, my skills as a pilot weren't that good. But when he saw this, I think it probably changed his opinion a lot."

It was a welcome relief.

According to the October 1999 issue of *Air Force* magazine (vol. 82, no.10), a panel of generals and other military experts convened by the Air Force Association to study the Kosovo War concluded that the "attacks on Serbian forces massed to counter" the KLA "in the latter days of the war were most important in convincing the Serbian army to relent." By June 9, the Serbs were ready to sign. The signing was to take place at 4 P.M. in a tent at Skopje, Macedonia. As a result, NATO put tight reins on air operations again. FAC-As had to be sure to get clearances to drop. Altitude restrictions were to be strictly adhered to. Nevertheless, the squadron scheduled missions as it always had. "They told us, 'We don't want to escalate this thing,'" said Bru. "Just go up there, and don't expect anything to happen."

Bru and Joey, with Dog and Wog on their wing, had the midday SCAR. After checking in, they got a report from the E-2 controller that a helicopter was coming south from Pristina. The E-2 told them that as soon as their Prowler arrived, they should take off after it. "I'm thinking, 'You're kidding me? The war's about to end.'" But they also still wanted that air-to-air kill.

As soon as the Prowler arrived, they went in looking. The weather was bad, and they spent considerable time searching, but the helo eluded them. "Probably set down by then." They started "snooping around" but were cautious because of the restrictions. Then the E-2 radioed that it had an SA-9 site it wanted them to hit. "Now, we're really surprised. This is completely different from what we expected," said Bru.

The SA-9 is a small SAM. This one was mounted on a "humvee"-type vehicle. They found it very close to the Skopje peace-signing site—perhaps ten miles away, just inside the Kosovo border. They radioed, " 'Are you sure you want us to hit this?' " The E-2, talking to higher authorities, said yes.

They were low on gas. "We're kind of casual about it," said Bru, "not wanting to screw it up at this point." Tanking was certainly prudent. They went. When they came back, the weather had gotten very bad. They had to go up to forty-five thousand feet for awhile to avoid it. When they came back down, the peace signing was just minutes away. But the answer was still yes.

Definitely yes.

"So we go, 'Well, okay,' " said Bru. "I look down at my watch, and it's about five minutes to four, and we're close enough in my opinion that they're going to hear the bombs . . . Somebody was talking to somebody who said it would be really nice if we kinda nudge them right up until the signing—at least that's my perception."

Whether that was the case or not, they began their runs. Bru and Joey's LANTIRN dysfunctioned, and Dog and Wog buddy-lased for them. In order to get a good guide, they had to go under the clouds—which put them below the ten-thousand-foot floor restriction—but they destroyed the site.

Theirs were the last bombs dropped in the Kosovo War.

"The party is over," wrote Squab in his diary.

Nineteen

The Aces flew several more days of missions in Kosovo, but they were mainly to show power. No bombs were dropped, no shots fired.

On June 11, Bru and others in the squadron flew CAP for American marines who were arriving on the ground to enforce the agreed-upon Serb military withdrawal. Russian troops made a surprise entrance at the Pristina airport, briefly raising tensions in the area, but prompting little concern in the ready room. The aviators knew they weren't going to be sent against the Russians unless something outrageous happened, which wasn't likely. The politicians wanted peace. Many of the younger Aces' minds were already on an upcoming training exercise in which a select detachment of them would crew their Tomcats against German MiG-29s — a formidable air-to-air test. Dogfighting was what the F-14 was made for and what most of its pilots and RIOs enjoyed doing the most. While Joey and the squadron leadership would have loved to have competed in the practice fights, the skipper had already decided that he would send mostly JOs and nuggets like Lupe. It would be a kind of payback to most of them for missing important missions at the war's beginning.

By 2 A.M. several nights later, a crowd of Aces was drinking and dancing in Dirty Nelly's, one of the loudest hair-on-fire night spots in Palma de Majorca, the beautiful Spanish island in the Mediterranean where the *Roosevelt* anchored for a needed postwar liberty. The current

Black Aces had been blooded, and they'd survived. Not one casualty. And they'd been part of a victory. It was certainly something to celebrate. The Irish-themed bar was an old favorite of Joey's from earlier cruises. But he and Dog were more like parents, nursing drinks separately around the dance floor and watching their "kids" having a good time. They were shepherding them, making sure none got into any serious trouble.

They need not have worried. The aviators were on good behavior. Razor, in a highlight, sang and led songs from the bandstand, his buddies swaying in drink-raising joy. They had participated in the longest airwar since Vietnam—arguably the first war ever won by air power alone. They'd done so in aging, thirty-year-old airplanes, not the state-of-the-art machines the public usually pictures. The Tomcats, although upgraded, had been in need of constant maintenance—and received just that from the squadron's unsung technicians, who toiled on long shifts in the carrier's hot, sweaty innards. The Aces had to break rules and be extremely innovative in the face of bomb and other shortages in order to do what they were asked. They had been restrained in their use of force. If they'd fought the war from fifteen thousand feet, as the politicians, afraid of body counts, had dictated, they probably would not have succeeded. But their leaders, despite the handicaps, were not going to be denied. "People do not understand our tenacity and resolve," said Dog. "We do not lose. We are very good. If somebody wants to come up and test our resolve, they are going to be sent home with their tail between their legs. With all the shortcomings talked about in the press, there is still no one to compare with us."

They had shown an extraordinary regard for innocent human life, and had sincerely risked their own lives, which is contrary to the war-mongering, brutish image of them often in the press. Various sources say that while they flew approximately 15 percent of the NATO sorties, they destroyed 30-some percent of the targets, dropping thousands of tons of ordnance in hundreds of combat missions. The cold hard statistics are classified, but the last entry in Squab's Kosovo diary gives an individual perspective:

```
This mission [was] very difficult. Being a FAC [A] with
troops on the ground would [have been] so much easier . . .
the Marines on the ground would [have done] most of the target
```

recce for us. . . . Our primary challenge [would have been] not [to] endanger the Marines we were supporting. [But without] the ground troops . . . the entire problem of reconnaissance and target identification fell to us. . . . [It] was an almost overwhelming task. . . . So why did we [succeed]? It became apparent fairly quickly that the success of the Navy in Kosovo and the success of the F-14 FAC [A] program relied on us being successful [at] targeting the fielded forces. . . . We worked very hard at cracking this nut. . . . [If we found revetments] and got ordnance off the strikers, it was tremendously relieving. Conversely, if we did not find any targets . . . we felt like failures. . . . I am convinced that it was the air campaign that brought Milosevic to the table. I don't believe it was the threat of a ground offensive because I do not believe that threat was credible. We weren't going to commit ground troops, plain and simple. . . . We may not actually have destroyed very many pieces of his war-fighting machine. This is largely due to the fact that almost all of his machine was cowering in holes and hiding spots which can be seen as a success if you like.

After Palma, the *Roosevelt* sped to the Persian Gulf, where the Aces helped enforce United Nations no-fly rules over Iraq. It wasn't a war; it was more like a border patrol or police action. But it was still against the hateful Saddam Hussein and the first time a modern carrier had fought in two combat zones during a single cruise. The Gulf had its perils. The heat was ghastly—sometimes 120 degrees on the flight deck, and worse below, if that can be imagined. Dog had a major inflight emergency but brought the crippled jet in. Periodically, they dropped bombs. Once, Dewar and Squab, after seniors went down, had to lead an important strike when they were only the spare. They wowed Joey and Bru by doing so. But mostly the squadron just went through the motions of bombing, performing all associated tasks except for the actual drop. There had to be a "triggering event" for that to be authorized. They used the runs as practice.

Several times Aces were involved in air-wing rope-a-dope traps to lure Iraqi MiGs into flying violations. The object was to have grounds to shoot them down. But the wily plans never bore fruit. On their last mission before returning home—a night hop—Wrex and Razor, true to their natures, filled their tanks after a routine mission and had a practice dogfight in the Arabian moonlight. The nugget RIOs in their backseats could only hold on. "Totally illegal. Totally fun," said Razor. "It was like, 'Who can get the fastest . . . the highest . . . just blowing it out?' "

It was a kind of farewell to what would possibly be their only combat cruise, a cruise they would never forget, a cruise that for the aviators would be jauntily remembered with phrases like "kick 'em in the Balkans" and "precision diplomacy."

There were other individual stories but nothing topping those about the war. The Aces, in Iraq, were honed and deadly—a fighter squadron at its peak. They had coalesced in Kosovo. When strikes were authorized, direct hits became the norm. In fact, 41 would later win the 1999 McClusky Award, given annually by the chief of Naval Operations to the best attack squadron in the navy. *The Best.* It would be a major and unique honor—the first time a squadron flying a Tomcat, basically a fighter plane, had ever won the award, which was named for a World War II naval aviator who led strikes sinking Japanese carriers in the Battle of Midway. Their competition would be major league—every Tomcat and Hornet squadron in the navy.

But winning the McClusky Award was still in the future when the *Roosevelt* left the gulf in mid-September. The Aces only knew they'd done their job. To Joey, that alone was a "tremendous satisfaction . . . I'm just fortunate. . . . I mean there are guys, and all they want to be is a fighter-squadron skipper. Not many guys get it. But to be successful . . . leading combat . . . I'll have that for the rest of my life. . . . And even more than combat is leading a squadron that feels good about themselves. . . . I told you how we were on the '97 cruise, guys not feeling good about the squadron, from the troopers to the officers. To transform that squadron from one that didn't feel good about themselves to one that really felt good about themselves was the biggest thing. Even more than combat."

The Aces' achievement bore witness to the fact that humans, not technology, were still the deciding factor in warfare. All the high-tech advantages believed to be possessed by America's flyers may not have mattered had the individual aviators not risen to the task. What would have happened had Bru not forced the issue and Joey not backed him? And CAG Lyle and Admiral Copeland, strong fighting commanders, had not given them their rein? The answer is speculative. But ask any fighting man, and he'll say that warriors, not their machines, are paramount—the major ingredient in any successful campaign.

The warriors had turned the tide.

Joey wouldn't get the top ranking among his peers. Slapshot got that. Joey got number two. But as Admiral Copeland would remark after the war, "Joey may not have been the number-one CO in the entire air wing. But at the end of the day, he was the number-one warfighter."

There could be no better compliment. And Joey's ranking would be good enough to get him what he wanted anyway—eventual assignment as a CAG, which he would be promised, after a year of graduate studies at Harvard, as a kind of perk for his special achievement. He and Bru would win Silver Stars along with other medals; Squab, a Distinguished Flying Cross, with the other FAC-As and Salami being honored, too.

Dog, who was instrumental in getting medals awarded to his squadron mates, would inherit the Aces, becoming CO after the squadron returned. Wog would go to Washington to work with space reconnaissance. Wrex went to Top Gun at Oceana; Razor to an adversary squadron at NAS Fallon, Nevada, the same base where Bru (who would become a minor legend in strike warfare for what he did), Squab, and Gooch went in other capacities. Dewar would go to the F-14 Replacement Air Group (RAG) at Oceana, where, among other duties, he would become a Tomcat demonstration pilot. Most of the younger Aces stayed with the squadron, moving up to take the places of the flyers ahead of them, who either left or advanced in the squadron in the navy's continual system of movement and replenishment. In doing so, they would become the hinges and senior and junior JOs to the squadron's newly assigned nuggets.

To Joey, nothing better exemplified the squadron's level of achievement than the fly-in the Aces performed when they arrived back at Oceana. He wanted it good, and he got it good.

As usual, things hadn't started out well. Bad weather, fueled by Hurricane Gert in the Atlantic south of them, threatened the arrival. But they launched. He was flying with Dog, his old friend. As they got close, they went into a wedge formation — eleven jets assembled like a triangle of bowling pins stacked in an alley. He and Dog were in the lead at the tip of the triangle. Keeping the formation tight was hard. It was also dangerous. At intervals, in an exacting cadence, he commanded pairs of Tomcats to peel off as the wedge flew over the field, starting with the rear outer tips of the triangle. "Guys can't see the other guys break, so they are trusting whoever is leading them to give them the right time."

The interval was every three seconds. "Just seeing all those planes around me and then telling them to break. 'Seven, eight. Break now. Three, four. Break now.' And just seeing them rip across the sky and land on parallel runways. All of them safely. I just thought, 'I really have a great squadron. . . .' "

They all came in together, parking in a row. They shut down their engines in unison, raised their canopies on command. "It went so picture perfect. . . . Then you see your little boy run out. I'd barely seen him since he was born."

Dog, climbing out, watched his wife and five-year-old daughter approach. "When [my daughter] came up to me, it was like she morphed . . . her face just went tragic, and she broke down and started to cry. If you look at her closely, she's in a fetal position. She just melted into my arms. And a moment after that picture was taken, she looked at her mother, who was standing behind her, and said, 'Mom, I'm not crying because Daddy gave me too big a hug, or I'm sad. I don't understand it. I'm crying because I'm happy.' "

Dog cried, too.

Aftermath

On June 18, 2000, roughly a year after the Kosovo War ended, Bill "Dewar" Dye, was killed in an air-show accident at NAS Willow Grove, Pennsylvania. He was flying a Tomcat. It is ironic as well as tragic that he would go through the entire war unscathed except for liberty cuts and nicks and then die in his airplane at home. But, of course, it underlies the danger that all aviators, especially military aviators, accept in pursuing their jobs.

Dewar was riding a crest. He'd finished the war as the number-one JO and later been picked for the navy's Tomcat demonstration team — an honor that goes only to the best Tomcat instructors available. He was hoping to become a member of the Blue Angels, the navy's premier demonstration team (they fly Hornets), for which he'd submitted a request heartily endorsed by Captain Lyle.

But it wasn't in the cards.

The accident occurred on a Sunday. It was Father's Day. Dewar's fifteen-month-old daughter, Kamryn, and his wife, Deborah, had driven the several hundred miles from Virginia Beach to see him in the show, which was performed Saturday and again on Sunday. His mother and father had come too. He and his backseater, David Bergstrom, another VF-101 instructor, had practiced the maneuver on Friday. The family had watched him do it on Saturday. It was a wave-off from a simulated carrier landing. The Tomcat would come in slowing in front of the crowd, then be waved off for another pass.

Neither his wife and daughter nor his parents had stayed for the Sunday show. Dewar and his wife were planning a Father's Day celebration that night back at Virginia Beach. She left in a car with Kamryn earlier that Sunday morning. Dewar was to do the show and then fly back late that afternoon. The couple had just celebrated their fifth wedding anniversary. They had been married shortly after he'd been winged at Pensacola and were very close, even though, in a sense, they were opposites. "It's ironic because I'm a social worker," said Deborah, still grieving nearly a year after the crash. "The joke between us was that I'm always out to save the world and he could always drop a bomb on it. So I think he was almost reserved sometimes, being unsure the family accepted what he did. . . . But we know the navy protects our country. They do such an amazing job." Not until after he'd returned from Kosovo had he been able to spend any time with little Kamryn. They'd induced Deborah's labor so that he could at least be there for the birth before he left.

So that night would have been Kamryn's first Father's Day celebration with her dad. The Tomcat came in low and slowing for the simulated approach. From the loudspeaker, the air show's audience heard the simulated wave-off and saw the Tomcat power skyward and away, presumably to come around and make another approach. But something went wrong. They were in one of the old A-models. Power didn't kick in fast. Eyewitness accounts vary, but all indicate that the fighter never really gained altitude as it should have. It was supposed to make a wide, sweeping turn back, its wings perpendicular to the ground. But it just kept turning over, and, inverted, it went into some woods just over the base's perimeter. It hit the ground in an area beyond some houses but before a sparse commercial mall housing a dentist's office and other small businesses. Residents heard the jet's roar above and looked out to see it slicing upside down and hitting in an explosion of fire. At that attitude, ejections, which reportedly did occur, were point-blank into the ground. Some residents believed that Dewar was deliberately trying to miss the houses before they crashed.

A report issued by the navy later blamed the accident on pilot error. It said that Dewar was too close to the ground and too slow when he did the maneuver and that consequently the plane stalled in the turn. But anybody who knew Dewar had to question that he was to blame.

He was among the Aces' best and most dependable pilots. The thing about Dewar was that he was a leader—the exact opposite of the hot-dogging, take-chances type of pilot like "Maverick" in the movie *Top Gun*. He simply would not have tolerated lax standards in any maneuver.

The issue of air-show safety is a controversial one. Those who don't believe Dewar was at fault, like his father, a retired New Jersey state trooper, believe that the navy overlooked the part played in the accident by the aging Tomcat. The navy did so, they say, to assure the public that air shows are not the culprit. An eight-hundred-page report is a damning document. But Dewar's sterling reputation and the record of the A-model Tomcats will always conjure questions.

They had a moving service for Dewar at the NAS Oceana Chapel of the Good Shepherd. Almost all the Aces were in attendance, plus about five hundred others. In the coming year, Bru and Dog would decide to leave the navy. Bru was dissatisfied with the demands on his family life, navy leadership, which he considered lacking, and the dearth of money for the military from Congress. Dog, after skippering the Aces, didn't relish flying a desk, which was where he saw his future if he stayed in. He was also angry over the denial of Kosovo medals to Aces who had flown combat while noncombatants had been overly decorated. Wog, who would frequent the Pentagon in his new job in space defense, and Toad, who was actually stationed there, would luckily escape harm in the shocking terrorist airliner-bombing of September 11, 2001—an attack that would make Bru reconsider his retirement. ("The chance to be involved in finishing this thing has me rethinking," he would say. But as of this writing he was still planning to leave the navy and team with Dog in a commercial "energy" venture.)

It was humid, and squadron members in the chapel as an honor guard wore their short-sleeved whites. Joey, choking back emotion, was the first to speak: Dewar was his "team captain," he said, the leader of the JOs, one of his best FAC-As. And he hated to fight him in air-to-air combat because "invariably I knew after three or four turns, I'd be looking behind the tail, and Dewar would be closing in to shoot us. We would get back from the hop, and Dewar would be there with that famous half smile of his. He wouldn't say a word, and he would be preparing the debrief board. And I guess I couldn't take it. And at times I would tell him just knock that crap off. And he would just start laughing. Dewar had an unbelievable laugh. And after I settled down, he would debrief us in his customary impeccable swifty style and show us how he humbled us."

Joey concluded with a story: After Iraq, the *Roosevelt* had a liberty in Rhodes, Greece. The squadron rented an old villa in the countryside. They could conduct their wrestling matches without scaring hotel guests. This was the time that Dewar decided he was going to climb a nearby mountain. Joey tried to talk him out of it because "I know I'm going to come back and have to organize a rescue party. But, of course, he went," leading the other lieutenants behind him. When Joey returned, Dewar, despite a cut hand, was triumphant. All of them had made it to the top and back. Dewar invited the skipper to go swimming with them. They jumped in cars and went to a picturesque cliff overlooking the Mediterranean. "We took turns jumping off and swimming around these small cliffs. I have to tell you it is one of the most cherished memories I have in my life because those lieutenants were so much fun to be around and they made me feel I was fifteen again."

Afterward, on the way back to the villa, they stopped at an outdoor restaurant and ordered Margaritas. "There we were in our wet swimming trunks, wet hair . . . drinking these terrible drinks with little monkey sticks as stirrers, all the time laughing, having a wonderful time. . . . In the center of all these happy men was Dewar, our team captain, laughing like he always did, making everybody feel good. That's how I will always remember and cherish him."

It was a picture of the Aces.

When the service ended, everyone in the chapel filed silently outside to wait for the missing-man fly-over. In the distance, four Tomcats appeared in a truncated V formation. Their wings were swept back with the hunch of angry war birds. They droned seemingly slowly forward. As they passed directly overhead, one of the jets peeled away, leaving a vacant space in the V.

It was the missing-man formation. Flying as Dewar was Wrex.

In that symbolic moment, all Joey's triumphant Aces were together again.

• • •

When Islamic terrorists flew suicide planes into the World Trade Center and the Pentagon on September 11, 2001, the newest roster of Black Aces was on its way to South Africa as part of Airwing 8, then deployed on the USS *Enterprise*. The air wing had just finished its latest cruise—the one after Kosovo—and was on its way home. Many of the senior Aces who had flown in Kosovo two years earlier had already rotated out of the squadron. But a core of junior officers from that campaign remained, as did Lt. Comdr. Dave "Beaker" Lobdell, one of the squadron's senior officers in 1999.

Comdr. Brian Gawne, a backseater who had come to VF-41 after Kosovo and had succeeded Dog, was the skipper. Gawne remembers: "I was walking down a passageway, and somebody came up to me and said a plane had just flown into the first tower at the trade center. I said, 'Plane?' I thought it was a Cesna [small plane] or something." He hurried to one of the ship's big-screen satellite feeds. "We were all just kind of stunned because of the damage. Then the second plane hit the other tower, and it was shock and disbelief. All of a sudden there was the realization that this wasn't an accident. That this was deliberate."

Lupe Lopez, one of the nugget junior officers from the Kosovo cruise, was now an Aces' second-cruise JO, seasoned and looked up to. He too was watching the attack on one of the carrier's television screens. "We were two days out of the Arabian Sea heading south," he remembers. "Everybody was just anticipating a good trip home." They'd spent most of the six-month cruise flying in Operation Southern Watch, enforcing United Nations no-fly restrictions over Iraq, and were looking forward to a leisurely voyage back to Oceana via a liberty stop in South Africa. It was to be the first time an American warship visited South Africa since sanctions there against apartheid, the policy of segregating native blacks, had been lifted. "We felt the ship turn and head back," he said. "They said, 'We need you on station. You've got the most experience.'"

The Black Aces, because of the expertise they had gained from Kosovo and Southern Watch, were to lead the bombing in Afghanistan. Their preparation had actually begun more than a year earlier in turnaround. "Our Kosovo guys were key since coming back from Kosovo," said Gawne. "We, of course, hadn't anticipated [the Islamic attacks]. But [before leaving on the present cruise] we knew we'd be doing Operation Southern Watch over Iraq. So we trained real hard to LANTIRN, practicing dropping precision-guided munitions, and pushed real hard on becoming FAC-As. The guys [remaining] from Kosovo were driving that. It paid off."

For the next few weeks, from September 11 to October 7, when the bombing of Taliban and Al-Qaeda sites in Afghanistan began, VF-41, still in their aging Tomcats, along with other planes of Airwing 8, flew reconnaissance missions, gathering all the information they could that would be needed when and if the War on Terrorism began. And when it did begin, said Lupe, VF-41 "led the way."

Aces spearheaded the first strikes. Gawne said, "We had the midnight-to-noon shift," which was called on the ship "Vampire Ops," and which was more stressful than day strikes. "That was our flying window." The war planners knew what they had in 41 and also put the Aces on some of the toughest targets—Al-Qaeda training camps, bunkers, and air defenses, all heavily defended. One of the first targets hit in the war was the Shindand Airbase in western Afghanistan. "They were storing a lot of aircraft there, radar and vehicles," said Lupe, who was on the mission. "It was pretty interesting. At least three SAMs were shot up and a ton of Triple-A. The higher-threat missiles were in Kosovo, but the elevations in Afghanistan were greater—it's a high desert—so their defensive fire got closer to our delivery altitudes."

But the result was similar to that in Kosovo. Aces crews, who returned to the United States in early November, hit 82 percent of what they targeted in the period they were there, which was somewhat less than a month. "That's high for anybody," said Gawne, and the best bombing scores in the air wing, added Lupe. The big difference between Kosovo and Afghanistan, in terms of strikes, said Slugz Kelly, another junior JO in Kosovo who, in Afghanistan, was in the thick of things, were the ranges involved. In Kosovo, it was a relatively short hop from the *Roosevelt* to Kosovo proper, something in the neighborhood of two hundred miles. In Afghanistan, the aging Tomcats were flying seven-to-eight-hundred miles one way, staying in the air 6-to-8 hours per mission, instead of the 2-to-3 hours normal in Kosovo, although FAC-A missions in Kosovo often took 5-to-6 hours.

Once the relatively few large and fixed targets in Afghanistan were destroyed, the United States had command of the skies and could bomb at will as long as they stayed out of Triple-A and SAM ranges. But with American special operations troops on the ground to help direct the bombing and fewer hard targets like tanks and vehicles, hunter-killer operations relying solely on spotters from the air don't appear to have been as prominent in Afghanistan as they were in Kosovo. But much of what happened is still secret. When Bru was contacted at "Strike U" in Fallon, Nevada, where he was finishing up his career, he said, "There's a lot I can't tell you," regarding the Afghanistan operations.

So the story is still unfolding. What can be said for sure is that carrier air wings and their various squadrons are becoming more valuable, as are fighter planes that can bomb. The hot spots, like terrorist camps, are more and more in remote areas far from U.S. landed bases. But U.S. carriers are never further than a few days away on the water and often can launch within hours of arriving on station. Such quick-strike ability can mean the difference between success and failure. More important, the United States is not deploying lots of troops rapidly. It can't. Bases and a large buildup at those bases are needed to support major troop deployments. And without forces on the ground, FAC-As and their search-and-destroy SCAR missions are going to be the best means of finding and killing enemy troops and their mobile weapons.

At the very least, if not primarily, FAC-As are going to continue to be needed.

Unmanned aerial vehicles have been used a lot in Afghanistan and promise to be used more in future wars. When the United States was bombing the Taliban and Al-Qaeda fighters at Tora Bora, their mountain hideout, UAVs were employed to sense escaping enemies scurrying away in the mountain's protective forests. The UAVs, using infrared detectors, could see heat from the humans under the forest canopy. In those cases, planes were summoned to fire at what had been found. But UAVs are easily shot down. And in cities and areas populated with *friendlies* as well as enemies, their sensors are not going to be enough. Humans, with their wide range of abilities, are going to have to be on the scene in cockpits to make the complicated decisions about whether the target is enemy or innocent. A remote viewer might miss something important, increasing the chances for error. For that reason alone,

FAC-A-trained fighter crews peering out of airplanes, making decisions about identification, and then firing the sophisticated weapons systems to kill valid targets, will still be needed. To a large extent what the Black Aces did in Kosovo laid the groundwork for the improvements that followed in Afghanistan.

The Aces themselves are leaving the Tomcats, which are to be phased out of the navy arsenal by 2010, with the aged A models going first. By the time this book is published, the squadron should have completed a transition into the new F/A-18 Super Hornet, a two-seat, longer-range version of the current single-seat fighter-bomber. Bigger and able to carry more ordnance, it will be a better bomber than the current Hornet. The Aces will be the first in the fleet to make the transition, which is perhaps an acknowledgment that they have earned the upgrade. In any case, until enemies can match the level of training, commitment, crew skill, and aeronautic sophistication of the United States, which doesn't appear likely anytime soon, the Super Hornets will continue the modern trend of navy fighter squadrons doing more bombing than dogfighting. And the Black Aces, if their past, now embellished by stellar performances in Kosovo and Afghanistan, is any indication, will continue to be among the best fighter squadrons in the U.S. Navy.

Roster of the Aces,

Their Commanders and Contemporaries (by Rank)

Battle Group Officers

Admiral Copeland — Rear Adm. William Winston "Mad Dog" Copeland, Jr., commander of the *Roosevelt* Battle Group; a former fighter pilot and Vietnam War MiG killer.

CAG — Capt. Dale E. "Sparky" Lyle, commander of the *Roosevelt's* Airwing 8; a pilot and Joey's immediate boss.

Contemporaries

"Slapshot" — Comdr. Ted Carter. Much-honored skipper of the Aces' sister squadron, the VF-14 Tophatters.

Aces' Senior Officers, Managers of the Squadron ("hinges")

"Joey" — Comdr. Joseph P. Aucoin. 42. The Aces' skipper and a RIO. A Desert Storm combat veteran with over four thousand hours in the cockpit.

"Dog"—Comdr. Jim J. Bauser. 40. Aces' XO (executive officer), next in line to command the Aces. Pilot and former marine from upstate New York.

"Wog"—Lt. Comdr. Steve R. Carroll. 38. Aces' operations officer. RIO. New Jersey native.

"Bru"—Lt. Comdr. Brian B. Brurud. 38. Aces' maintenance officer. Pilot and bombing expert. From Bartlesville, Oklahoma.

"Loose"—Lt. Comdr. Louis T. Cannon. 35. RIO. Aces' only black aviator. From Washington, D.C.

"Alvin"—Lt. Comdr. John R. Young. 34. Pilot. Assistant administration officer, next in line to take over operations. From Seaford, Delaware.

"Beaker"—Lt. Comdr. Dave J. Lobdell. 33. Pilot. Assistant operations officer and former F-117 Stealth pilot in an air force exchange program. Born in Waukegan, Illinois.

"Double"—Lt. Comdr. Eric S. Pfister. 30s. RIO. Administration officer. From San Diego, California.

Aces' Junior Officers (JOs)

"Mo"—Lt. Ron E. Vaught. 32. RIO. Born in Redondo Beach, California.

"Toadboy" or "Toad"—Lt. James F. Skarbek. 32. RIO. Quality assurance officer. From Baltimore, Maryland.

"Salami"—Lt. Frank H. Silebi. 31. Pilot. From Bethlehem, Pennsylvania.

"Gooch"—Lt. J. Greg DeGruccio. 31. Pilot. Training officer. Born in Chandler, Arizona.

"Thing"—Lt. Doug A. Thien. 30s. RIO. Born in Alaska, raised in Iowa.

"Razor"—Lt. Ken W. Shick. 30. Pilot. Air-to-air training officer. From Hanover, Pennsylvania.

"Wrex"—Lt. R. Keith Harrison. 29. Pilot. From Houston, Texas.

"Dewar"—Lt. William J. Dey. 30. Pilot. From Hightstown, New Jersey.

"Meat"—Lt. Brian M. Fleisher. 29. Pilot. Born in Cincinnati, Ohio.

"Pappy"—Lt. Eric J. Anduze. 29. Pilot. Born and raised in Puerto Rico.

"Squab"—Lt. Clay G. Williams. 30. RIO. Born in Sedalia, Missouri, raised in Texas.

"Brain"—Lt. G. Merle Perry. 28. Pilot. From Durham, North Carolina.

"Money"—Lt. Doug R. Halter. Late 20s. RIO. Born in New England, grew up in Cherry Hill, New Jersey.

"Mentul"—Lt. Tim A. Challingsworth. 27. RIO. Born in Pennsylvania.

Aces' New JOs ("Nuggets")

"Rhino"—Lt. Kurt A. Rhineheimer. Late 20s. RIO. Public information officer. Born in Van Nuys, California, grew up in New Jersey and Arizona.

"Moto"—Lt. Ed J. Mayle. 26. RIO. Born in Ohio, near Akron.

"Jack" or "Tab"—Lt. James A. Corlett. 27. Pilot. Born in Naples, Italy, grew up in Idaho and Cleveland, Ohio.

"Lupe"—Lt. Marcus Lopez. 27. Pilot. Born in Rhode Island.

"T-Bone"—Lt. J. Eric Tidwell. 28. RIO. Born in Jacksonville, Florida.

"Slugz"—Lt. (jg) John F. Kelly. RIO.

Aces' Nonaviator Officers

"Gunner"—Lt. (jg) T. A. Phillips. 36. Ordnance officer. Former enlisted. Born in New Orleans.

"Topper"—Lt. (jg) Kyle L. Leese. 27. Intelligence officer. Born in Camden, New Jersey.

"Mookie"—Lt. (jg) Christian A. Stover. Maintenance.

Warrant Officer Roger Elkins. Maintenance. Born in Cincinnati, Ohio.

Aces' Officers Not Mentioned in the Book, All First-Cruisers

ENS Douglas E. Houser. Maintenance.

ENS Mellany Hamilton-Coleman. Material Control Officer. The squadron's only female officer.

ENS Nick Greven. Intelligence.

Glossary of Terms

AAA — antiaircraft artillery, usually called "Triple-A"

ABCCC (ABTripleC) — Airborne Command and Control Center

ACM — air combat maneuvering, also called air-to-air fighting, or dog-fighting

AIM-54 missile — see "Phoenix"

AIMC — air interdiction mission commander — strike leader

ALE — U.S. designation for airborne countermeasures such as chaff and flares

AOM — All Officers Meeting

APC — armored personnel carrier. Tracked vehicle, like a tank, used to transport troops

ATO — air tasking order (the official air missions written and defined and sent to the units to be flown)

AWACS — Airborne Warning and Control System aircraft. The plane is a converted Boeing 707 with all types of electronic surveillance and control gear to detect hostile aircraft and direct fighters in the battle areas. Flown by the air force

BAI — battlefield air interdiction, a type of mission flown by the squadron; usually accompanying a SCAR mission

BDA — bomb damage assessment

Bogey — confirmed enemy aircraft

Bolter — Term used to indicate a missed landing on the carrier, resulting in the plane having to lift off at the last moment for another try. Usually, the plane is in some way dangerous in its approach. Or it may be that its tailhook has not caught one of the four arresting wires, which it must in order to land securely. Those in control of the landing tell the pilot to bolter, or he encounters some kind of problem just before the literal touchdown. In either case, the pilot instantly powers the plane into maximum speed so that he can lift off and try again. No one wants a bolter, but they happen, increasingly as landing conditions get worse.

BOQ—Bachelor's Officers Quarters

CAG—commander, air group; head of the air wing

CAOC—Combined Air Operations Center at Vicenza, Italy, which selected targets and directed the war

CAP—Combat Air Patrol. The term refers to a mission in which a fighter stations itself in position, usually flying a repeat "racetrack" pattern to guard strikers from enemy attack by air.

CAS—close air support—mission type where the bomber goes in close, usually at the direction of a FAC-A

chaff—Various types of decoy debris emitted by planes to confuse enemy radars that may be homing on them. The enemy radar, from either another plane or a ground missile launcher, will hopefully lock on the chaff and not on the plane.

CO—commanding officer, often used in reference to the head of a squadron

COD—carrier onboard delivery, the plane that brings mail and other supplies to the ship

CVIC—Carrier intelligence center. "CV" designates "carrier"

DFCS—Digital Flight Control System

division—a flight of four aircraft; two elements or "sections" of two planes each

DMPI—Designated Mean Point of Impact—the aim point or place you put the bomb on the target, sometimes written "dimpy"

ESC—escort, a type of mission flown by the squadron

FAC-A—Forward Air Controller Airborne. Name for an aircrew member who has been trained in the skill of directing air strikes on ground targets from the cockpit. The airborne forward air controller usually orbits an area, spots targets, identifies them, and directs other aircraft to bomb them. A FAC-A usually does his stuff on a SCAR mission. In the Kosovo War, SCAR missions were also called KEZ Ops.

feet dry—Navy slang for flying over land from the ocean. At the moment the aircraft flies over land, it is said to be "feet dry."

feet wet—Navy slang for exiting land for the ocean. At the moment the aircraft is back over water, it is said to be "feet wet."

FLIR—Forward-Looking Infrared Radar, a screen that is part of the LANTIRN and that shows target images in the cockpit. The RIO has one in his backseat. The image shows the terrain and targets in an infrared picture.

FOD—foreign object damage—Anything on the deck or in the plane that could damage its parts. These are usually little pieces of metal on the deck. Periodically, all hands will move slowly along the deck looking for FOD. But they can be in the engines or cockpit as well as elsewhere.

FTI—frequency transmitted intelligence

GBU-10—two-thousand-pound Paveway laser-guided bomb

GBU-12—five-hundred-pound Paveway laser-guided bomb

GBU-16—thousand-pound Paveway laser-guided bomb

GBU-24—two-thousand-pound "penetrator" bomb made to go through reinforced concrete bunkers

GPS—Global Positioning System—a satellite-directed navigation aid. With the right equipment, a ship or aircraft can tell almost exactly where it is at any time.

gunner—Navy term for ordnance officer. Often the officer's call sign is "Gunner." Each squadron has a gunner, and the air wing has a gunner.

HARM—High-speed radiation missile shot by Prowlers and Hornets at enemy radars and SAM sites. HARMs home in on radiation.

Hinges—nickname for the lieutenant commanders and higher officers who run a squadron

HVAAP ("have-a-pee")—High Value Airborne Asset Protection—a mission on a strike package in which a fighter protects an important aircraft against enemy fighters, normally a Prowler, when it goes into enemy territory.

IFF—Identification, Friend or Foe—transponder in airplane that tells others who you are and allows you to identify another plane. Uses codes.

IO — intelligence officer

IR — infrared

IZLID — Infrared Zoom Laser Illuminator Designator, a powerful hand-held laser light used to designate targets

JO — junior officer — a term used to designate the middle echelon of officers in the squadron, mostly lieutenants, who are between the inexperienced "nuggets" — ensigns — and the O4s — lieutenant commanders

JTFX — Joint Task Force Exercises — the last work-up before cruise

KEZ — Kosovo Engagement Zone

KEZ Ops — Kosovo Engagement Zone Operations. SCAR or FAC-A missions sent out to find and kill Serb Army fielded forces. As the war continued, SCAR missions became "KEZ Ops," for the area they were being flown in.

K9 — Missions, mini-strikes, smaller than the Alpha Strikes but larger than FAC-A. After the initial large strikes flown by the air wing, their fixed strikes were against smaller targets such as radio towers, bridges, and smaller supply and fueling hubs, which were the only fixed targets left in Kosovo.

LANTIRN — Low-Altitude Navigation and Targeting Infrared for Night — a pod on the airplane that allows the crew to see the target and bomb it at night

LGB — laser-guided bomb

LMAVs — laser-guided Maverick missiles

LSO — Landing signal officer. Positioned at the stern of the carrier, these officers aid, guide, and grade pilots landing on the carrier

MANPAD — small, shoulder-fired SAM

Maverick — Air-to-ground, laser-guided rocket missile with wings, fins, and a motor carried by Hornets. Once released, it flies itself to the laser spot. The missile is specially made to destroy armored vehicles like tanks.

MAWTS — Marine Air Weapons and Tactics Squadron

MO — Maintenance officer. Along with the XO and Ops O, MO is one of the most important positions in the squadron under the skipper.

NAS — Naval Air Station

NFO — Naval flight officer. The nonpilot aviator receives his wings as an NFO, and then, depending on the warplane he is assigned, he becomes a RIO, navigator, or other designation. In a Tomcat, an NFO becomes a RIO.

Nugget—brand-new aviator or officer, with no experience, usually fresh from one of the training squadrons

NVGs—night-vision goggles

O4—lieutenant commander (Lt. Comdr.)

O5—commander (Comdr.)

Ops O—Operations officer. One of the most important department heads

Paveway—Air force code name for a family of laser-guided bombs. So far, there are three series of the bombs: Paveway I, II, and III, each representing improvements over the last. The Paveway I series was developed during the Vietnam War.

Phoenix—long-range air-to-air missile used by the Tomcat, technically called the AIM-54 missile

Podgorica—Capital of Montenegro, code-named "Mexico." A large airfield used by the Serbs is in its vicinity.

POL—petroleum, oil, lubricants—usually used in referring to storage for same

QAO—quality assurance officer—ground job in, for instance, maintenance

QB—"Quarterback"—name given to first SCAR missions using FAC-A-trained crews

RAG—replacement air group—training squadron in a particular airplane from which a nugget graduates before going to his fleet squadron. For instance, there are F-14 and F/A-18 RAGs.

RHAW—Radar Homing and Warning Receiver—a device in the cockpit that alerts crew to enemy radars targeting them and tells them what the threat is

RIO—Radar intercept officer, also called "backseater." A RIO or any nonpilot receives his wings as a naval flight officer (NFO). He then becomes a particular type of aviation crew member, such as RIO, navigator, or electronic warfare officer, depending on the warplane he flies in. The F-14 has only a pilot and a RIO.

SA-6—Russian SAM frequently used in Kosovo

SA-10—large Russian SAM thought to be in Kosovo

SAM—Surface-to-air antiaircraft missile. There are various types, from shoulder-launched to large missiles shot from heavy platforms. A

SAM is identified individually with the preface SA-(numeral). For instance, "SA-6"

SCAR—Strike Coordinated Armed Reconnaissance. The type of mission run by FAC-A-trained crews hunting and striking Serb "fielded forces." As the war continued, SCAR missions were called "KEZ Ops," for the area—Kosovo—that they were being flown in.

SEAD—suppression of enemy air defense

section—a flight of two planes

Super JO—A junior officer who is in his second tour. The seniority usually makes the JO a leader.

TARPS—Tactical Air Reconnaissance Pod System—a pod on the airplane with which intelligence pictures are taken; also the name of an intelligence mission using the pod

TLAM—Tomahawk Land Attack Missile, fired by ships

TOT—time on target—the time airplanes are supposed to arrive at the target, part of the synchronization of strikes

Triple-A—antiaircraft artillery, also called AAA

UAV—unmanned aerial vehicle, used for reconnaissance

VID—visual identification—most frequently used in reference to getting close enough to an enemy plane to visually identify its hostile origin

XO—executive officer—next in line in command after the skipper, generally the officer being groomed to become skipper when the current skipper leaves